W9-BIV-376

DATE DUE

SMOKING
THE STORY BEHIND THE HAZE

SMOKING
THE STORY BEHIND THE HAZE

Edward L. Koven

Nova Science Publishers, Inc.
New York

Art Director: Maria Ester Hawrys
Assistant Director: Elenor Kallberg
Graphics: Susan A. Boriotti and Frank Grucci
Manuscript Coordinator: Phylis Gaynor
Book Production: Gavin Aghamore, Joanne Bennette,
Michele Keller, Christine Mathosian
and Tammy Sauter
Circulation: Iyatunde Abdullah, Cathy DeGregory and
Annette Hellinger

Library of Congress Cataloging–in–Publication Data
available upon request

ISBN 1-56072-401-3
© *1996 Nova Science Publishers, Inc.*
 6080 Jericho Turnpike, Suite 207
 Commack, New York 11725
 Tele. 516-499-3103 Fax 516-499-3146
 E Mail Novasci1@aol.com

Printed in the United States of America

DEDICATION

This book is dedicated to my wife Bonnie, my daughters Janet and Deborah, and the millions of human beings around the world who have died from poisonous tobacco smoke and secondary tobacco smoke and their families.

CONTENTS

Chapter   Page

DEDICATION   v

FOREWORD   ix

ABOUT THE AUTHOR   xv

I.   A Glance at the History of the Tobacco Toll   1

II.   Medical - The Medicine Men, Not Tobacco Men   17

III.   Deadly Endorsements   37

IV.   Sound Smoking Advice   65

V.   One Cartoon = 1,000 Anti-Tobacco Words   83

VI.   Courting the Tobacco Industry   97

VII.   Saving 419,000 Lives and Up to $100 Billion
        A Year Through Preventive Health Care   107

VIII.   Smoking is a Form of Child and Spouse Abuse   115

IX.   Ban Tobacco Advertising   123

X.   A Program to Prevent Minors Smoking and
        Using Tobacco - to Combat Tobacco Industry
        Efforts to Addict Minors to Poisonous
        Tobacco Smoke   133

XI.   Ban Smoking in Public Places   147

XII. Pinpointing the Fumes   163

      A.   Eliminate Tobacco PACs   163

      B.   Tobacco Exports - Foreign Exploitation by
           the Tobacco Industry   167

      C.   Subsidizing Tobacco   171

      D.   Exploitation of Blacks - "They Used to Make
           Us Pick It. Now They Want Us to Smoke It."   172

      E.   Exploitation of Women by the
           Tobacco Industry   175

CONCLUSION   181

SUBJECT INDEX   189

FOREWORD

During the past few years I discovered that there was a deadly, but little known tobacco war raging throughout the United States and around the world. The casualties are enormous. Approximately three million human beings are dying prematurely each year around the world from the enemy, including nearly a half million Americans. Estimates are that by the year 2020 ten million human beings will prematurely perish each year due to enemy smoke and fire of which over four million will be Americans. The enemy is the American tobacco industry. Hopefully some of the ideas set forth in this book may serve as counterattack weapons in health-conscious humanity's war against the amoral tobacco industry.

My challenge has been to formulate an approach for exposing the magnitude of the tobacco war and setting forth ideas to reduce the casualties. The setting of my daily routine in recent years – which has been getting up early, often before dawn, and jogging along an isolated trail for 45 minutes to an hour – has facilitated this process. I formulate and coalesce thoughts while running endless miles whether the temperature is in the 80s or the wind chill is subzero. Inhaling the usually crisp, clear, and smokefree air seems to stimulate the flow of ideas. My mind can wander and create without the buzzing of a phone or other distracting intrusions.

It was during these runs permeated by complete freedom of thought that many of the ideas emerged that found their way into this book. This relatively clear outdoor air I inhaled inspired me to try to find ways to encourage people to enjoy and inhale healthier smokefree indoor air where they live, work, and dine. I hope this book helps encourage all readers to take steps to improve the quality of the air we breathe through the reduction or elimination of tobacco smoke or secondary tobacco smoke.

My interest in the smoking problem was sparked initially as a young boy in the late 1940s and early 1950s when I was subjected to a double dose of secondary tobacco smoke from my chain smoking parents in apartments in Chicago and Evanston, Illinois. The fumes from my parents' cigarettes irritated my eyes, nose and throat and became worse when the family would travel in our 1936 Oldsmobile or 1948 Pontiac.

Over the years a number of my heavy smoking relatives became ill or died from what appeared to be the constant stream of smoke which permeated their households. My heavy smoking uncle on my mother's side, with whom I had a number of memorable boyhood trips, died prematurely at age 60 in 1976 from a heart attack undoubtedly brought on by smoking. My two to three pack-a-day smoking father passed away in 1988 from emphysema and several strokes apparently caused by a lifetime of chain smoking. My mother, who died January 3, 1996, miraculously survived for more than 80 years, but the quality of her life had been greatly reduced from many years of smoking.

But the final spark which launched my desire to write <u>Fuming</u> came as a result of my handling a smoking-in-the-workplace case in 1990 when I served as an attorney with the Department of Health and Human Services (HHS) in Chicago. In that arbitration case I attempted to defend a nonsmoking policy where the union was attempting to reinstate smoking in the workplace based on language in the collective bargaining agreement. During the course of the defense of the nonsmoking policy, I called upon James Repace, a health physicist with the Environmental Protection Agency and author of numerous indoor air quality articles, to be an expert witness. His insights such as pointing out that smoking in the workplace would turn our work areas into "gas chambers" helped me become more aware of the breadth and depth of the smoking problem.

The more I learned about the dangers of smoking to both the smokers and those exposed to the poisonous tobacco smoke, the angrier I became. The anger was not directed so much at the nation's 46 million smokers, but the tobacco industry which has and is leading our youth down the path of lifetime tobacco addiction. The tobacco companies appear to be placing corporate profits ahead of the health of our nation's children and adults.

We live in a world where the most distant nations are separated by merely hours by air rather than oceans that took weeks to cross. It is a small world after all with problems afflicting one nation frequently being identical to problems facing others. The premature death of about three million human beings a year, including over 400,000 Americans, from tobacco smoke and secondary tobacco smoke, is a major problem facing most nations. Recently I noticed that smoking in public places has been banned in Shanghai and Sao Paulo, but flourishes in most American cities. Although our government warns Americans of the dangers of poisonous tobacco smoke, I find it blatantly hypocritical that our country encourages the exportation of tobacco products that are responsible for the premature death of about 2.5 million human beings a year other than Americans.

My heart reaches out to a five-year-old asthmatic child who must grow up in a home environment permeated with the toxins and carcinogens of secondary tobacco smoke, many restaurant workers who must breathe poisonous tobacco smoke eight hours a day, and the numerous international airline flight attendants who are risking their lives breathing passengers' secondary tobacco smoke in order to earn a living.

My research has convinced me that it will be quite difficult for lifelong smokers to stop. The only effective solution to the smoking problem is to find a way or ways to convince our elementary, junior high, and high school students not to start smoking thereby avoiding the path to lifetime tobacco addiction. The students are the primary source used to replace the nearly half million Americans who prematurely die each year from tobacco smoke and secondary tobacco smoke and the many more who become seriously ill.

President Bill Clinton appeared to agree with this conclusion when on August 10, 1995, he concurred with the Food and Drug Administration (FDA) findings that nicotine in cigarettes should be declared to be an addictive drug and endorsed the proposed regulations that FDA administer pertaining to the sale and distribution of nicotine-containing cigarettes and smokeless tobacco products to children and adolescents. The ultimate solution may hinge on the elimination of tobacco ads geared towards young people such as the Joe Camel and "Slims" ads. It appears that the tobacco industry and their PACs have been and will be pouring huge sums into the political coffers of members of Congress and state legislators to thwart the implementation of these findings.

As we head into the 1996 Presidential campaign and await the 1998 Congressional elections, as well as the year 2000 Presidential campaign, the regulation of tobacco to protect American children and nonsmoking adults who constitute more than 80% of our population to be free from the carcinogens and toxins of poisonous tobacco smoke should be a significant political election year issue. An objective review of the reputable medical and scientific evidence leads one to conclude that regulation of tobacco is essential to protect the health and safety of every American, especially our grade school and high school students. President Clinton should be commended for his concern about the health of the younger persons in our country being ruined by tobacco and his willingness to confront the all-powerful tobacco industry on this issue. Tobacco company spin control cannot minimize the leadership of the President of the United States on this issue. Unfortunately the same cannot be said for House Minority leader Richard Gephardt of Missouri who received $65,258 from the tobacco industry from January 1985 through September 1995 and Speaker of the House Newt Gingrich who received $53,500 from the same source during the same period.

After a number of my letters to newspaper and magazine editors regarding smoking were published, a colleague in the Public Health Service, Carl Andrianopoli, convinced me to write a book on the subject. With the strong encouragement of Carl, Deputy HHS Chicago Regional Director Hiroshi Kanno, attorneys Anne Galkin and Fran Pergericht in HHS, and Cher Klemme in the HHS Chicago Regional Personnel Office, I undertook the challenge of trying to set forth the smoking problem in as creative and readable manner as possible and to set forth proposed solutions. I am grateful for their help.

My goals have been to set forth facts and propose solutions designed to improve the quality of life and save the lives of both the nation's 46 million smokers and 200 million nonsmokers exposed to secondary tobacco smoke and to portray a picture designed to encourage young people not to start smoking. If this book positively impacts on one person, all the effort would have been worthwhile.

I would like to express my appreciation for the perspective and insights provided by Eppie "Ann Landers" Lederer, Abigail "Dear Abby" Van Buren, and Jack Mabley for permitting me to reprint their sage advice on many aspects of the smoking problem. And I would like to thank the outstanding cartoonists for their unique portrayals of numerous facets of the smoking/health problem – Steve Benson, Chip Bok, Adrian Carson, Jack Higgins, Gary Larson, Dick Locher, Mike Peters, Milt Priggie, Gary Trudeau, and Don Wright.

As a result of this four-year project, my wife Bonnie has seen far less of me on weekends and evenings and my daughters, Janet and Deborah, at times have wondered about my existence. I thank them most of all for their patience and tolerance, but also for not smoking. I hope they will permit me to reemerge as a full-time family member.

Finally, I would like to express my appreciation for the efforts of the many men and women in the medical, scientific and health professions over the past 70 years whose smoking research and perseverance against one of the most powerful lobbies in the world –

the tobacco lobby – helped make former Surgeon General Dr. C. Everett Koop's goal of a smoke-free society by the year 2000 an achievable objective. These men and women are the real heroes in the war against smoking.

Edward L. Koven

November 1996

ABOUT THE AUTHOR

Edward L. Koven is a 55-year-old attorney who resides with his wife Bonnie in Highland Park, Illinois. His more than 150 commentaries, articles, and letters on smoking issues have appeared in over 25 publications during the past five years.

A Glance at the History of the Tobacco Toll

Almost every American has experienced a close family member or friend dying or becoming seriously ill from smoking or the secondhand effects of smoking. Despite the fact that nearly a half million Americans die prematurely from tobacco smoke and secondary tobacco smoke each year and many more become seriously ill, the amoral tobacco companies appear to be unconcerned. They are replacing their dying and sick customers by recruiting and enticing our nation's grade school and high school children through Joe Camel and Virginia Slims type ads as well as exporting a poisonous product to foreign customers.

The tobacco industry appears impervious to the health disaster it has inflicted upon more than 46 million American current smokers, many more former or deceased smokers, their children and spouses who live or lived with them, and the remainder of the more than 200 million nonsmoking Americans subject to poisonous secondary tobacco smoke. The tobacco industry's production and sale of a lethal consumer product that when used as intended is likely to kill users or render them seriously ill leaves me fuming. Whether you find yourself upset, angry, aggravated or fuming, every American has an opportunity to help eradicate the preventible health problems from poisonous tobacco smoke and secondary tobacco by such activities as contacting legislators to support anti-smoking laws, boycotting restaurants which permit smoking, keeping children out of public places where smoking is permitted, and boycotting non-tobacco products made by tobacco companies.

My ultimate goal is to provide smokers with reasons for stopping and potential smokers, mainly our youth, reasons for not starting. A brief history of the smoking problem should provide the foundation for reaching this goal.

The 1990 census reveals that there are 248,709,873 living Americans.[1] A total of 63,604,432 or approximately 25.6% are under 18.[2] Of the 185,105,441 adults, approximately 75% or 138,829,080 do not smoke.[3] That leaves 46,276,361 adults and a portion of those minors under 18 who smoke as the smokers in the United States. Approximately 200 million Americans do not smoke.

Tobacco smoke is the cause of approximately 419,000 premature deaths each year of American smokers from cancer, heart disease, emphysema, and other diseases and illnesses.[4] In addition, it has been estimated that approximately 53,000 American nonsmokers die prematurely each year from secondary or involuntary tobacco smoke, also known as passive smoke,[5] which is exposure from the smoke emitted by the burning end of cigarettes, cigars, and pipes between and during puffs and exhaled smoke from the smoker. Thus, approximately 472,000 Americans die prematurely each year from tobacco smoke. This figure does not take into account the toll from smokeless tobacco estimated to be about 8,000 a year.[6]

Based on recent mortality figures, about 47.2 million Americans will die prematurely from tobacco smoke and secondary tobacco smoke the next century. Multiplying the American projection by five or six will result in the projection of the number of human beings around the world who will die prematurely from tobacco smoke and secondary tobacco smoke during the next century - between 243 and 292 million deaths. In fact, the World Health Organization projects at the current smoking rate that in 2020 ten million human beings will die year each year from tobacco smoke and secondary tobacco smoke.[7] This extrapolates out to a billion human beings a century. If something is not done to reduce human exposure to the toxins and carcinogens in poisonous tobacco smoke and secondary tobacco smoke, the cumulative carnage will be a holocaust that would be unsurpassed in the history of civilization.

Moreover, millions of Americans and human beings around the world have become and will become seriously ill from tobacco smoke and secondary tobacco smoke. Major operations for varied conditions such as lung cancer, heart impairments and broken bones from avoidable osteoporosis could have been avoided along with the huge preventable medical costs that have overwhelmed our health care system. Unlike other drugs such as alcohol (with the exception of drunk driving), secondary tobacco smoke endangers the health and lives of millions of innocent victims who are frequently unable to avoid smokefree work places or recreational facilities.

Tobacco is the only consumer product that when used exactly as the manufacturer intends causes death and disease. The following major tobacco companies in the United States appear to have knowingly produced a product that has caused millions of preventable deaths and illnesses – Philip Morris, Inc., R.J. Reynolds Nabisco, Inc., Brown and Williamson Tobacco Corporation, American Tobacco Company, Lorillard, U.S. Tobacco Company, and Culbro Inc. These companies have been collectively described as the "Merchants of Death."[8]

Occasionally even one of the descendants of a tobacco company founder feels compelled to warn the public of the dangers of the industry's lethal product. The grandson of the founder of the R.J. Reynolds Tobacco Company made the following public-service spot:[9]

> My name is Patrick Reynolds. My grandfather, R.J. Reynolds, founded the tobacco company that makes Camels, Winstons, and Salems. We've all heard the tobacco industry say there are no ill effects caused by smoking. Well, they ought to look at the R.J. Reynolds family.
>
> My grandfather chewed tobacco and died of cancer. My father, R.J. Reynolds, Jr., smoked heavily and died of emphysema. My mother smoked and had emphysema and heart disease. My two aunts, also heavy smokers, died of emphysema and cancer. Currently three of my older brothers who smoke have emphysema. I smoked for 10 years and have small-airways lung disease.
>
> Now tell me. Do you think the cigarette companies are being truthful when they say smoking isn't harmful?

What was so obvious to the grandson of R.J. Reynolds has been known to observant human beings for almost four centuries. King James I in his 1604 *Counterblast to Tobacco* observed that "Smoking is a custom loathsome to the eye, hateful to the nose, harmful to the brain, and dangerous to the lungs."[10] These harmful effects perceptively set forth by King James I leave the nonsmoker who often must breathe the tobacco smoke "fuming" or very angry.

For nearly 400 years the nonsmoking men and women on this planet have been unsuccessful in channeling their fuming into constructive ways in eliminating the harmful impact of tobacco smoke and secondary tobacco smoke. The primary purpose of this book is to identify and explore areas which may be subject to more successful attacks and zeroing in on those areas for the sake of children and three quarters of the American adult population who do not smoke. A brief examination of the historical development of tobacco places in perspective possible ways to prevent the merchants of death, the tobacco companies, from continuing to carry out the greatest holocaust in the history of civilization.

The deadly smoking habit began around 1700-2000 B.C. when men and women would light paper tubes containing granulated tobacco weed and inhale the resulting smoke in their lungs.[11] Europeans first saw tobacco in 1492 when Christopher Columbus and his crew members observed that Cuban natives lit dried tobacco leaves and breathed their smoke. In 1518, Spanish explorers in Mexico noticed Aztecs smoking tobacco through hollow reeds. The explorers tried it thereby "bumming" the first cigarette. Jean Nicot, the French ambassador to Portugal, shipped tobacco to France in 1558 for studies on the healing power of tobacco as a cancer cure. Tobacco ingredients have been subsequently found to be a cancer cause rather than a cure. Nicot's place in history was assured when scientists named a toxic substance in tobacco, nicotine, after him.

John Rolfe planted the world's first commercial tobacco crop in Jamestown, Virginia, in 1612. After losing New York City to the British in 1776, George Washington pleaded for help to the army by saying "if you can't send money, send tobacco." In 1843, a French tobacco company began manufacturing Spanish papaletes and named them "cigarettes" in 1843.

In 1875, R.J. Reynolds started a chewing tobacco company in Winston-Salem, North Carolina. Six years later a patent was issued for a machine with a capacity for producing over 100,000 cigarettes a day. The invention of a cigarette matchbook in 1892 was important in popularizing cigarette use. Camels was introduced by R.J. Reynolds in 1913. Camels took their image from Old Joe, a dromedary with the Barnum & Bailey Circus that travelled through North Carolina. Liggett & Myers came out with Chesterfield in 1915 and the American Tobacco Company followed with Lucky Strike in 1916.

The Commander of the United States forces in World War I, General John Pershing, cabled Washington in 1918 that "tobacco is as indispensable as the daily ration; we must have thousands of tons of it without delay." The first time a woman was shown smoking was in a 1919 ad for Lorillard's Helmar cigarettes. The expression "smoke-filled room" describes the behind-the-scenes political maneuvering that helped secure Warren Harding's 1920 Republican Presidential nomination, as reported in the February 21, 1920 New York Times.[12]

Lung cancer was initially recognized in 1923 by American medical authorities as a disease. The number of deaths attributed to lung cancer grew from under 1,000 in 1923 to over 147,000 in 1990. Reader's Digest published an article in November 1924 entitled "Does Tobacco Injure the Human Body?" Over the next 66 years, Reader's Digest published almost 100 articles on smoking and health including "Are you a Man or a Smoke Stack," "Cancer by the Carton," "You've Come the Wrong Way, Baby!," and "So You Want to Burn to Death!".

An English physician, F.E. Tylecote, reported in the medical journal *Lancet* in 1927 that in nearly every lung cancer case he had seen or known about, the party smoked. Although unscientific and anecdotal, it was one of the initial efforts to explain the lung cancer increase.

Tobacco was one of the seven basic commodities to qualify for price supports under the Franklin Roosevelt Administration's Agricultural Adjustment Act of 1933.

National magazines in 1936 began carrying full page ads asserting that "more doctors smoke Camels than any other cigarette." Since Camels were the top-selling cigarette at the time, the claim could have been made for most occupations.

The American Medical Association Journal reported in 1936 that in a study involving 135 men with lung cancer, 90 percent were chronic smokers. The same year a Tulane School of Medicine physician concluded that cigarettes might be a "major cause" of lung cancer since most of his lung cancer patients smoked.

A John Hopkins University biology professor, Raymond Pearl, reported in 1938 based on a sample of 6,813 individuals that smoking affects lifespan. He observed that 68% of nonsmokers lived beyond age 60 while only 46% of heavy smokers reached age 60. Despite increased medical concerns, the cigarette companies promoted their products as health enhancing. Camels were advertised as relieving fatigue and aiding digestion, Kools claimed to protect against the common cold, Lucky Strikes were the favorite of athletes, and Old Gold bragged "not a cough in a carload."

President Roosevelt during World War II declared tobacco an essential crop and tobacco growers were given draft deferments. One of the postwar hit songs was "Smoke, Smoke, Smoke" recorded in 1947 by Tex Williams. One of the lines goes "I've been smoking 'em all my life and ain't dead yet."

A 1949 Gallup Poll revealed that just over half of Americans believed cigarette smoking was bad for one's health. When the same question was posed in a 1978 Gallup Poll, nine out of ten responded affirmatively, which apparently included many smokers.

Arthur Godfrey assured his 1952 national television audience that smoking "will make you feel better." A heavy smoker, he died of emphysema in 1983 after prior lung cancer surgery.

A 1953 American Cancer Society study showed that the death rate of smokers was 68 percent higher than for nonsmokers. The Tobacco Industry Research Committee, a self-serving arm of the tobacco industry, reported there was "no proof" that cigarette smoking is a cause of lung cancer. At the 1954 American Medical Association annual convention, the American Cancer Society reported that the death rate from cancer among male smokers is 75 percent higher than for nonsmokers.

The Federal Trade Commission in 1955 banned health claims in cigarette advertising. A committee appointed by the National Heart and Cancer Institutes, the American Heart Association, and the American Cancer Society in 1957 stated for the first time the existence of a direct cause-and-effect relationship between cigarette smoking and lung cancer.

Humphrey Bogart, the well-known star of the movie classic *Casablanca* who gave smoking a tough guy image, died of throat cancer at age 57 in 1957.

Senator Richard Neuberger of Oregon, a heavy cigarette smoker, died of lung cancer in 1960 at age 48. His wife, Maurine, won a special election to fill the vacancy and raised the issue of banning cigarette advertising. Movie star Gary Cooper of "High Noon" fame, who endorsed Chesterfields, died of lung cancer in 1961 at age 60.

The British Royal College of Physicians of London reported in 1961 that "cigarette smoking is a cause of lung cancer, and bronchitis, and probably contributes to the development of coronary heart disease and various other less common diseases."

In response to a reporter's random unexpected question at a May 1962 press conference and at Senator Maurine Neuberger's urging, President John F. Kennedy established an Advisory Committee on Smoking and Health headed by Surgeon General Luther Terry to ascertain whether cigarette smoking caused cancer.[13] The Advisory Committee was comprised of ten eminent biomedical scientists. Surgeon General Terry released a 387-page report on January 11, 1964 entitled "Smoking and Health" concluding that smoking was a major cause of lung cancer in men and was a contributing cause of many forms of chronic lung disease.

Nat King Cole, the popular cigarette smoking crooner and father of Natalie Cole, died of lung cancer in 1965 at age 45.

In response to the issuance of the 1964 Surgeon General's Report "Smoking and Health," the Federal Trade Commission issued Trade Regulation Rules on Cigarette Labeling and Advertising, which effective

January 1, 1966, required that all cigarette packages carry the warning "Caution - Cigarette Smoking May be Hazardous to Your Health"

Senator Robert F. Kennedy told the First World Conference on Smoking and Health in New York City on September 11, 1967:[14]

> Each year cigarettes kill more Americans than were killed in World War I, the Korean War, and Vietnam combined; nearly as many died in battle in World War II. Each year cigarettes kill five times more Americans than do traffic accidents. Lung cancer alone kills as many as die on the road. *The cigarette industry is peddling a deadly weapon. It is dealing in people's lives for financial gain.* . (Emphasis added)

Senate Minority Leader Everett McKinley Dirksen of Illinois died in 1969 shortly after a lung cancer operation. Among his last words were, "Give me a cigarette."

William Talman, who played Hamilton Burger on the Perry Mason television show, made a commercial in 1969 telling viewers:

> I have lung cancer. Take some advice about smoking and losing from someone who's been doing both for years. If you haven't smoked, don't start. If you do smoke, quit. Don't be a loser.

Mr. Talman died prior to the commercial being shown.

The Federal Trade Commission persuaded Congress in 1970 to upgrade the 1971 cigarette package warnings to say that cigarette smoking is "dangerous" and to ban all cigarette radio and television advertising effective January 2, 1971.[15] The Supreme Court upheld the legislation banning radio and television cigarette advertising in 1971.[16]

In 1971 the British Royal College of Physicians of London, in its second report, "Smoking and Health Now," referred to the annual toll caused by cigarette smoking as "the present holocaust." [17]

Airlines in 1973 were required to have separate seating areas for smokers and nonsmokers on domestic flights.

Actor John Wayne, who once described himself as a "Camel fan 'going' on 24 years," died from cancer at age 67 in 1979, 15 years after he had a lung removed. Jesse Owens, who started smoking after winning three gold medals in the 1936 Olympics in Berlin, died of lung cancer at age 67 in 1980.

Joseph A. Califano, Jr., Secretary of Health, Education and Welfare during the Carter administration, warned in 1978 that smoking is "slow motion suicide."[18] An HEW survey during Secretary Califano's tenure revealed that nearly four million teens and subteens were regular smokers.[19]

Secretary Califano was apparently forced to resign before the 1980 election partially because of his anti-smoking activities.

Department of Health and Human Services Acting Assistant Health Secretary Dr. Edward Brandt testified in 1983 as follows before a Congressional committee:[20]

> Cigarette smoking is clearly the single most important preventable cause of premature illness and death in the United States. Estimates of the number of deaths related to smoking exceed 300,000 annually. One may compare this figure with the 105,000 deaths that occur each year as a result of all injuries, 20,000 deaths from homicides, or the 40,000 infant deaths.

Congress in 1984 required all cigarette manufacturers and advertisers to have one of the following four warnings on each pack of cigarettes or advertisements to be rotated quarterly:[21]

SURGEON GENERAL'S WARNING: Smoking Causes Lung
    Cancer, Heart Disease, and Emphysema;

SURGEON GENERAL'S WARNING: Quitting Smoking

    'Now Greatly Reduces Serious Health Risks;'

SURGEON GENERAL'S WARNING: Pregnant Women Who

    'Smoke Risk Fetal Injury and Premature Birth;'

SURGEON GENERAL'S WARNING: Cigarette Smoke
    Contains Carbon Monoxide

Actor Yul Brynner best known for his role in "The King and I" and who began smoking at age 12 died of lung cancer in 1985 at age 65. Just before his death he taped the following television spot to be released after his death:[22]

> I really wanted to make a commercial when I discovered that I was that sick and my time was so limited. To make a commercial that says, simply, "Now that I'm gone, I tell you, Don't smoke. Whatever you do, just don't smoke." If I could take back that smoking, I wouldn't be talking about any cancer. I'm convinced of that.

Surgeon General Dr. C. Everett Koop in a 1986 report entitled "The Health Consequences of Involuntary Smoking" documented that nonsmokers face serious health risks if exposed to the smoke of others.[23]

Smoking was banned on all domestic airline flights of less than two hours in 1988.

Patrick Reynolds, the grandson of R.J. Reynolds, testified on July 18, 1986, before the House of Representatives' Energy and Commerce Committee's Subcommittee on Health and Environment as follows:[24]

> When my grandfather began making cigarettes he did not know that they caused heart disease, lung disease and cancer....Am I biting the hand that feeds me? If the hand that once fed me is the tobacco industry, then that same hand has killed millions of people and may kill millions more.

Reynolds pledged to help reach Surgeon General Koop's goal of a "smoke-free society by the year 2000."

Surgeon General Koop reported in 1989 that smoking takes 390,000 American lives each year and that the average male smoker is 15 times more likely to die from lung cancer than a nonsmoker.[25]

Sammy Davis, Jr., a multi-talented entertainer who often performed with cigarette in hand, died in 1990 at age 65 of throat cancer. He quit smoking nine months before his death, but smoked two packs a day most of his life.

The General Accounting Office, the investigative arm of the United States Congress, issued a report on May 15, 1990 entitled "Dichotomy Between U.S. Tobacco Export and Antismoking Initiatives" which pointed out:[26]

> In some ways, a policy level conflict exists between U.S. trade goals and health policy objectives in regard to the export of tobacco products. On the one hand, federal resources are used to facilitate the export of U.S. tobacco and tobacco products, while on the other hand the federal government has directed a major antismoking effort and is a participant in the international antismoking movement.

The World Health Organization in 1990 estimated that if smoking continued at the current levels, worldwide annual deaths from smoking would increase from the current three million to over ten million by the year 2020.[27]

Smoking was banned on most domestic airline flights in 1990.

The American Medical Association in a December 4, 1990 statement to the Environmental Protection Agency recommended that environmental tobacco smoke be classified as a human carcinogen, a substance that produces cancer. In the last paragraph of its statement, the American Medical Association said the following about the tobacco industry:[28]

We know of no other industry which would be allowed to produce a product which kills so many. It is now clear that *tobacco is lethal, not only to those who use it as intended by the manufacturer but to those who have not assumed those risks.* (Emphasis added)

Dr. Louis Sullivan, former Secretary of Health and Human Services, in early 1991 submitted a proposed executive order to the George Bush White House seeking to ban smoking in all federal buildings.[29] The proposed executive order was not implemented. Secretary Sullivan also advised parents that "I can't think of a more compelling reason for parents to quit smoking than ensuring their children's chance for a healthy life."[30]

After examining portions of two buildings containing federal offices in a major city downtown area where smoking was not permitted, a health physicist knowledgeable in indoor air pollution testified in a July 1991 administrative proceeding.[31] When asked what would happen if smoking were to be initiated in these facilities, the expert said the work areas would be turned into "gas chambers." The "gas chamber" observation is consistent with what airline passengers and crews were subjected to before smoking was banned on domestic flights and what they are being subjected to on most international flights. The "gas chamber" analogy is consistent with a February 1, 1991 Federal Court of Appeals decision holding that a nonsmoking prisoner's exposure to secondary tobacco smoke from a smoking cellmate could constitute cruel and unusual punishment in violation of the Eighth Amendment of the Constitution. *McKinney v. Anderson*, 924 F.2d 1500 (9th Cir. 1991). The case was appealed to the United States Supreme Court. The Supreme Court on June 18, 1993 affirmed or upheld the Court of Appeals decision. *Helling v. McKinney*, 113 S. Ct. 2475 (1993)

A December 1991 review at Manchester University in England of 143 scientific studies concluded that children who are exposed to routine cigarette smoke are more likely to suffer from at least 50 different illnesses including asthma, bronchitis, sudden death syndrome, middle ear infection and adolescent meningitis.[32] Dr. Alan Luskin of the Rush Medical Center in Chicago in June 1992[33] and Dr. William Cahan of the Memorial Sloan-Kettering Cancer Center in New York in August 1992[34] expressed the opinion that parents who smoke in the presence of children are guilty of child abuse. Parental exposure of children to the toxins and carcinogens of secondary tobacco smoke is cruel and unusual punishment to these millions of innocent children.

New Jersey Federal District Court Judge H. Lee Sarokin on February 6, 1992 in *Haines v. Liggett Group, Inc.,* 140 F.R.D. 681,683 (D. N.J. 1992), said that "the tobacco industry may be the king of concealment and disinformation."

During his campaign in June 1992, President Bill Clinton issued the following statement with regard to his record and position on smoking:[35]

> I strongly believe that we must continue education and awareness programs addressing the serious health risks of using tobacco products. A Clinton Administration will consider any new scientific evidence about tobacco addiction that would merit strengthening existing or placing new warning labels on packaging and advertisements. As President, I would certainly be willing to open a dialogue with other nations about the possibility of banning smoking on international commercial passenger airline flights.

> As Governor of Arkansas, I have played an active role in tobacco related issues. I am particularly concerned about tobacco usage among young people. I have signed legislation making it illegal to place tobacco vending machines in public places that are accessible to people under 18 years of age and prohibiting the free distribution of tobacco products in public areas around schools and playgrounds or to any person under 18 years of age.

> Workplace smoking is also a very important issue. I have signed a law requiring all state agencies to implement a smoking policy for their general office space. I vetoed a bill that would have prohibited employers from hiring only non-smokers and potentially given smokers rights in the workplace itself, which I believe is inappropriate. While Americans plainly may smoke in many circumstances, smoking is an acquired behavior and given the overwhelming evidence of the toll it takes every year in disease and death, it should not be accorded legal protection like freedom of speech, nor should smokers be a protected class like those who have been wrongly discriminated against because of race, sex, age or physical handicaps.

> I personally am not now and have never been a smoker.

President Clinton on August 10, 1995 proposed comprehensive regulations in an effort to curtail teenage smoking including banning vending machine sales, banning brand-name sponsorship of sporting events, requiring cigarette buyers to prove they are 18 or older and requiring the tobacco industry to spend at least $150 million annually in a campaign to deter young persons from smoking.[36] The President said the measures were necessary in order to curb the recent rapid growth of tobacco use among young persons.[37] The Chief Executive pointed out at the August 10, 1995 news conference that "Cigarettes and smokeless tobacco are harmful, highly addictive and aggressively marketed to our young people. The evidence is overwhelming, and the threat is immediate."[38] The regulations were finalized August 28, 1996. 61 Fed. Reg. 44396-44618.

President Clinton is the first President to ban smoking in the White House and in February 1994 backed legislation banning smoking in all buildings used by the public. However, he has not approved an executive order banning smoking in all federal buildings and has perhaps created a false image by being photographed with a cigar in his mouth on more than one occasion.

Wayne McLaren, the Marlboro Man, died July 25, 1992, of lung cancer at age 51. His mother said that some of his last words were, "Tobacco will kill you, and I am living proof of it."[39]

Eddie Kendricks of the Temptations died of lung cancer on October 5, 1992 at age 52. He attributed his illness to 30 years of smoking.[40]

Scientists at the Environmental Protection Agency in June 1992 released a draft report analyzing how secondary tobacco smoke or passive smoking adversely affects respiratory health.[41] The draft report warned that each year environmental tobacco smoke causes 3,000 lung-cancer deaths, contributes from 150,000 to 300,000 respiratory infections in babies, triggers 8,000 to 26,000 new cases of asthma in previously unaffected children, and exacerbates symptoms in 400,000 to one million asthmatic children.[42] The report was adopted in final revised form by the Environmental Protection Agency in December 1992 and released in January 1993.

In 1994 the American Medical Association agreed with Dr. David Kessler, Commissioner of the Food and Drug Administration, in calling for the regulation of nicotine as a drug.[43]

Men and women have been warned of the dangers of tobacco smoke since King James I *Counterblast to Tobacco* in 1604. Some medical authorities as early as 1923 and 1924 saw the dangers of tobacco smoke, but the cigarette companies ignored the warnings and continued to produce a lethal product. They paid movie stars and athletes to glorify the alleged virtues of smoking. Many physicians ignored the mounting evidence and implicitly or explicitly supported the tobacco industry.

When as a child in the late 1940s I saw both my parents coughing and wheezing from smoking more than two packs of cigarettes a day, I wondered how any human being could survive in a cloud of smoke which irritated his or her eyes, nose and throat. I warned my parents that smoking would kill them. My father's response was that he would rather live fewer years and experience the "joys" of smoking. After developing emphysema and incurring several strokes, undoubtedly smoking related, my father eventually succumbed to poisonous tobacco smoke. The quality of my mother's life was greatly diminished through her shortness of breath attributable to lung and heart problems caused by smoking.

One gets angry or fumes when seeing the wasted opportunities to save human lives the past 390 years since King James I observed that "smoking is a custom loathsome to the eye, hateful to the nose, harmful to the brain, and dangerous to the lungs." Americans largely ignored the numerous Reader's Digest articles beginning in 1924 about the harmful effects of smoking and health. We ignored the 1927 Lancet medical journal article observing that in almost every case of lung cancer, the patient smoked. We largely downplayed similar findings in a 1936 American Medical Association Journal article and findings by a physician at the Tulane School of Medicine. The 1938 findings of a John Hopkins University biology professor indicating shorter life spans for smokers were cast aside. We overlooked the fact that a number of heavy smoking athletes and entertainers were dying of lung cancer. Not much was done when a 1949 Gallup Poll revealed that more than 50 percent of Americans believed smoking was harmful to their health. Neither a 1953 American Cancer Society study showing the death rate of smokers was 68 percent higher than for nonsmokers nor a similar study a year later indicating the death rate for smokers was 75% higher had a marked impact on smoking.

Despite the mounting evidence of smoking being a major cause of cancer, it took a reporter's presidential news conference random and unexpected question for which President John F. Kennedy atypically was not prepared and did not have an answer to bring the Federal health machinery to bear on this deadly problem. The advisory committee established by President Kennedy largely in response to the reporter's question concluded in early 1964 that smoking was a major cause of lung cancer in men and contributed to many forms of chronic lung disease. Warnings on cigarette packages and other advertisements followed as well as banning radio and television ads in 1971. Eventually smoking was banned on most domestic airline flights.

The Surgeon General in 1986 issued a report documenting that nonsmokers face serious health risks if exposed to smoke of others. My observations as a young boy 35 years earlier were confirmed by the Surgeon General. It was not surprising when the American Medical Association in December 1990 emphasized that tobacco is lethal.

Fortunately the published results of these studies have resulted in the reduction of adult smokers from 40 percent in 1964 to 25.5% in 1990.[44] However, more than 46 million adults and a significant number of minors still smoke. Each year nearly a half million Americans and three million human beings around the world die prematurely from tobacco smoke and secondary tobacco smoke and many more are rendered seriously ill.

This premature termination of human lives and suffering from unnecessary illnesses leaves me fuming. Producing and advertising a product that when used exactly as the manufacturer intends causing the premature death of nearly a half million Americans and rendering many more seriously ill leaves me fuming. Losing members of one's family, friends and co-workers to avoidable tobacco-related death or serious illness makes me fume. Exposing 200 million nonsmoking Americans to toxins and carcinogens from poisonous tobacco smoke leaves me fuming. The attempt by tobacco companies to mislead the American public about the health impact of smoking for more than half a century makes me angry. The tobacco companies' preying on minors through Joe Camel type ads, on women through "you've come a long way baby" and "Slims" type ads, and on minorities, makes be fume. The tobacco PACs and lobbyists who make monetary contributions to nearly half the members of Congress hoping to prevent needed legislation to heavily tax cigarettes, ban tobacco advertising, prohibit smoking in public facilities and encourage stricter enforcement of tougher laws prohibiting the sale and access of tobacco to minors leave me fuming. It is no wonder that the tobacco companies have been referred to as the merchants of death.

The primary purpose of this book is to set forth insights and ideas that can be utilized against the tobacco industry in order to help save lives, prevent human beings from succumbing to unnecessary serious illnesses, and in so doing perhaps alleviating the health care cost crisis which was estimated to be $939.9 billion in 1993.[45] Every nonsmoker in this country can help meet these goals and make Dr. Koop's goal of a "smoke-free society by the year 2000" a reality.

ENDNOTES

[1] The World Almanac – 1993, p. 387.

[2] *Id.*, at p. 385.

[3] Morbidity and Mortality Weekly Report, Centers for Disease Control and Prevention, 4/2/93, Vol. 42, No. 12, pp. 230-233, reported that an estimated 25.7% of adults in 1991 were current smokers.

[4] Morbidity and Mortality Weekly Report, Centers for Disease Control and Prevention, reported in "Substance Abuse: The Nation's Number One Health Problem," prepared by the Institute for Health Policy, Brandeis University for The Robert Wood Johnson Foundation, Princeton, New Jersey, 10/93, pp. 32-33.

[5] "Passive Smoking and Heart Disease," Stanton A. Glantz, Ph.D., and William W. Parmley, M.D., American Heart Association, *Circulation*, Vol. 83, No. 1, 1/91, p. 10.

[6] Feinstein, John, "A Baseball Tradition – Chewing Tobacco – That Can Be Deadly," Health Section, Washington Post, 10-19-93, pp. 12-15 at `15.

[7] Mintz, Morton, "Tobacco Roads – Delivering Death to the Third World," Progressive, 5/91, pp. 24-26 at 25.

[8] White, Larry, Merchants of Death, Beech Tree Books, 1988, p. 21.

[9] Tobias, Andrew, Kids Say Don't Smoke (Smokefree Educational Services, Inc.), Workman Publishing Company, Inc., 1991; Reynolds, Patrick and Shachtman, Tom, The Gilded Leaf, Little, Brown and Company, 1989, pp. 315-316.

[10] Tobias, Andrew, supra.

[11] The references of historical developments by year, unless otherwise indicated, come from "Tobacco Road," William Ecenbarger, Philadelphia Inquirer Magazine, 11/17/91, p. 16 et seq., at p. 17.

[12] Bartlett, John and Kaplan, Justine, Bartlett's Familiar Quotations, Little, Brown and Company, Sixteenth Edition (1992), p. 582.

[13] Meyer, Dr. John A., "Cigarette Century," American Heritage, 12/92.

[14] New York State Journal of Medicine, Vol. 83, No. 13, 12/83, p. 1249.

[15] Public Law 91-222, Public Health Cigarette Smoking Act of 1969.

[16] Capitol Broadcasting Co. v. Acting Attorney General, 405 U.S. 1000 (1972), (mem.), aff'd. sub. nom. Capitol Broadcasting v. Mitchell, 333 F. Supp. 582 (D. D.C. 1971).

[17] Taylor, Peter, The Smoke Ring – Tobacco, Money & Multi-National Politics; Pantheon Books, 1984, p. xiv.

[18] Califano, Joseph A., Jr., Governing America, Simon & Schuster, 1981, p. 185.

[19] Id. at p. 195.

[20] See footnote 11, "Tobacco Road" at p. 35.

[21] P.L. 98-474, 15 U.S.C. §1331, Comprehensive Smoking Education Act.

[22] Meyer, Dr. John A., Lung Cancer Chronicles, Rutgers University Press 1990, p. ix.

[23] U.S. Department of Health and Human Services, The Health Consequences of Involuntary Smoking. A Report of the Surgeon General (1986).

[24] Reynolds, Patrick and Shachtman, Tom, The Gilded Leaf, Little Brown & Company (1989), p. 316.

[25] "Secondhand Smoke" Pamphlet, Association for Nonsmokers – Minnesota, 8/91.

[26] "Dichotomy Between U.S. Tobacco Export and Antismoking Initiatives," General Accounting Office, 5/15/90.

[27] Mintz, Morton, "Tobacco Roads – Delivering Death to the Third World," supra at footnote 7.

[28] Statement of the AMA to the EPA Science Advisory Board, Indoor Air Quality and Total Human Exposure Committee, December 4, 1990.

[29] "No Smoking Policy Proposed for All Federal Buildings," Federal Times, 4/8/91, p. 3; "Sullivan firing up antismoking debate," Minneapolis Star Tribune, 4/28/91, p. 10A; "Health chief wants ban on smoking in federal buildings," Chicago Tribune, 3/7/91, Sec. 1.

[30] "Secondhand Smoke" Pamphlet, supra.

[31] The examination was conducted by James L. Repace, a health physicist and Senior Analyst in the Air Policy Office of the U.S. Environmental Protection Agency.

[32] "Kids get sick from second-hand smoke," Gary-Post Tribune, 1/7/92, p. A5, referring to an article in the Journal for the Association of Nonsmokers Rights entitled "Children and Passive Smoking," by Anne Charlton, 12/91.

[33] "Asthma – Deadly but Treatable," Time, 6/22/92, p. 62.

[34] "Smoking Issue Is Heating Up Custody Suits," Wall Street Journal, 8/17/92, p. B1.

[35] Fall 1992, SmokeFree Air.

[36] "Clinton Proposes Widespread Curbs on Young Smokers," New York Times, 8/11/95, A-1, 18-19.

[37] Id.

[38] Id.

[39] "'Marlboro Man' Wayne McLaren, 51, Lung Cancer Victim," Chicago Sun-Times, 7/25/92, p. 37.

[40] "Eddie Kendricks, 52; Sang Falsetto with Temptations," Chicago Sun-Times, 10/7/92, p. 79.

[41] United States Environmental Protection Agency, Office of Research and Development, Office of Air and Radiation, "Respiratory Health Effects of Passive Smoking: Lung Cancer and Other Disorders," SAB Review Draft, 5/92.

[42] United States Environmental Protection Agency, Office of Research and Development, Office of Air and Radiation, "Respiratory Health Effects of Passive Smoking: Lung Cancer and Other Disorders," 12/92.

[43] Tobacco on Trial, 2/95, p. 3.

[44] See Footnote 3.

[45] "Health-care costs: The bad news just keeps getting worse," Joan Beck, Chicago Tribune, 1/7/93, Sec. 1, p. 23.

II

MEDICAL - THE MEDICINE MEN,
NOT TOBACCO MEN

Ihave occasionally heard an irritated person say that "smoking makes me sick." There is far more wisdom engrained in that complaint than one may realize. Smoking not only makes one sick in nearly every way imaginable, but tobacco smoke and secondary tobacco smoke are responsible for the premature deaths of nearly a half million Americans and three million human beings around the world each year.

The danger of smoking has not been a newly discovered secret. As previously pointed out, King James I in his 1604 *Counterblast to Tobacco* observed that "Smoking is a custom loathsome to the eye, hateful to the nose, harmful to the brain, and dangerous to the lungs."[1] This astute observation was reinforced and illustrated by Gary Trudeau in his Doonesbury cartoon, wherein a Dartmouth Medical College Physiology Professor pointed out in a medical textbook in 1885 that smoking is harmful to every aspect of the body.[2] A growing number of articles starting in the November 1924 Readers Digest entitled "Does Tobacco Injure the Human Body?"[3] warned Americans of the dangers of smoking. In response to the issuance of the 1964 Surgeon General's Report "Smoking and Health," effective January 1, 1966 all cigarette packages had to contain the warning to consumers that cigarette smoking "may be hazardous to your health."[4]

The Assistant Secretary for Health of the Department of Health and Human Services testified before Congress in 1983 that "Cigarette smoking is clearly the single most important preventable cause of premature illness and death in the United States."[5] Congress in 1984 required cigarette manufacturers and advertisers to have one of four warnings on each pack or an advertisement warning that smoking causes lung cancer, heart disease and emphysema, as well as risks of fetal injury and premature birth for pregnant women.[6]

Former Surgeon General Koop warned in a 1986 report entitled "The Health Consequences of Involuntary Smoking" that nonsmokers face serious health risks if exposed to the smoke of others.[7] A December 1991 review at Manchester University in England of 143 studies concluded that children who are exposed to routine cigarette smoke are more likely to suffer from at least 50 different illnesses.[8] The Environmental Protection Agency in December 1992 classified secondary tobacco smoke as a Class A carcinogen that each year causes 3,000 lung-cancer deaths, contributes from 150,000 to 300,000 respiratory infections in babies, triggers 8,000 to 20,000 new cases of asthma in previously unaffected children, and exacerbates symptoms in 400,000 to one million asthmatic children.[9]

As a young boy I remember the tobacco company commercials bragging that they were not medicine men, but tobacco men. Unfortunately, too many persons listened to those commercials and other similar ads rather than to knowledgeable physicians. They regretfully relied on the tobacco men and ignored the medicine men warnings. Many died prematurely or became seriously ill. They suffered needlessly from lung cancer, emphysema, and heart disease. They risked other forms of cancer, osteoporosis, asthma, and other illnesses and diseases. They endangered the health and lives of their unborn children and their children. Unfortunately, they only listened to the tobacco men.

I am reminded of the story of the fellow on his death bed for whom they had given up all hope. Suddenly he took a turn – for the nurse! Why? He decided to give up smoking and had new hope. Unfortunately most smoking-related illnesses do not have this happy ending. The endings too frequently are enveloped in agony and trauma for the victims and their loved ones.

A vivid summary of the dangers of smoking is contained in an award-winning poster by Decatur, Illinois eighth-grader Adrian Carson in the 1993 American Medical Association- Surgeon General poster contest. Mr. Carson's poster depicts 26 reasons in alphabetical order why smoking is harmful including cancer risks, emphysema, and weakened lungs. See Chapter V, "One Cartoon Equals 1,000 Anti-Tobacco Words," footnote 12.[10] Many school children are far more cognizant and concerned with the dangers of tobacco and tobacco smoke than their parents. Children have good reasons to be concerned.

A 1992 study showed that sudden infant death syndrome is associated with smoking during pregnancy. After congenital abnormalities, sudden infant death syndrome is the most common cause of infant death in the United States and it is the leading cause of death among infants over a month old.[11] One of the strongest risk factors is maternal smoking during pregnancy. Past studies have consistently shown a two-fold to four-fold higher risk of sudden infant death syndrome among infants whose mothers smoked during pregnancy compared with infants whose mothers did not smoke even after controlling for other factors.[12] A recent study showed that children whose mothers smoke during pregnancy had significantly lower IQ scores than the children of nonsmokers.[13]

The Dartmouth Medical College physiology professor was correct when he pointed out in 1885 that smoking is injurious to many parts of the body - many not even dreamed of and others known for many years.[14] Hopefully, recent studies linking diseases and illnesses to smoking and implicating a wide variety of lesser publicized illnesses and diseases will encourage smokers to stop and nonsmoking minorities and women to resist the temptation of dangerous tobacco industry products.

1. LUNG CANCER

There are a few occasions in a lifetime that are more devastating than when a person is informed by his or her physician that he or she has cancer. The victim is stunned as are family and close friends. The question "why me?" is frequently asked. There is often no readily ascertainable answer. And then what could he or she have done to prevent this frightening and often terminal illness. The answer to this question is frequently summarized in just two words - "stop smoking."

One of the major cancer killers is lung cancer with over 140,000 Americans dying of this horrible illness each year. Smoking is a major cause of lung cancer. The American Cancer Society estimated that there would be 161,000 new cases of lung cancer diagnosed in 1991 and 143,000 deaths.[15] Lung cancer is the leading preventable cause of death in the United States. Studies going back to the 1920s have linked smoking with lung cancer.

Despite overwhelming scientific and medical evidence, the tobacco industry continues to dispute this linkage. The tobacco companies appear to be arguing that since there are other causes of lung cancer, the linkage has not been absolutely proven. The smoking-lung cancer linkage has been proven beyond any reasonable doubt, the standard which we use to prove guilt in criminal cases which can result in executions. If it were 90 percent certain that the brakes in a certain make of car were defective, the vehicles would be recalled. If there were a 90 percent chance that a drug might cause deformities in a human being, that drug would be immediately pulled off the market. And if there were a 90 percent chance that a child's toy could cause an eye injury, the toy would be recalled. The tobacco industry wants special treatment. It wants an absolute certainty standard. The tobacco industry wants carte blanche permission to play tobacco roulette with the health of over 200 million nonsmoking and 46 million smoking Americans regardless of the cancer risk.

There is no question from a scientific or medical standpoint that smoking enormously increases the risk of lung cancer. Tobacco companies apparently do not care. They have fought nearly every effort to eliminate or confine the use of tobacco products. They have fought the elimination of smoking in restaurants, airplanes and other public facilities. They have lobbied hard against the elimination or restriction of Joe Camel types of advertising that get kids hooked on cigarettes at an early age. They have fought hard to stave off federal and state cigarette tax increases which would discourage people from stopping smoking for economic reasons. The tobacco companies do not appear to care who or how many human beings die from lung cancer. Instead of discouraging smoking in the household, through Joe Camel type ads they encourage kids smoking or approve their smoking.

The primary concern of tobacco companies is profit. Ask the families and friends of Yul Brynner and John Wayne what they think of the tobacco industry's concern about human life. The same question should have been asked of tobacco family member Patrick Reynolds. Every tobacco industry official should be required to spend a week in a hospital ward or a nursing home with lung cancer patients and their families. Perhaps their consciences would become activated and their perspective of making money at any cost would change.

Hopefully some day the United States will be a kinder and gentler nation. Then we will not permit the premature killing off of nearly a half million Americans each year through tobacco smoke and secondary tobacco smoke and export death and disease through American tobacco products. Notwithstanding First Amendment rights, American have the right to breathe air free from carcinogens and toxins of poisonous tobacco smoke and secondary tobacco smoke as to minimize the risk of serious diseases such has lung cancer. Exposure of secondary tobacco smoke to nonsmokers also violates a fundamental moral principle, the Seventh Commandment, which says "Thou shalt not kill."

Former HEW Secretary Califano in 1978 called smoking "slow-motion suicide."[16] The process starts when the carcinogens and toxins from tobacco smoke enter one's lungs with the initial puff of one's first cigarette and frequently comes to a premature conclusion shortly after a cough or gasp from the last cigarette.

The American Cancer Society reported in February 1990 that smoking is responsible for more than 87% of lung cancer cases overall, smoking increases the risk of cancer tenfold, and smoking has made lung cancer the number one cancer killer of American women.[17] Smoking is specifically related to 80% of emphysema and 75% of chronic bronchitis cases.

The Surgeon General estimated in 1989 that smoking is responsible for more than one of every six deaths in the United States and that accounted for 87% of lung cancer deaths in males and 75% in females in 1985.[18] The Environmental Protection Agency in December 1992 estimated that approximately 3,800 annual lung cancer deaths are attributable to environmental tobacco smoke in the United States.[19]

An industry that produces a lethal consumer product that when used as intended causes death or serious illness or disease should be characterized as immoral or amoral. Elected public officials who accept tobacco industry and tobacco PAC money, of which nearly half of Congress does, and fails to take the necessary steps to eradicate this country's tobacco holocaust are likewise immoral or amoral. Tobacco industry officials and those elected officials in their hip pockets are a plague on our society. The killing and rendering seriously ill adults and children through the selfish, self-serving and unconscionable spreading of poisonous secondary tobacco smoke should no longer be tolerated. The nation's over 200 million nonsmokers should unify to eradicate smoking and slow down the spread of dreaded diseases such as lung cancer.

2. OTHER CANCERS

Although the focus thus far has been on lung cancer, studies have shown a linkage between smoking and other cancers. For example, a study reported in the February 1994 Journal of the National Cancer Institute (NCI) found strong evidence that cigarette smoking can lead to colon or rectal cancer in both men and women.[20] The NCI Journal editorial noted other studies have shown linkages between smoking and cancers of the pancreas, bladder, and kidney.[21]

It is not surprising after knowing for years that smoking is a leading cause of lung cancer that researchers have also concluded that smoking is a cause of adult leukemia, a cancer arising in the body's blood-forming tissues.

The lead author of a 1993 report, Ross Brownson of the Missouri Department of Health, analyzed 15 studies since the 1970's.[22] The incidence of acute nyloid leukemia, an adult leukemia, in smokers was 40% greater than in nonsmokers. The incidence in smokers for all leukemias was 30% greater than in nonsmokers and in people who smoked 20 or more cigarettes a day the risk was increased by sixty percent.

3. HEART

There has been a great deal of publicity linking smoking to lung cancer. Less attention has been given to the linkage between smoking and heart disease.

The American Heart Association reported in 1992 that a smokers' risk of heart attack is more than twice that of nonsmokers.[23] A recent Oxford University study revealed that smokers in their 30's and 40's have five times as many heart attacks as nonsmokers in the same age group.[24] The British Study also found that smokers in their 50's tripled the risk of heart attack and those in their 60's and 70's doubled that risk.[25] Cigarette smoking is the biggest risk factor for sudden cardiac death. Smokers who have a heart attack are more likely to die and die suddenly (within an hour) than nonsmokers.

Recent studies indicate that chronic exposure to secondary tobacco smoke increases the risk of heart disease.[26] Smoking is also the biggest risk factor for peripheral vascular disease which involves the narrowing of blood vessels carrying blood to leg and arm muscles.

Inhaling cigarette smoke has several temporary adverse effects on the heart and blood vessels.[27] The nicotine in tobacco smoke increases a person's blood pressure, heart rate, the amount of blood pumped into the heart, and blood flow in the heart arteries. Nicotine also causes narrowing of arm and leg arteries.

Carbon monoxide gets into the blood, reducing the amount of oxygen available to the heart and the rest of the body.[28] Tobacco smoke causes blood platelets to become sticky and cluster, shortens platelet survival, decreases clotting time, and increases blood thickness. It appears that smoking does to the heart what a blindfold would do for a driver - enormously increases the chances of a preventable disaster.

Smoking is a major risk factor of peripheral muscular disease, the narrowing of blood vessels that carry blood to the arms and legs.[29] If a blood clot blocks a narrowed artery, the result could be damage to or a loss of a leg. Diabetes is a major risk factor for peripheral vascular disease. Diabetics who smoke increase the risk of peripheral vascular disease.

Arteriosclerosis occurs when deposits build up on the inner walls of the arteries, narrowing the blood vessels and reducing their elasticity.[30] Arteries clogged with fatty deposits are a major cause of stroke and heart attack. Hardening of the heart arteries occurs more often in smokers than in nonsmokers and when it occurs, it tends to be more severe.

The three major risk factors of heart attack are cigarette smoking, high blood pressure and high levels of fat (e.g. cholesterol).[31] The risk of a heart attack increases the more a person smokes. Individuals who smoke a pack a day have more than twice the risk of persons who never smoked. Those who smoke two or more packs a day have a risk of heart attack three times greater than nonsmokers. Moreover, smokers have less of a chance of surviving a heart attack than nonsmokers.

Smoking is the primary cause of chronic lung diseases - chronic bronchitis and emphysema.[32] These chronic lung diseases place additional pressure on the heart when heart disease is present and may result in heart failure.

Of the nearly half million premature deaths due to tobacco smoke and secondary tobacco smoke each year, it has been estimated that anywhere from 115,000 to 200,000 were attributable to cardiovascular disease.[33] This does not include the hundreds of thousands of victims who survive, but who are seriously ill. It has been estimated that over 70 million Americans have one or more forms of heart or blood vessel disease including 63.4 million with high blood pressure, 6.2 million with coronary artery disease, three million who have survived a stroke, and 1.3 million with rheumatic heart disease. Millions of heart or blood vessel disease victims and their families could have been spared the pain, agony, and personal loss that cardiovascular disease imposes if only the smokers had not believed the misrepresentations and deceptions of the tobacco companies. To paraphrase a line in a well-known song, heartache does bring heartbreak. The cigarette companies and tobacco industry have brought heartache and heartbreak to millions of American families through their being a primary cause of heart disease.

4. STROKE

A stroke is one of the most devastating illnesses from both a physical and mental standpoint. It is the third leading cause of death of Americans behind only heart disease and cancer.[34] A stroke frequently results in paralysis and loss of mental function. It invariably results in a lowering of one's quality of life. About a half million persons suffer a stroke each year and about 30% die from strokes.[35] It is the third leading cause of death frequently has a devastating impact on victims' families.[36]

Smoking can be a significant cause of a stroke. Strokes occur when a blood vessel carrying oxygen to the brain clogs or bursts. Nerve cells die within minutes, causing the part of the body they control not to function. Paralysis frequently results.

A 1991 British study concluded that middle-aged men who have high blood pressure and smoke more than 20 cigarettes daily are ten times more likely to suffer a stroke than nonsmokers with normal blood pressure.[37] Smokers with normal blood pressure increase their risk of stroke to 2.5 times that of nonsmokers.

A 1993 Finnish study found that the most serious strokes which usually result in death or permanent paralysis were more than seven times likely to hit men who smoked more than 20 cigarettes a day than men who had never smoked.[38] A recent Harvard study confirmed that cigarette smoking is a major cause of hemorrhage stroke among women and smoking cessation leads to a decline in risk.

Every smoker and minor contemplating smoking should visit a hospital stroke rehabilitation floor or similar nursing home section. The sight may convince them that Marlboro country is just one's local cemetery.

5. CHRONIC OBSTRUCTIVE PULMONARY DISEASE (COPD) (EMPHYSEMA AND CHRONIC BRONCHITIS)

Emphysema is a chronic lung disease which most frequently occurs after many years of smoking.[39] It affects more than 1.6 million Americans. As emphysema progresses, the victim's lungs become scarred and filled with useless air sacs that crowd out healthy tissue, making breathing difficult.

Chronic obstructive pulmonary disease encompasses patients with emphysema or chronic bronchitis.[40] In most cases the symptoms include a history of cigarette smoking, chronic cough and sputum production in chronic bronchitis and dyspnea in emphysema, airflow limitations on pulmonary function testing, and rhonchi, decreased intensity of breath sounds, and prolonged expiration on physical examination.[41] About ten million Americans have chronic obstructive pulmonary disease.[42]

The following concise summary of the relationship between chronic obstructive pulmonary disease and cigarette smoking is contained in a well known medical treatise:[43]

The first report of the Surgeon General regarding the effects of cigarette smoking appeared in *Smoking and Health* in 1964. The Surgeon General deemed cigarette smoking the principal cause of chronic bronchitis and suggested a relationship to emphysema. Cigarette smoking was judged to exceed atmospheric pollution and environmental exposures as a cause of COPD.[44] Since then further studies have strengthened that conclusion.

Cigarette smoking is presently the single most important preventable environmental factor contributing to illness, disability, and death in the United States and is the main cause of COPD. Compared with nonsmokers, cigarette smokers have higher death rates from chronic bronchitis and emphysema, and an increased prevalence of respiratory symptoms and decreased performance on pulmonary function tests can be detected among smokers, even in the younger age groups. The difference becomes more marked as the number of cigarettes smoked increases. Many studies have shown a very low incidence of COPD in nonsmokers and a relatively high incidence in heavy smokers (20 or more cigarettes daily). Cigarette smokers without symptoms have more evidence of small airways dysfunction than do nonsmokers and about ten times greater risk than nonsmokers of dying from COPD.

In 1986, 71,099 Americans died from chronic obstructive pulmonary disease.[45] Cigarette smoking accounts for most mortality associated with chronic obstructive pulmonary disease.[46]

Every smoker and minor contemplating smoking should visit emphysema and chronic bronchitis patients in nursing homes. Listening to their coughing or labored breathing should be enough to convince them to stop smoking or not to start smoking.

6. ASTHMA

About 15 million Americans suffer from asthma, a chronic condition of the airways of the lungs.[47] The symptoms are wheezing, coughing, and thick mucus in the lungs with chest tightness.[48] An estimated two to five million American children suffer from the lung problem.[49]

A recent study revealed strong new evidence that secondary tobacco smoke causes or worsens the condition in children.[50] The study measured cotinine, a chemical which is a byproduct of nicotine, in their urine. When the doctors counted the number of asthma attacks each child had suffered during the preceding year, they discovered that youngsters exposed to the most secondary tobacco smoke had 70% more attacks compared to children with little or no exposure.

A 1992 study indicated that asthma is the most chronic disease in child-hood and is the leading cause of days lost from school.[51] A survey published in the Archives of Internal Medicine disclosed that 78% of asthma sufferers said that cigarette smoke aggravates their symptoms, while one-third reported exposure to it at home.[52]

The Supreme Court has on many occasions defined what constitutes cruel and unusual punishment including the recent *Helling* decision wherein the court held that placing a nonsmoking prisoner in a cell with a smoker could constitute cruel and unusual punishment in violation of the Eighth Amendment of the Constitution. *Helling* v. *McKinney*, 113 S.Ct. 2475 (1993). A parent subjecting an asthmatic child suffering from constriction of the airways to secondary tobacco smoke in the home or car would appear to constitute a form of child abuse tantamount to cruel and unusual punishment that could trigger a serious attack. To subject any of the 15 million asthmatic Americans to secondary tobacco smoke in a home, restaurant, shopping mall, or other public facility is cruel and inhumane. The right of 15 million asthmatic Americans to breathe is more important than the right of 46 million smoking Americans to spread the carcinogens and toxins of poisonous tobacco smoke in the air in which we breathe.

7. OSTEOPOROSIS

The tobacco industry appears to have geared a substantial amount of its advertising towards attracting women to make up for a portion of the nearly half million Americans who die prematurely each year from tobacco smoke and secondary tobacco smoke. The industry has been silent about one health problem aggravated by smoking that primarily strikes women, osteoporosis.

A two-year study published in the April 1991 Journal of Bone and Mineral Research showed that smoking accelerates bone loss in older women and increases the risk of osteoporosis.[53]

A study reported in the May 1, 1992 Annals of Internal Medicine concludes that estrogen's benefits of preventing bone fractures in older women is wiped out for women who smoke.[54] The National Osteoporosis Foundation advised that women who smoke and take estrogen should stop smoking.[55] Post menopausal women constitute about 70% of the 300,000 Americans who break a hip each year. About 15 to 20 million Americans suffer from osteoporosis which can lead to life threatening pelvic fractures and spinal deformations. Stopping smoking and not starting smoking might help American women avoid this crippling and sometimes fatal disease.

A study reported in the February 10, 1994 New England Journal of Medicine found "compelling evidence of an association between smoking and reduced bone density in women."[56] In a related editorial, it was recommended that doctors tell smokers about the damage they are doing to their bones.

The number of costly hospitalizations and amount of painful suffering could have been avoided by the victims not smoking will never be precisely known, but the medical evidence indicates it is substantial. Despite the influence of Joe Camel type advertising, hopefully the younger generations will learn from the mistakes of their parents and grandparents.

8. HEALING BROKEN BONES

Few events are more frustrating than breaking a bone. Frequently one is cast for six weeks with the inevitable slowing down and curtailment of some activities. Each passing day is one less of normal activity and when the regular prescribed course of healing is completed, there is an easing into the normalcy of activity.

The healing scenario for smokers is frequently more protracted. A study presented in February 1992 at the American Academy of Orthopedic Surgeon's annual meeting confirmed that cigarette smoking may delay the healing of broken bones. It took smokers 50% longer to heal from surgically treated osteomyelitis than nonsmokers.[57] One physician speculated that the nicotine in cigarettes may reduce blood-vessel development which is needed for bone regeneration.

Make no bones about it. Smoking appears to delay bone healing.

9. FOR THE SPECIAL ATTENTION OF WOMEN

Since 1984 one of the four current cigarette label warnings has been "Pregnant Women Who Smoke Risk Fetal injury and Premature Birth." Recent medical findings support the warnings and other smoking-related dangers for women and/or their children.

The United States Centers for Disease Control reported in August 1992 that women who smoke while pregnant are more than twice as likely to deliver underweight babies as mothers who do not smoke.[58] The Centers for Disease Control reported that 11.5% of babies born to smokers were underweight at birth compared with 5.6% for non-smoking mothers.[59] Children whose mothers smoked during pregnancy had significantly lower

IQ scores than the children of nonsmoking mothers according to a study released in February 1994.[60]

A 1992 study at the Baylor College of Medicine revealed that cigarette smoking reduced the production of breast milk to a little more than half the normal rate.[61] Judy Hopkinson, head author of the report, stated that "I think women who smoke cigarettes really need to know that, if they want to successfully breast feed, they're stacking the cards against themselves by continuing to smoke."

A 1991 study at the Medical College of Virginia concluded that women who were smokers or former smokers were more than twice as likely to get urinary incontinence.[62] Dr. Thomas Thorton, a Chicago physician and expert on tobacco-related disease, said the tie makes sense because the bladder and kidneys process cigarette poisons. The physician pointed out that incontinence or the inability to control urine flow may result from nerve or tissue damage. Women of all ages should be quite reluctant to run out and buy a pack of Virginia Slims or any other brand of cigarettes when objectively viewing the severe negative health impact of smoking on members of the female sex.

10. THE BACK

Smoking is a pain in the neck and back.

A study presented at the American Academy of Orthopedic Surgeons meeting in San Francisco in February 1993 suggested that smoking at least a pack of cigarettes a day triples the risk of surgery for a herniated disc while quitting smoking reduces the risks.[63] Discs act as shock absorbers between spinal vertebrae. The findings revealed smoking quadrupled the risk of a serious upper back or neck disc problem and triples the risk for lower back disc problems. Ex-smokers who had not smoked for more than five years had a risk no higher than persons who never smoked. Medical experts believe smoking may cause damage to the back by reducing blood flow to vertebrae, which supply the discs.[64]

Millions of Americans suffer from painful back and neck problems. Many smokers appear to have the choice of smoking in agony or quitting and enjoying a life free or freer of pain. One wonders if smokers with back problems are aware of this important option. Clearly, the tobacco companies through Joe Camel type ads are not informing them of this important health news. Hopefully their physicians and orthopedic surgeons are providing smokers with this vital information.

11. DEPRESSION

It is quite depressing to realize that almost a half million Americans die prematurely each year from tobacco smoke and secondary tobacco smoke and many more Americans become seriously ill. It has been estimated that at least three million human beings around the world die prematurely every year from tobacco smoke and secondary tobacco smoke.

If it is depressing for outside observers to view this avoidable human tragedy, it is not difficult to imagine the impact on the victims and their families. One word sums up these feelings - depression. A recent study out of the Medical College of Virginia in Richmond showed that the incidence of serious depression steadily increases with the number of cigarettes smoked.[65]

The results make sense. If one were to engage in a life-threatening habit such as smoking and began to experience some of the preliminary symptoms of one or more of the numerous smoking related illnesses – e.g., frequent coughing or shortness of breath – there would be a tendency to become depressed.

12. RHEUMATOID ARTHRITIS

It is interesting to observe that some of the pain and suffering in our lives could have been avoided. A Finnish research team reported in 1992 that male smokers are almost eight times more likely to develop rheumatoid arthritis than nonsmokers and about four times more likely than ex-smokers.[66] The Arthritis Foundation estimates that about 2.1 million Americans and 15 million men around the world suffer from this crippling disease.[67]

Since similar findings were not found with women, tobacco smoke may trigger the production of rheumatoid factors which in combination with male hormones, may contribute to the development of arthritis.[68] It appears that smoking makes symptoms such as joint pain and swelling worse in rheumatoid arthritis sufferers.

The study did not deal with the impact of secondary tobacco smoke on rheumatoid arthritis sufferers. Many studies show that smoking kills. This study shows that smoking leads to pain. Tobacco industry spin control spokespersons will contend that these medical findings and those relating to other illnesses are not absolute certainties. In this country we execute human beings who are "guilty beyond a reasonable doubt." The "beyond a reasonable doubt" standard appears to be met in this rheumatoid arthritis study. The standards demanded by the tobacco industry are much higher than government agencies' requirements for recall of foods, medicines, beverages, cars and children's toys posing health or safety risks.

13. EYES

Few of us stop to think about that line "smoke gets in your eyes," from a well-known song. The tobacco companies would like Americans to remember the song, but overlook what happens to a person after tobacco smoke gets into his or her eyes. The lesson to be learned by farsighted Americans who want to minimize eye problems as they get older is not to smoke.

Of course, cigarette smoke irritates eyes and causes tearing. A young child can convey this information. So it was not surprising when in separate studies researchers from Harvard Medical School and Brigham and Woman's Hospital in Boston found that men who smoked a pack or more of cigarettes a day were twice as likely to develop cataracts than non-smokers.[69]

A John Hopkins University scientist reported in April 1993 that smokers are three times more likely than nonsmokers or ex-smokers to progress from minor to serious cataract problems.[70] The more one smokes, the greater the risk of cataracts. The scientist reported that 5.5 million Americans have vision-obstructing cataracts. The annual national health care bill to remove the cataracts amounts to $2.4 billion, funds that could be better utilized insuring the 37 million uninsured Americans and for a meaningful health care reform program with a sound and adequate financial base.

The American Academy of Ophthalmology reported that "smoking is especially bothersome" for a condition called "dry eyes" where some persons do not produce enough tears to keep the eye wet and comfortable.[71]

Two of a person's most precious gifts are the eyes that facilitate a much greater enjoyment of life. The tobacco companies are producing a product that appears to be endangering one's vision, especially as the aging process takes hold. The lesson to be learned by far-sighted Americans who want to minimize eye problems as they get older is do not smoke.

14. DENTAL

Few persons look forward to a trip to the dentist's office. Too often one comes away from the dentist with the sad realization that the pain and expense could have been avoided or minimized if only one took better care of his or her teeth and followed the frequently ignored advice of the dentist.

Not surprisingly smoking aggravates the problem of dental care. Just look at the stained teeth of smokers.

A recent study at the State University of New York at Buffalo showed that smoking is the second leading risk factor for severe gum disease with only aging being greater.[72] The study found that the more one smokes, the greater the risk of gum disease.

The American Dental Association points out that gum disease is a leading cause of tooth loss in adults and smokers are more likely to have severe gum disease than nonsmokers.[73] Smokers have larger deposits of tartar on their teeth than nonsmokers. It has been reported that a number of periodontists will not perform certain procedures on smokers because smoking interferes with healing.[74] Finally, smokers have a much higher risk of developing oral cancer than nonsmokers.[75]

Put that in your pipe, but don't smoke it. Smoking greatly increases the chances of that feared trip to the dentist and greater dental expenses.

15. A NEW WRINKLE

One of the latest wrinkles about smoking concerns "wrinkles." Studies have found that smoking ages the skin of smokers more rapidly than non-smokers. Women who are concerned about appearances as they age should take note. In appearance, smokers age more rapidly than nonsmokers. The next time you attend a high school reunion check out this observation.

A 1991 University of Utah study revealed that smoking more than triples the average person's likelihood of premature facial wrinkling.[76] Dr. Thomas Kotke of the Mayo Clinic stated that "you're going to be old and ugly before your time if you smoke."[77] Women and teenage girls take heed! The changes occur as a result of loss of elasticity and the stricture that supports the skin which leads to the wrinkling. This is not necessarily a picture which complements Virginia Slims ads.

It appears that the news about the adverse effects of smoking is getting uglier with new wrinkles all the time - premature death, serious illness, disease, pain, and premature aging.

16. BUERGER'S DISEASE

The circulation of secondary tobacco smoke in the indoor air we breathe may not be as harmful as the circulation of tobacco smoke within the human body.

A disease not widely known by the general public involves blockage of circulation in the arms and legs from inflammation of blood vessel linings

known as Buerger's Disease.[78] Chest pain is a symptom. Most persons with
Buerger's Disease smoke. When the patient quits smoking, the vessel inflammation and circulation problems usually stop. New vessels might be
created to serve the previously deprived tissue and symptoms subside.

Acute stage Buerger's Disease patients who continue to smoke may in-
cur so much tissue damage that amputation may be required.[79]

17. GRAVES DISEASE

Most people probably had never heard of Grave's disease, an auto immune
disorder that causes thyroid and eye problems, until newspaper stories revealed that former President George Bush and his wife Barbara suffered
from the illness. About 1% to 2% of Americans suffer from the disease in
their lifetime.[80] A Dutch study published in the Journal of the American
Medical Association in January 1993 revealed that smoking increases the
risk of Graves eye disease characterized by protruding eyeballs by about
eight times and doubled the risk of Graves hyperthyroidism.[81] Study results indicate that smoking may have a specific effect on the eye muscles.

The lyric "when smoke gets in your eyes" may lose some of its beauty
to smokers with Graves disease and their families.

18. ESOPHAGUS

Smoking kills kids and injuries others. Unfortunately the young children
are powerless to avoid secondary tobacco smoke's 43 carcinogens and toxins from smoking parents.

One of the more than 50 illnesses to which children are exposed from
secondary tobacco smoke is inflammation of the esophagus. A five-year
University of Toronto study showed the risk of esophygitis increased six-
fold if one parent smokes and seven-fold if both smoke compared to nonsmoking families.[82] What rational parent would knowingly expose his or
her child to avoidable health problems? Unfortunately too many parents
place the "pleasures" of smoking ahead of their children's health.

A CONCLUSORY NOTE

Homespun philosopher Will Rogers once said "The only thing good about tobacco is that it chases the mosquitoes away, which goes to show that mosquitoes are smarter than people."[83] I never realized how billions of insects could be so smart and 46 million smokers so dumb.

Smokers who have read this chapter and continue to smoke might be interested in learning that a cigarette has been defined as "a fire at one end, a fool at the other, and a bit of tobacco in between."[84] The 46 million Americans who continue to smoke and risk lung cancer, heart disease, emphysema, and many other serious illnesses and diseases are the fools.

ENDNOTES

[1] Tobias, Andrew, and Smokefree Educational Services, Workman Publishing Company, Inc., 1991.

[2] Doonesbury cartoon, by Gary Trudeau, Chicago Tribune, Sunday comic section, 5/16/93, *infra* at Chapter V.

[3] "Does Tobacco Injure the Human Body?", Readers Digest, 11/24.

[4] P.L. 89-92, Federal Cigarette Labeling and Advertising Act.

[5] Department of Health and Human Services Acting Assistant Secretary Dr. Edward Brandt reported at "Tobacco Road," William Ecenbarger, Philadelphia Inquirer Magazine, 11/17/91, *supra* at p. 35.

[6] P.L. 98-474, 15 U.S.C. §1331, Comprehensive Smoking Education Act.

[7] U.S. Department of Health and Human Services, The Health Consequences of Involuntary Smoking (1986). A Report of the Surgeon General.

[8] "Kids get sick from second-hand smoke," Gary-Post Tribune, 1/7/92, p. A5, referring to an article in the Journal for the Association of Nonsmokers Rights entitled "Children and Passive Smoking," by Anne Charlton, 12/91.

[9] United States Environmental Protection Agency, Office of Research and Development, Office of Air and Radiation, "Respiratory Health Effects of Passive Smoking: Lung Cancer and Other Disorders," 12/92.

[10] American Medical Association News Release, 5/26/93.

[11] Schoendorf, MD, MPH, and Kiely, John L., Ph.D., "Relationship of Sudden Infant Death Syndrome to Maternal Smoking During and After Pregnancy," Pediatrics, Vol. 90, No. 6, 12/92, p. 905.

[12] *Id.*

[13] "Smoking while pregnant can lower IQ of children," Chicago Tribune, Sec. 1, p. 6, 2/11/94; "Smoking moms' children test below norm," Daily Herald, Sec. 1, p. 3, 2/11/94; "Pregnant and Smoking," Daily Herald editorial, Sec. 1, p. 8, 2/12/94.

[14] See footnote 2 – *Infra* at Chapter V.

[15] "Lung Cancer and Smoking Trends in the United States over the Past 25 Years," A Cancer Journal for Clinicians, May/June 1991, Vol. 41, no. 3, p. 107.

[16] Califano, Joseph A., Jr., *Governing America*, Simon and Schuster, 1981, p. 185.

[17] American Cancer Society, Cancer Response System, #2522, reviewed 2/8/90, reprinted 4/26/91.

[18] U.S. Department of Health and Human Services, *Reducing the Health Consequences of Smoking: 25 Years of Progress. A Report of the Surgeon General.* U.S. Department of Health and Human Services, Public Health Service, Centers for Disease Control, Center for Chronic Disease Prevention and Health Promotion, Office on Smoking and Health, 1989.

[19] *Supra* at footnote 9.

[20] "Smoking linked to two more cancers," South Bend Tribune, 2/2/94, p. A4.

[21] Id.

[22] "Smoking May Increase Risk of Adult Leukemia," Chicago Sun-Times, 2/22/93, p. 7; "Smoking and Leukemia," Chicago Sun-Times, 3/1/93, p. 2A.

[23] "Heart and Stroke Facts," American Heart Association, 1992, p. 19.

[24] "Fivefold Increase in Heart Risk is Reported for Some Smokers, New York Times, 8/18/95, p. A-20.

[25] Id.

[26] "Passive Smoking and Heart Disease," Stanton A. Glantz, Ph.D., and William W. Parmley, M.D., American Heart Association, Vol. 83, No. 1, 10.

[27] "Smoking and Heart Disease," American Heart Association, 1986.

[28] Id.

[29] Id.

[30] Id.

[31] Id.

[32] Id.

[33] Id.

[34] "Ex-smokers' stroke risk stays higher for 20 years, study says," Washington Times, 5/10/95, p. A 11.

[35] "High stroke risk in men who smoke, study says," Chicago Sun-Times, 5/10/91, p. 3.

[36] Id.

[37] "Fast Treatment Helps Ease Stroke's Impact," Chicago Sun-Times, 12/20/92, p. 53.

[38] "Deadly risks – Smoking, heavy drinking tied to a virulent form of stroke," Chicago Tribune, 6/13/93, Sec. 5, p. 9.

[39] Current Medical Diagnosis & Treatment, Appleton & Lange, 1993, p. 197.

[40] Id.

[41] Id.

[42] Id.

[43] Stein, Jay, Internal Medicine, Little, Brown and Company, Second Edition (1987), p. 643.

[44] Id. COPD is the acronym for chronic obstructive pulmonary disease.

[45] United States Department of Health and Human Services, Centers for Disease Control, Chronic Disease and Health Promotion Reprints from the MMWR, 1985-1989, Volume 2, Tobacco Topics, p. 61.

[46] Id.

[47] "Asthma, Deadly . . . But Treatable," Time, 6/22/92, p. 61.

[48] "A Breath-Taking Ordeal," Chicago Sun-Times, 5/24/93, p. 3B.

[49] "Children's Exposure to Tobacco Smoke is Found to Cause or Worsen Asthma," Washington Post, 6/10/93, p. A5.

[50] "Association Between Exposure to Environmental Tobacco Smoke and Exacerbation of Asthma in Children," New England Journal of Medicine, 6/10/93, pp. 1665-69.

[51] "Asthma called worst chronic illness for kids," Chicago Tribune, Sec. 1, p. 2, 11/6/92.

[52] The John Hopkins Medical Center- Health after 50, Vol. 4, Issue 12, 2/93, p. 1.

[53] "Smokers Lose Estrogen Benefit," Washington Post, 5/5/92; "Smoking Eliminates the Protective Effect of Oral Estrogens on the Risk for Hip Fracture Among Women," Annals of Internal Medicine, 5/1/92, pp. 716-721.

[54] "Cigarettes and Estrogen," New York Times, 5/5/92, p. C4.

[55] See footnote 50.

[56] "The Bone Density of Female Twins Discordent for Tobacco Use," New England Journal of Medicine, 2/10/94, pp. 387-392.

[57] "Smoking may delay healing of broken bones," Chicago Sun-Times, 2/24/92, p. 10.

[58] "CDC: Smoking while pregnant hikes risk of underweight baby," Chicago Tribune, Evening-Health, 8/4/92, p. 7.

[59] *Id.*

[60] *Supra* at footnote 13.

[61] "Smoking Cuts Breast Milk by Half in Study," Chicago Sun-Times, 12/7/92, p. 8A.

[62] "Female incontinence tied to smoking," Chicago Sun-Times, 6/6/91, p. 12.

[63] "Smoking worsens bad backs," USA Today, 2/22/93, p. 1A.

[64] *Id.*

[65] "Genetics May Link Smoking, Depression," Chicago Sun-Times, 2/11/93, p. 8.

[66] "Men's Smoking Tied to Arthritis," Chicago Sun-Times, 12/13/92, p. 39.

[67] *Id.*

[68] *Id.*

[69] "Another Worry for Smokers: Cataracts," Chicago Sun-Times, 8/26/92, p. 25.

[70] "Smoking and drinking raise cataract risk," USA Today, 4/29/93, p. 1-D.

[71] "Dry Eye" pamphlet, American Academy of Ophthalmology, 7/91.

[72] "Yet Another Reason to Quit," Chicago Tribune Evening-Health, 7/16/93, p. 7.

[73] "Smoking & Oral Health," pamphlet, American Dental Association, 1991.

[74] Wanning, Esther, *Meditations for Surviving Without Cigarettes*, Avon Books, 1994, p. 99.

[75] *Supra*, see footnote 73.

[76] "Study shows new wrinkle for smokers," Chicago Tribune, 5/15/91, Sec. 1, p. 13.

[77] *Id.*

[78] "Buerger's Disease Affects Circulation in Smokers," Chicago Sun-Times, 2/26/93, p. 37.

[79] The Merck Manual, Sixteenth Edition, pp. 582-583 (1992).

[80] "Smoking may spur Graves' disease onset," USA Today, 1/27/93, p. 1D.

[81] "Smoking and Risk of Graves' Disease," Journal of the American Medical Association, 1/27/93, pp. 479-482.

[82] "Smokers' children prone to esophagus illness," Chicago Tribune, 5/4/93, Sec. 1, p. 12.

[83] *Supra* at footnote 74, p. 225.

[84] *Supra* at footnote 74, p. 39.

III

DEADLY ENDORSEMENTS

Americans have grown up to the sounds and pictures of famous entertainers and public figures endorsing cigarettes and other tobacco products. A number of these stars were our heroes who we sought to emulate. Others, such as the rugged Marlboro Man, created the All-American image. Unfortunately, most admirers fell short of achieving the substantive stardom and only succeeded in emulating one detrimental aspect of their idol's life, his or her addiction to smoking.

Doctors say that the nicotine in tobacco smoke is more addictive than alcohol or hard drugs.[1] Quitting the smoking habit may be more difficult than quitting the alcohol or drug scene. In order for the tobacco industry to make up for the nearly half million premature deaths and many more serious illnesses due to smoking each year, tobacco companies have to entice minors, women, minorities and foreign customers. Many of today's adult smokers were hooked by endorsements 30, 40, 50 and 60 years ago. What some of these famous users, endorsers, and facilitators said about tobacco in their later years and how others have fared with this poisonous product should be of interest to the nation's 46 million smokers and more than 200 million nonsmokers, including millions of impressionable children and teenagers, who are frequently exposed to the carcinogens and toxins in secondary tobacco smoke.

Since the early 1920s when information was forthcoming linking tobacco with lung cancer, Americans have been bombarded with pro-smoking propaganda and images from celebrities who realized belatedly the severe health dangers of smoking or conquered the addictive habit in time.

The insights of many of the following celebrities showing (a) the harmful side of the tobacco picture too late and wanting others to benefit from their mistakes of starting and continuing smoking and (b) those who stopped smoking in time to save their lives should be instructive.

The following personalities are living or dying examples of what tobacco can do to you or how you can set aside this lethal weapon and save your health.

A. THE WORLD OF ENTERTAINMENT

1. CLAUDE AKINS

Actor Claude Akins was born in 1926. His career spanned numerous Broadway, movie and television appearances. When smoking appeared to be jeopardizing his career, he quit for the following reasons:[2]

> For 20 or 30 years, I smoked a couple of packs a day. I was always quitting and then starting again. I did it a thousand times.

> Then about 10 years ago, I developed a sore throat which doctors thought might have resulted from smoking. "If they cut out my voice box, where will I be?" ... So I quit permanently.

Akins died January 27, 1994, at age 67 from cancer.[3] He probably would have been with us today if he had not started smoking or had quit earlier.

Persons who must speak a lot in their vocations, e.g., teachers, trial lawyers, and broadcasters, might benefit form Mr. Akins' insights.

2. DESI ARNAZ

Desi Arnaz was the co-star of the popular *I Love Lucy* television series from 1951 to 1957 while married to comedienne Lucille Ball.[4] The *I Love Lucy* show was the favorite comedy series of millions of Americans. Arnaz was also a director of *Lucy* and *The Lucille Ball Show* and headed Desilu Studios before its sale to Paramount.

A heavy smoker, Arnaz succumbed to lung cancer at age 71. He would have been among the first to tell all Americans that a premature death from lung cancer caused by the carcinogens and toxins in poisonous tobacco smoke is not funny.

3. LUCILLE BALL

Lucille Ball was one of the most popular and funniest comediennes ever to appear on television. She co-starred with her husband Desi Arnaz in the television comedy series *I Love Lucy* from 1951 to 1957. She continued the same type of character in the television comedies *The Lucy Show* from 1962 to 1968 and *Here's Lucy* from 1968 to 1974.

A heavy smoker, she died of a heart attack in 1989 at age 77.[5] Ball's smoking apparently robbed her of additional years of enjoyment of life and her friends and audiences of her charm and wit.

4. LEONARD BERNSTEIN

The multi-talented Leonard Bernstein was an outstanding conductor, composer, and pianist. He was the first American musical director of the New York Philharmonic Orchestra from 1958 to 1969.

He will best be remembered for his musicals including *On the Town* (1944), *Wonderful Town* (1953), *Candide* (1956), and *West Side Story* (1957).[6] Some believe that *West Side Story* with his Romeo and Juliet theme between the black and Puerto Rican gangs might be the best musical ever produced. Bernstein composed *Mass* for the 1971 opening of the John F. Kennedy Center for the Performing Arts in Washington, D.C. His young person television concerts helped convey to children his love and knowledge of music.

Bernstein died prematurely in 1990 at age 72 due to lung cancer and emphysema.[7] The October 12, 1990 New York Daily News sadly noted that "a lifetime of cigarettes had ravaged the maestro - yet he continued to smoke."[8]

Tobacco smoke robbed Bernstein of many more productive years and prematurely deprived millions of Americans, young and old, of the conducting, composing, and teachings of an American musical genius. The cancer stick, also known as the cigarette, forced the maestro to lay down another stick, his baton. Bernstein was victimized by the merchants of death, the American tobacco companies.

5. ART BLAKEY

The New York Daily News reported on October 21, 1990 "(t)wo days after (Leonard)Bernstein died, jazz great Art Blakey, yet another heavy smoker, died of lung cancer," at age 71.[9] Blakey was a drummer and band leader for more than four decades. His octet called the Jazz Messengers was the springboard for such jazz musicians as Chuck Magionne, Wynton Marsalis, and Woody Shaw. Art Blakey had many more years of musical treats in store for young musicians and his fans. The tobacco industry's beat of premature death from cigarette smoke cut short his career.

6. YUL BRYNNER

Yul Brynner, a Swiss citizen, achieved great fame as the bald-headed King of Siam in the Rogers and Hammerstein *The King and I* musical on Broadway in 1951 and in film in 1956. He starred in nearly 20 films from 1956 to 1976 winning the Best Actor Oscar in 1956 for *The King and I.* Brynner died from lung cancer on October 10, 1985 at age 65.[10] In a 1985 American Cancer Society ad recorded just weeks before his death to be aired after his death, Brynner said:[11]

> If I could take back that smoking, we wouldn't be talking about any cancer now. I'm convinced of that. ... Now that I'm gone, I tell you don't smoke, whatever you do, just don't smoke.

Brynner had been on tour from 1981 to 1985 reviving *The King and I* until shortly before his death.

If Brynner had not smoked, many more Americans would have seen his spectacular performance in *The King and I,* and if Americans had listened to his 1985 "just don't smoke" warning, the annual premature American death toll of nearly a half million from smoking would have greatly declined.

Perhaps a decade from now, Yul Brynner admirers will look back and say that his most valuable contribution to Americans was his 1985 warning against smoking. The memorable performance of *The King and I* would have to take second place.

7. NAT "KING" COLE

Nat "King" Cole was an American pianist and singer with cigarettes in hand or close by whose career was sadly cut short at age 45 in 1965 due to lung cancer most likely caused by chain smoking.[12] In the early 1940s he was considered one of the nation's leading jazz pianists. His numerous vocal hits included "It's Only a Paper Moon" (1943), "Nature Boy" (1948),

"Mona Lisa" (1950), and "Unforgettable" (1951). His soft and relaxed singing style has contributed to his continued popularity more than 30 years after his premature death from the carcinogens of tobacco smoke.

Natalie Cole, his successful singing daughter, in 1992 revived her father's oldies in the top-selling album "Unforgettable." Modern technology superimposed Nat King Cole's 1951 rendition of "Unforgettable" over his daughter's recent rendition resulting in a unique and memorable musical experience.

Cole portrayed composer W.C. Handy in the film *St. Louis Blues* in 1958.[13]

If it had not been for smoking, Nat "King" Cole may have given his fans many more years of unforgettable musical experiences and had a chance to enjoy seeing his daughter reach full musical stardom.

8. GARY COOPER

Gary Cooper was a well-known actor who appeared in nearly 100 films. His best known roles were as a cowboy in films such as *The Virginian* (1929) and *The Westerner* (1940) portraying the courageous pioneer of the American West.[14] He represented a common American fighting evil in films such as *Meet John Friendly* (1941) and *Friendly Persuasion* (1956). Cooper won Academy Awards as best actor for his performance in *Sergeant York* (1941) and *High Noon* (1952), the latter ending with one of the most memorable shoot-outs in the history of western films.

Although financially benefitting from his endorsement of Chesterfield cigarettes, Cooper succumbed prematurely to the fallout of lung cancer from years of heavy smoking at age 60 in 1961.[15] Cigarettes robbed movie fans of many more films by this superb actor.

9. SAMMY DAVIS, JR.

Sammy Davis, Jr., an outstanding and versatile entertainer, died prematurely at age 65 in 1990 from throat cancer.[16] People Magazine reported on January 29, 1990, that "when diagnosed, he broke his 50-year, pack-and-a-half-a-day habit."[17] He was well known for his shows, films, recordings, stage career, cabaret appearances, and television appearances. He received a special citation in 1974 from the National Academy of Television Arts and Sciences for contributions to television entertainment.

Davis had that rare ingredient of showmanship. I was fortunate to see him on his last performance of a run around 1960 at the Elmwood Casino in Windsor, Ontario. With unlimited enthusiasm, energy, and talent interspersed with maximum showmanship, Davis said at the outset of the midnight show that he would perform all night because he had an early morning flight. For four hours he sang, tap-danced, played instruments, and cracked jokes becoming stronger and better as the night wore on. He loved entertaining and the audience loved him. Al Jolson is the only other male performer I have seen or heard whose showmanship and talent could completely capture an audience.

When advised he had cancer, Davis said:[18]

> My throat was raw. If I touched it, my hand would come away with blood.
> I was losing weight. I couldn't eat. Everything looked like mush.

Cigarettes robbed Sammy Davis, Jr. of many years of doing what he loved, entertaining audiences. His smoking deprived many persons around the world of seeing an entertainer who personified showmanship.

10. KIRK DOUGLAS

Actor Kirk Douglas played the lead role in the majority of the 60 films he made.[19] He was nominated for the Best Actor for *Champion* in 1949, for *The Bad and the Beautiful* in 1952 and for *Lust for Life* in 1956. One of his sons, Michael Douglas, is an accomplished actor-producer.

Kirk Douglas' following views on the Hollywood influence on his smoking is quite revealing:[20]

> When my father, who was a Russian immigrant, decided to stop smoking, he used to carry a cigarette around with him. Whenever he felt the urge to smoke he would take it out, look at it and ask himself, "Who's stronger, you or me?" Then he'd say, "*I'm* stronger." And he'd put the cigarette back. He made it a contest between him and the smoke - sort of a battle of wills - and it worked. He carried that cigarette around until he had knocked the hell out of it. I was in my teens then, but later on, when I wanted to give up smoking, I would think of how my father did it and it helped me. Smoking for me was one of the earliest corruptions of Hollywood. I had to smoke for my first movie part and I never had before. They just gave me a cigarette and kept taking close-ups saying, "Inhale!" I was sick as a dog. After that I started smoking on my own and soon I was averaging about 2 1/2 packs a day. For actors, smoking is a prop, a crutch. When in doubt in a scene, they reach for a cigarette. It gives them something to do with their hands. I think the same thing is true with people in ordinary life. When you feel insecure, smoking gives you something to do. Then one day I said, I don't think I like

it; its just a habit. So, with my father's example to help me, I stopped cold. For ten years now I haven't smoked a cigarette - offscreen or on. And I don't think its detracted at all from my virile image. I kind of agree with that nun who was offered a cigarette and said, "No thank you. One habit is enough." The nun was wearing *her* habit. I'm not going to tell you what mine is.

Hollywood entertains, but it also conveys powerful images. Through film it has conveyed the belief that smoking is "macho" meaning some type of male/female power/sex symbol. The health of many moviegoers has been damaged, if not ruined, by wanting to imitate the macho image portrayed on the screen. The tobacco companies have adroitly exploited this weakness. Douglas saved his health by quitting his 2 1/2 pack-a-day smoking habit and has indicated that killing yourself with cigarettes is not necessary to attain the macho image. Hopefully his life-saving words will convey the thought that success in and out of Hollywood or in any profession need not be due to the carcinogens and toxins in poisonous tobacco smoke.

11. BARBARA FELDON

Actress Barbara Feldon has performed on the stage, in movies, and in numerous television series during her more than 50 years.[21] A few years ago she described her decision to give up smoking as follows:[22]

The first time I stopped smoking was easy for me. But then, six months later, I took a trip to Europe. On the plane, I thought well, since I had no trouble giving it up, I'll just smoke on my vacation and after I get home, I'll stop again. But I couldn't do it that time and I went on smoking for months. Then a friend of mine, who was the son of a doctor, told me that his father had taken him to the hospital to watch him dissect the lungs of someone who had died of lung cancer. And my friend said he would never touch another cigarette as long as he lived, and that everyone in cancer research at that hospital had stopped. That convinced me that smoking was terribly dangerous. And I didn't have the feeling that "it's going to get the other guy." I was sure it was to be me. So, I decided to quit again. I set up a fantasy situation: I was standing in front of a firing squad and they said, "If you smoke a cigarette we won't fire." But I refused to smoke. In other words, going back was completely, totally out of the question. I gave myself no "just-this-once" kind of thing. I killed cigarettes forever. I expected to want them, but I never for a moment thought I would weaken. I knew that I could chew my nails right down to my elbow, but that my puritanical background would rise up in a bristling mass and say, "Too bad!" That was eight years ago and I haven't smoked since.

Perhaps if all nurses and physicians in the medical community could similarly convey specific examples of smoking causing death and/or serious illness with the accompanying suffering and pain to the patients and loved ones, and to their smoking family members and friends, the number of smokers would decrease and many lives could be saved.

13. GLENN FORD

Actor Glenn Ford made more than 70 films in a career spanning about five decades.[23] He was named the number one box office star in America by the Motion Picture Herald-Fan Poll in 1958, the year after he appeared in *Cowboy, Imitation General* and *The Sheepman*. After he quit smoking, Ford said:[24]

Smoking is just a terrible dirty habit....It was once glamorous, but now it is nuisance and one that no longer interests me.

A story might illustrate how actors like Ford might help alleviate the smoking problem with young people. In the fall of 1961 I took a course in ethics at Northwestern University from Professor Paul Schilpp, a brilliant scholar who left Germany in the 1930's after Hitler gained power. During the ethics course Nazi Lieutenant Colonel Adolf Eichman was being tried for the mass murder of Jews during the World War II Holocaust. One day Professor Schilpp asked the class what would be the appropriate punishment for Eichman. Almost everyone said "execution". Surprisingly, Professor Schilpp believed that the appropriate penalty would be locking Eichman in a cell for the rest of his life showing narrated films of his atrocities 24 hours a day until he was driven out of his mind. Tobacco company executives producing a product that kills when used as intended deserve similar treatment. The final days of a lung cancer or emphysema tobacco victim are somewhat reminiscent of the agonizing scenes in Steven Spielberg's Holocaust movie "Schindler's List." In 1971, the British Royal College of Physicians of London referred to the annual toll caused by cigarette smoking as "the present holocaust."[25]

Likewise, every grade school and high school student as well as addicted smokers should be shown films of patients dying in hospitals from lung cancer, emphysema, heart disease, and other diseases caused by smoking. There should be dual-purpose student field trips to hospitals and nursing homes - one purpose being comforting and spending time with the ill and the other being seeing first hand the painful and tragic results of smoking. The hospital narrations, just like Professor Schilpp's example, of coughing, screaming, moaning and crying should be included. The narrators should include articulate actresses and actors like Glen Ford. Tobacco company executives and members of their Boards of Directors such as Clinton transition team head Vernon Jordan might benefit from a similar experience. If Americans die from smoking at the present rate, an estimated 42 million Americans will die from tobacco smoke and secondary tobacco smoke the next century, a potential holocaust that would be unsurpassed in the history of civilization.

13. EVA GABOR

Comedienne Eva Gabor comes from a slightly different perspective concerning the adverse impact of smoking. Gabor says:[26]

> Somebody very close to me died from cancer of the lung and I said, "Okay, that's it. I've had my last cigarette." After that they would have tasted to me like poison. I'd like to be that strong about lying on the floor and rolling to get rid of my fanny, or not eating midnight snacks, but I'd rather use my will power on not smoking. My slogan is, "I'd rather be fat and alive than thin and dead." Smoking I find most unfeminine and unattractive. I mean, who likes to kiss a chimney? And if a man has to smoke to feel masculine, I feel sorry for him. A man is a man and a cigarette isn't going to make him one. I can't bear the thought of a woman reaching for a cigarette first thing in the morning. I mean, why should any man like that? My big sadness is my husband whom I love and adore. I can't make him quit smoking because he's high strung and when pressure starts he reaches for cigarettes. With your own husband you can be a pest just so long and then he tells you, "Enough, already."

My wife would always notice when I walked through the smoking car on the Chicago and North Western railway commuter train. The 10 to 15 seconds it took me to walk through this gas chamber type rail car were enough for the tobacco smoke to penetrate my clothing. Smoking may appear to be macho to some, but it is physically unpleasant to most of the more than 200 million nonsmoking Americans.

14. LARRY GATLIN

Country Western singer Larry Gatlin succinctly warned that "(S)omeone told me that cigarettes kill you. I didn't want to die, so I quit. Thank God!"[27] Unfortunately about three million human beings around the world, including about 419,000 Americans, who die prematurely each year from smoking are not as perceptive as Gatlin. They ignore the numerous reports that permeate our media each year of new studies linking smoking with a myriad of health problems. If the advice of Gatlin were followed, the premature deaths of over 40 million Americans and 300 million human beings around the world would be saved in the next century. Perhaps that is why the British Royal College of Medicine in 1971 referred to the annual toll caused by cigarette smoking as "the present holocaust,"[28] why former U.S. Department of Health, Education and Welfare Secretary Joseph A. Califano, Jr., warned in 1978 that smoking is "slow motion suicide" and designated it as "Public Health Enemy Number One,"[29] and the American Medical Association in 1990 said "tobacco is lethal."[30]

Fortunately, like Larry Gatlin millions of Americans are bypassing the tobacco company spin controllers and are getting the message. Tobacco smoke is poison and it kills. Larry Gatlin got the message and is alive.

15. LARRY HAGMAN

Actor Larry Hagman, son of the late Broadway star Mary Martin, is best known for his portrayal of J.R. Ewing in *Dallas*, a CBS Friday night serial for over 12 years. Though the character was disreputable and even hateful, Hagman made him fascinating, a remarkable achievement in a program that was essentially a soap opera. The talented star of Dallas discussed his efforts to quit smoking,[31]

> I quit smoking for about the tenth time on January 1, 1965. But that time was different ... my New Year's resolution finally took. I was smoking about two packs a day and had been trying to quit for two years... ever since a doctor in Italy showed me an X-ray of my lungs ranting "Morte, Morte," to make me understand what I was doing to my body. Then, when the surgeon general released his report linking smoking with lung cancer, I knew I wouldn't continue poisoning myself.

Hagman's equating tobacco smoke with poison at the time the Surgeon General issued his 1964 report was quite insightful. The Environmental Protection Agency issued a report on January 7, 1993 concluding that passive or environmental tobacco smoke was a Class A human carcinogen in the same category as asbestos, radon, and benzene.[32] In other words, tobacco smoke is poison just as Hagman indicated. And as former HEW Secretary Joseph A. Califano, Jr., warned in 1978, smoking is "slow motion suicide."[33] If Hagman had not quit smoking in 1965, he may have never lived to perform his career-topping role as J.R. Ewing in *Dallas*.

16. WAYLON JENNINGS

Waylon Jennings is a well-known country - music singer, songwriter, and guitarist. In the late 1950s he played electric bass in Buddy Holly's band and subsequently formed his own band, the Waylons. In the 1970s he teamed up with Willie Nelson and his Austin "outlaws." He has made recordings with his wife, Jessi Colter. His career has undoubtedly been prolonged by his quitting smoking which he described as follows:[34]

> The most amazing thing is how quickly your lungs clear up after you quit smoking. In less than two months my lungs were as clean as someone's who had never smoked. When it comes to quitting smoking, try to keep in mind there are four or five rough days of withdrawals and then after that you just have to quit reaching for them. The only advice I have for someone who wants to quit smoking is to just do it and don't dwell on it.

One wonders how long a singing voice such as Waylon Jennings' can be subjected to tobacco poisons before the vocal chords or larynx becomes irreparably damaged or diseased.

17. EDDIE KENDRICKS

Eddie Kendricks, an original member of the Temptations, died of lung cancer on October 5, 1992 at age 52.[35] A year prior to his death he had a cancerous lung removed. He attributed his illness to 30 years of smoking.

The Temptations were one of the top male singing groups in the 1960s. Cigarette smoking prematurely cut short Kendricks' career in his prime time of life and deprived his fans of many years of musical enjoyment. Kendrick's smoking expedited a trip to his final resting place which may be Marlboro Country.

18. SALLY KIRKLAND

All actresses are concerned about their appearances. Actress Sally Kirkland discussed the relationship between smoking and one's appearance by observing:[36]

> I used to smoke in my early years, but when I got into nutrition, I knew it was time to stop. I have never felt or looked better and I attribute it to no more cigarettes. I also encourage all of my friends to stop.

Kirkland could also have mentioned that studies have shown that smokers tend to have more wrinkles earlier and appear to age earlier. Kirkland would be an articulate spokesperson for the more than 100 million American women who do not smoke and the approximately 20 million women who smoke - to refute the Virginia Slims "You've come a long way baby" sex appeal ads. Perhaps the counter Virginia Slims ads should say "You'll age a lot quicker and get six feet under a lot faster" by smoking.

19. MICHAEL LANDON

Michael Landon, an actor best known for his leading role in *Little House on the Prairie* from 1974 to 1982, died in 1991 from liver and pancreatic cancer at age 53.[37] It was many young person's favorite television program during this period. Throughout his career Landon strove to create thought provoking and optimistic themes. He also acted on *Bonanza* and *Highway to Heaven* from 1984 to 1988.

Upon Landon's death, the Associated Press reported on July 2, 1991 that "cigarette smoking is the leading risk factor for pancreatic cancer with smokers twice as likely to get it as nonsmokers." Landon was a former four-pack a day smoker.[38] He appeared in numerous films, television programs and television specials. Landon received the 1982 Academy Founders Award from the National Academy of Television Arts and Sciences. Cigarette smoking prematurely deprived a generation of Americans of this outstanding actor.

20. CHRIS LEMON

Actor Chris Lemon said the following about quitting smoking:[39]

> I quit smoking because my wife asked me to. Now I feel better, look better, and smell better. The effects were instantaneous. I gained some weight, but through exercise I took it off.

Stopping smoking is a critical step toward improvement of health. However, a proper diet and a medically approved exercise program as alluded to by Lemon will help refute the "weight gain" argument frequently propounded by smokers to justify continuation of their harmful habit.

21. PATTY LOVELESS

Singer Patty Loveless was also concerned about the impact of smoking on her appearance. She described her concerns as follows:[40]

> I smoked during my teen years. I finally quit smoking because someone who really cared about me kept discouraging me. Eventually, I became so annoyed by the way the cigarette smoke made my hair and clothes smell, that I was able to quit cold turkey. Now being around smoke really bothers me, especially when I'm playing in a small club.

My wife and I went to Minneapolis for a family celebration in the spring of 1992. We were put up in a refurbished motel. When we opened the door of the poorly ventilated room, it felt as if we had entered a gas chamber filled with cigarette smoke.

Patty Loveless' description of a small nightclub is comparable to an airplane, railroad car, restaurant, or sports arena that permits smoking. Contrary to the Virginia Slims "you've come a long way baby," smelly hair and clothes are hardly coming a long way. Cigarette smoke is a poison. Poisoning oneself and others as well as smelling up one's body and clothes is the opposite of coming a long way. Smoking is coming a longer way and a faster way to a grave in the local cemetery, which some have referred to as Marlboro Country.

22. SHIRLEY MACLAINE

Shirley MacLaine is one of the most versatile, energetic, and well-known actresses of the twentieth century. She received an Oscar for the Best Actress Academy Award for *Terms of Endearment* in 1983 after being nominated in 1958 for *Some Came Running*, in 1960 for *The Apartment*, in 1963 for *Irma LaDouce*, and in 1977 for *Turning Point*.[41] MacLaine appears to say more with her eyes and facial expressions than many actresses say with their voices. With her endless energy she found time to be a best-selling author, a television and film producer, and a political activist. As a former smoker, the multitalented star said:[42]

As a dancer, I have much more energy from not smoking - And a lot of friends who are thankful as well.

23. JOHNNY MATHIS

Chances are that Johnny Mathis, one of the outstanding popular music singers of the second half of the twentieth century, would neither have been a singer nor have been alive if he had continued smoking. Mathis said:[43]

I never did smoke a great deal, but early in my career, I realized that a singer shouldn't smoke at all, so I quit. If I hadn't quit, I probably wouldn't be able to sing today. In fact, I might not even be here.

On another occasion Mathis described in greater detail his struggle to stop smoking:[44]

My voice was in such terrible condition that I couldn't sing an open "ah" vowel. I really didn't know whether the tones were going to come out at all and I had a rasp which I'd never had before because the essence of my singing has always been nice, clear tones. So finally after a rough concert tour I decided that I would smoke my last cigarette ever on the plane going home. It was one of he hardest things I've ever had to do, because I am by nature a little on the nervous side. Afterwards I almost became an alcoholic and I was pretty well smashed by about four o'clock every day. This went on for about a month and a half and then I decided that was no good either and cut out the booze too. But I ballooned up 15 pounds and my brother and sister said, "If you're going to look like this you'd better go back to smoking because you're going to ruin your career." Even so, I stuck with it. I believe that people have to have a "do or die" reason to quit and I had one: Singing is three quarters of my life and I was scared to death that I wouldn't be able to sing again and wouldn't be able to live the way I wanted to. Once the anxieties were over I felt like a new person. I've had dreams that I was smoking with my friends and was hooked again. Believe me, those dreams were awful! I'd wake up in a cold sweat because I've been told that if you stop something and then get back on it again, you're hooked for life. I've never gone back.

When you turn on a radio station and hear some of Mathis' old hits such as "Chances Are," "Wonderful-Wonderful," "Misty" and "It's Not for Me to Say,"[45] you realize that cigarettes were not able to prematurely cut short his magnificent career. However, one wonders how many thousands of careers tobacco smoke prematurely shortened. Apparently the tobacco companies do not care, for as one ad said, they are tobacco men - not medicine men.

24. JENNIFER O'NEILL

Actress Jennifer O'Neill made her film debut at age 21 in 1970 and has starred in numerous television and film productions.[46] She was the 1975 female Star of the Year from the National Association of Theatre Owners for *The Reincarnation of Peter Proud.* Her career has broadened to include screen-writing, producing and composing. O'Neill has a cogent reason for stopping smoking:[47]

> When your body is like a fine tuned engine, you don't want to put the wrong chemicals in it. I thought of that and quit smoking.

If she could have anticipated the findings of the January 7, 1993 Environmental Protection Agency report classifying secondary tobacco smoke as a Class A carcinogen like asbestos, benzene and radon, O'Neill may have substituted "poison" for "chemicals" in her statement.

25. R.T. OSLIN

R.T. Oslin, a singer and songwriter, said that:[48]

> After smoking for many years, I finally had enough of the taste, smell and the look. It was no longer cool for an 80s lady to be engulfed in a cloud of smoke.

To put it another way, the tobacco odor not only stinks, but also kills. And if looks could kill, clearly a tobacco odor can kill. Tobacco smoke and secondary tobacco smoke kill nearly a half million "stinkin" Americans a year.

By the way, look closely at two groups of comparably aged women -- one group that smokes and the other that does not smoke. Notice the comparable wrinkling of their skin. The smokers generally have far more wrinkles.

26. TONY RANDALL

Tony Randall is a well-known television actor best known as the humorous Felix Unger in The Odd Couple from 1970 through 1975 though his television career dates back to One Man's Family (1950-52) and Mr. Peepers (1952-55) in which he played a secondary role to Wally Cox.[49] Randall explained as follows how he would not have had an acting career if he continued smoking:[50]

> When I got out of the Army I started to study voice under the GI Bill which paid for four years of training in anything you chose. My teacher said, "Stop smoking. There's no point in your trying to train your voice if you're going to smoke." So I quit. What you need in order to do it, is someone to impose his will on you. Then it's easy. Once you've really accepted the idea, you can't shed it; it's like posthypnotic suggestion. That's what I try to do for my friends. I *order* them to quit smoking. Jack Klugman has stopped. Actually, no one smokes in *The Odd Couple* set. Not one cigarette for all our 60 people! No, it's not fear of God. It's fear of *me*. The person who makes it stick can't be afraid of being disliked. But I haven't been able to make my wife stop. When she tries, she gets so irritable that I'd rather she smoked. She doesn't smoke around me, though. She goes up to the bathroom which is the only room in the house where cigarettes are allowed. I don't mind when Johnny Carson lights up when I come on his show because that's for laughs. But generally, when people start puffing, I just get up and go.

I never dated a girl who smoked and today I doubt if I would hire a smoker. Millions of men have followed my dating principle. Many employers will not hire a smoker - for health, fire safety, and loss of smoke-break time reasons. Randall's first wife died of cancer in 1992 and apparently was not one of the lucky smokers who beat the odds against succumbing prematurely to the carcinogens and toxins of poisonous tobacco smoke.[51]

27. CLIFF ROBERTSON

Cliff Robertson has numerous television and theater credits and won the 1969 Academy Award for the best male actor for *Charly*.[52] He was blacklisted for three years by the movie studios for blowing the whistle on Columbia Studio President David Begelman's embezzlement in the late 1970s. He weathered that storm and embarked on a second movie career. He movingly tells how his five-year-old daughter warned him about dying from smoking:[53]

Ten years ago one of my daughters - she was five then - called me in tears one day and said, "Daddy, I don't want you to die." I said, "Why do you say that, dear?" And she said, "Well, if you smoke, I'm afraid you're going to die." She said she'd heard something on television about it. I wouldn't lie to her, so I said, "I'm not going to promise I'll quit, but I will cut down." And that's when I first cut down to a pack and a half a day. Up until then I'd smoked about 2 1/2 packs. Then when I was writing, directing and acting in *J.W. Coop* and was under terrific pressure, a friend said, "If you have what it takes to quit when you're under pressure, once it's over you'll know you can stay off under any conditions." So I thought: Now's the time. And I did it. But five months after I had finished the film and the pressure was off, I started smoking again. The biggest problem was the reflex action: when an important long-distance telephone call comes in or there's an office crisis, you reach for a cigarette. When I was trying to write, that was also tough. So, kind of like a child, I secretly made a little pact with myself. Cold turkey hadn't work for me so I decided to phase out of smoking gradually, without that big announcement to embarrass me every time I had a cigarette. The second thing I said was I won't buy any more cigarettes. If I have to bum cigarettes from people, you're bound to cut down on smoking....And that worked. My smoking comes to about ten cigarettes a week now and I'm satisfied with this. (Maybe you don't think that's really "quitting," but as a man who used to burn up 10 smokes a day, I do).

As Robertson points out, many smokers realize that smoking is harmful. However, the addictive nature of tobacco makes quitting very difficult for many smokers. That's why its important that children and teens never begin this addictive habit and why the Joe Camel and Virginia Slims successful appeals to our nation's youth have been devastating.

If more parents listened to their children's warnings about smoking and stopped smoking - not just cut down like Robertson, there would be fewer premature deaths. If more children listened to the news items on radio and television about the serious hazards of tobacco smoke and secondary tobacco smoke, our children would be a lot healthier and they would grow up to be healthier and longer lived adults.

28. SARAH VAUGHN

Jazz and popular singer Sarah Vaughn died prematurely of lung cancer at age 66 in 1990.[54] It was reported in March 1989 that Vaughn was "smoking feverishly."[55]

Vaughn tended to treat her voice more as a jazz instrument than as a vehicle for lyrics. One of her biggest hits was "Broken-hearted Melody" in

1959. Her broken-hearted fans were prematurely robbed of years of recording and entertainment because of her smoking.

29. JOHN WAYNE

If there was ever a macho man in motion pictures, John "Duke" Wayne was the one. He won the Academy Award for Best Actor for *Sands of Iwo Jima* in 1949 and *True Grit* in 1969.[56] Even after lung cancer was diagnosed in 1964, the three to five-pack-a-day smoker since the 1930s did not give up the fatal habit.[57] The macho actor who was a compulsive smoker of a popular brand of unfiltered cigarettes (Camels) and liked them so much he did advertisements for the tobacco company.

Dan Jennings, who interviewed the Duke in the October 27, 1962 Saturday Evening Post, observed:[58]

> As he talked, frequently cussing and using the same grim drawl that had cowed badmen from Fort Dodge to Tombstone, he compulsively lighted one cigarette after another. "So maybe it's six months off the end of my life," he said, opening the day's fifth pack, "but they're not going to kill me."

They did kill the Duke. His smoke-ravaged remains rest in Marlboro Country, a local cemetery, where they were prematurely put to rest in 1979 at age 72 due primarily to his smoking three to five packs of cigarettes a day for more than 30 years.

Like hundreds of thousands of Americans who start smoking each year because it is the macho thing and a comparable number who die prematurely each year from smoking, Wayne believed he was stronger than the carcinogens and toxins in poisonous tobacco smoke. Unfortunately for Wayne and his fans, toughness does not mean a thing when lung cancer strikes. For the Duke, smoking was truly "slow motion suicide."

30. MARY WELLS

Singer Mary Wells died in 1992 at age 49 after a long bout with cancer.[59] Two years earlier the two-pack a day smoker underwent surgery for cancer of the larynx. Cancer of the larynx is normally tragic, but it is even more so when it strikes a well-known singer. The Motown recording star was best known for her rendition of "My Guy" in the early 1960s. Wells is another example of dying proof of what former Department of Health, Education

and Welfare Secretary Joseph A. Califano, Jr., called smoking - "slow-motion suicide."

31. HANK WILLIAMS, JR.

Country-music singer, guitarist, and songwriter Hank Williams, Jr., was the son of the famous Hank Williams who died on New Year's Day in 1953 due to a heart attack accompanied by whiskey and pills.[60] Describing his quitting smoking, Hank Williams, Jr., said:[61]

> A little over a year ago, I was out in the mountains on an extended hunting trip. After two or three weeks of breathing nothing but mountain air, I walked into my office, and for the first time ever, the smell of stale cigarette smoke got to me. At that moment I realized what a filthy habit it was and quit cold turkey. I can't ever remember feeling this good.

About 40 years ago my smoking father-in-law was hiking in the Colorado Rockies and had a similar experience. Enjoying the fresh air, he put out his last cigarette, said smoking was crazy, and did not light up during the last 25 years of his life. Hank Williams, Jr., my father-in-law, and millions of Americans have come to realize that enjoyment of our relatively clear air and tobacco smoke are incompatible.

B. THE WORLD OF POLITICS

1. EVERETT MCKINLEY DIRKSEN

Senator Everett McKinley Dirksen, A Republican United States Senator from Illinois from 1950 to 1969 and Senate minority leader the last 10 years, was a chain smoker who died of lung cancer at age 73.[62] He was a showman and skilled orator who I once observed getting down on his knees to emphasize a point while delivering a speech in the Senate.

One of Dirksen's greatest concerns during his final illness was getting another cigarette. Tobacco smoke prematurely deprived 11 million Illinois citizens of one of its most effective and powerful leaders who worked effectively with both Democratic and Republican administrations.

2. LYNDON BAINES JOHNSON

Lyndon Baines Johnson served as the 36th President of the United States
from 1963 to 1969. He assumed office after the assassination of President
John F. Kennedy on November 23, 1963. Born in Texas in 1908, Johnson
worked his way up to the United States House of Representatives in 1937,
was elected to the United States Senate in 1948, became Senate majority
leader in 1955 and was elected Vice President in 1960.[63] He succumbed to
a fatal heart attack on January 22, 1973.[64]

Prior to suffering a heart attack in 1955, Johnson smoked two to three
packs of cigarettes a day.[65] After suffering a major heart attack in July
1955, Johnson gave up cigarettes and went on a diet. Upon recovery, he resumed his post as Senate majority leader, and subsequently served as Vice
President and President. Johnson shocked the nation on March 31, 1968
when he said he would not run for reelection most likely because of his actions in Viet Nam which greatly reduced his popularity at home. In late
1971 he resumed smoking up to two packs a day. He suffered another heart
attack in 1972, slowly recovered, and rarely left his ranch. His fatal heart
attack occurred January 22, 1973. Smoking even kills former presidents.
Nobody is immune.

Who knows how the course of modern American history would have
evolved if Johnson had not stopped smoking after his major heart attack in
1955. Most likely he would have had another attack and died before becoming Vice President in 1961 and President in 1963. And perhaps the nation's agony over Viet Nam for which such a large share of responsibility
rests with Johnson could have been avoided. However, Johnson's stopping
smoking in 1955 greatly enhanced his career and by starting up again in
late 1971 he committed slow-motion suicide.

3. PATRICIA NIXON

Former First Lady Patricia Nixon was a recent victim among the nearly
half million Americans who die from tobacco smoke and secondary tobacco smoke each year.

A heavy smoker who never smoked in public, she had suffered from
lung disease for several years and was hospitalized for emphysema when
cancer was discovered.[66] She was representative of a large group of closet
smokers who confine the carcinogens and toxins to themselves rather than
to others.

The Patricia Nixon case is illustrative that smoking not only decreases one's longevity, but also greatly reduces the quality of life during the final years.

C. THE WORLD OF ENDORSERS

1. DAVID GOERLITZ

David Goerlitz became known as "The Winston Man" by appearing in Winston advertisements for R.J. Reynolds.[67] For 24 years he smoked three packs a day.

The New York City Tribune reported that Goerlitz apologized to school children on February 8, 1989 for pushing "the deadliest drug of all." He told fifth-grade students at Public School 63 in Manhattan that "the image that I projected is nothing but a bunch of lies made up by ad executives and the tobacco industry."[68]

Goerlitz quit smoking at age 38 in 1988 after visiting his cancer-ridden brother in a hospital. He noticed many other cancer patients in their 30s and 40s with tubes sticking out of their bodies. When Goerlitz asked what caused so much suffering, the doctors replied "smoking." When Goerlitz asked a tobacco company executive why he didn't smoke, he replied "Are you kidding? We reserve that right for the young, the poor, the black and the stupid."[69]

Goerlitz summarized his career as the Winston Man and his attitude towards smoking as follows:[70]

> As the Winston man, I helped move Winstons from fourth to second place in cigarette sales in the United States and I began to feel guilty, because people were accusing me of encouraging young people to develop a habit that would kill them. You know cigarettes are the only products manufactured in the country which, if used according to the manufacturer's directions, will kill you.

> Boys would see me as the Winston Man climbing mountains, doing all sorts of exciting things, and they'd think that if they smoke they'd be like me. They didn't know they were looking at a physical wreck. Smoking was ruining my health even though I didn't realize it at first.

> Anyway, I quit my job as the Winston Man. Then after my brother died of cancer and I began to develop obvious health problems, I quit smoking. I smoked for 24 years, and as a result haven't been able to taste food for

seven years. In addition, I'm paralyzed on one side and doctors blame this on my smoking.

No wonder the tobacco companies are sometimes referred to as the merchants of death. Hopefully the message Goerlitz conveyed to the fifth-graders at Public School 63 in Manhattan can be effectively communicated to every child in the country.

2. WAYNE MCCLAREN

Wayne McLaren, known as the "Marlboro Man," succumbed to lung cancer after a two-year illness at age 51 on July 22, 1992.[71] McLaren smoked a pack-and-a-half a day for about 25 years. His mother said that some of his last words were "tobacco will kill you, and I am living proof of it."[72]

In the spring before he died, he appeared before a shareholders meeting of Philip Morris, maker of Marlboros, to attempt to persuade the tobacco giant to limit its cigarette advertising.[73] When he appeared before the combined Houses of the Massachusetts Legislature in March 1992 in support of an increased cigarette sales tax to pay for health education, he said, "I started to smoke in my early teens because it seemed to be the thing to do, a rite of passage to adulthood." Shortly thereafter he told a British news broadcaster that "If I was responsible for making one person smoke, maybe I can be responsible for making two of them quit."

McLaren was the living and dying proof that smoking causes lung cancer and how tobacco companies promote misleading advertising. For McLaren, Marlboro Country was a premature trip to the local cemetery. Tobacco smoke is poison and poisons kill. Cigarette advertising is the craft of camouflaging and concealing a quicker trip to the local cemetery known as Marlboro Country. About 200 million American nonsmokers and some of the 46 million smokers can thank McLaren for his late-life concern by trying to educate people about the horrors of cigarette smoke in his dying months.

3. ALAN LANDERS

Alan Landers, a former advertising model for Winston cigarettes and Tiparillo cigars, blames his two episodes of lung cancer and the paralysis of his vocal cords for a year, on his 2-1/2 pack-a-day smoking habit.[74] Landers was the gentleman in the "Should a gentleman offer a lady a

Tiparillo?" ad campaign and in the late 1960s was featured in an ad campaign with the slogan "Down home with Winston cigarettes."[75]

Landers is trying to get the message across to teenagers that "cigarettes definitely kill you." He pointed out that the warnings on cigarette packages "didn't tell you the truth. They didn't tell you cigarettes cause lung cancer, emphysema, and heart attacks."[76]

After losing his smoking grandfather, aunt and uncle to lung cancer, the former smoking model says "I'm angry at the cigarette companies." He angrily reflects:[77]

> I wound up with lung cancer twice. They perpetrated a lie, which has really screwed my life up. I'm grateful to be alive, but it has been torture.

Like David Goerlitz, Wayne McClaren, and Lucky Strike woman Janet Sackman who lost her larynx and part of a lung to cancer,[78] Landers is trying to warn persons of the deadly effect of smoking. It is significant that the current message of former tobacco pitchmen and pitchwomen is to either stop smoking or not to start if you want to have a chance to live a normal and healthy life.

D. NEWS AND VIEWS

1. LARRY KING

One of America's best known talk show hosts, Larry King, gave up smoking after a heart attack in the late 1980s.[79] In his book "Tell Me More," King admitted that he "smoked too long" and does not miss smoking at all.[80]

The famous talk show host relates a story from the heavy smoking Bob Uecker, a sportscaster and former major league ballplayer. After five years of not smoking, Uecker picked up a cigarette for a couple of drags and said, "How did I ever smoke this shit? In fact, it tastes worse than shit."[81]

King asked former Surgeon General Dr. C. Everett Koop why he was so vehemently against the tobacco industry.[82] Koop unhesitatingly said, "Because of the sleaze." What he meant by sleaze is:

> Because they continue to say that no one has conclusively linked cigarette smoking to lung cancer and that no one has conclusively linked smoking to heart disease, when more than fifty-five scientific papers have been published supporting my position that they *are* linked. And because they say,

"We're not trying to entice young people to start smoking. We only want them to switch brands." That's garbage.

Larry King is probably alive today pursuing his vocation as one of America's top talk show hosts because he heeded the heart attack warning and gave up smoking. Unfortunately many persons fail to heed similar warnings.

2. EDWARD R. MURROW

Edward R. Murrow may go down as the outstanding radio and television broadcaster and television series narrator of the twentieth century. He served as the Director of the U.S. Information Agency from 1961 to 1964.[83] His "See It Now" program attack on Senator Joseph R. McCarthy in 1954, whose investigations of Communist influences in the government had caused a national controversy, played a significant role in the downfall of the Wisconsin Senator, and may have helped prevent similar unsubstantiated future savage attacks.

A cigarette in hand was Murrow's trademark. However, he was unable to overcome addiction to smoking which caused his premature death in 1965 at age 57. Had Murrow covered just one more story during his career - the dangers of smoking - he may have stopped smoking, saved many lives, and devoted those extra years to making additional meaningful contributions to the United States. His premature departure due to excessive smoking deprived Americans of many more years of insightful reports and service to his country.

3. HARRY REASONER

For many years millions of Americans gathered around their television sets each Sunday evening to see Harry Reasoner along with founding co-editor Mike Wallace on *60 Minutes*. USA Today on August 12, 1991 said that Andy Rooney called Harry Reasoner the "smartest correspondent" he ever knew, but also perhaps the "dumbest" because he continued to smoke after a lung operation. Reasoner died of a heart attack at age 68 in 1991[84] undoubtedly attributable at least, in part, to smoking.

How many dummies do you know who have continued to smoke after a serious warning? How many dummy parents continue to smoke in the home after learning that secondary tobacco smoke will jeopardize their children's health?

4. JIM LEHRER

Jim Lehrer of Public Television's McNeil-Lehrer News Hour was an addicted smoker for 30 years when he had a heart attack on December 11, 1983 at age 49.[85] Even on the way to the hospital he had a cigarette. Lehrer was one of the lucky survivors and not one of the 419,000 smokers who die prematurely each year from tobacco smoke.

Lehrer has not had a puff on a cigarette or any other kind of tobacco for more than ten years since his December 1983 heart attack. And when he is not insightfully informing the nation of the day's events, he bikes, plays tennis, watches his diet, and takes a daily nap.[86]

E. THE SAD CONCLUSION

These are a few of the many more celebrities who should be mentioned in passing who succumbed to smoking:

Steve McQueen at age 50 due to lung cancer;
Babe Ruth at age 53 due to throat cancer;
Betty Grable at age 57 due to lung cancer;
Humphrey Bogart at age 57 from throat cancer;
Chet Huntley at age 63 due to lung cancer;
Walt Disney at age 65 from lung cancer;
Jackie Gleason at age 71 from heart disease and lung cancer;
Ed Sullivan at age 72 from lung cancer.

They say the bigger you are the harder you fall. Hopefully today's celebrities, sports heroes and politicians will join the anti-smoking bandwagon. Perhaps Bill Clinton and Michael Jordan can be persuaded to throw away their cigars. They will have learned the sad lessons from the sufferings of their predecessors ravaged from the carcinogens and toxins of poisonous tobacco smoke. They will have learned there is no glory and there are no spotlights when dying of emphysema, lung cancer, throat cancer, stroke, and heart disease caused by smoking.

ENDNOTES

[1] Taylor, C. Barr, M.D., and Killen, Joel D., Ph.D., *The Facts About Smoking*, Consumer Reports Books, 1991, pp. 32, 37.

[2] Heart Corps, "Famous Quitters," February 1990, p. 32.

[3] "Claude Akins, 67, A Supporting Actor in Many Noted Films," New York Times, 1/29/94, p. 11.

[4] 1991 World Book.

[5] Tobacco Hall of Shame 1991, Roswell Park Cancer Institute, Buffalo, New York.

[6] 1991 World Book.

[7] *Id.* at footnote 5.

[8] *Id.*

[9] *Id.*

[10] 1986 World Book Yearbook; *Id.* at footnote 5.

[11] See footnote 2, at p. 33.

[12] Tobacco Hall of Shame 1991, Roswell Park Cancer Institute, Buffalo, New York.

[13] World Book 1991.

[14] World Book 1991.

[15] "Tobacco Road," William Ecenbarger, Philadelphia Inquirer Magazine, 11/17/91, p. 16 et seq..

[16] "I'm Just Lucky To Be Alive," People Magazine, January 29, 1990, pp. 33-35.

[17] *Id.*

[18] Tobias, Andrew, and Smokefree Educational Services, *Kids Say Don't Smoke*, Workman Publishing Company, 1991.

[19] Contemporary Theatre, Film, and Television, Gale Research, Inc., Volume 7, pp. 103-104 (1989).

[20] "How I Quit Smoking," compiled by Lynn Minton.

[21] Contemporary Theatre, Film, and Television, Gale Research, Inc., Volume 6, p. 130 (1989).

[22] See footnote 20.

[23] Contemporary Theatre, Film, and Television, Gale Research Company, Volume 3, pp. 155-56 (1986).

[24] Heart Corps, "Famous Quitters," February 1990, p. 32.

[25] Taylor, Peter, *The Smoke Ring – Tobacco, Money & Multi-National Politics*, Pantheon Books, 1984, p. xiv.

[26] See footnote 20.

[27] Heart Corps, "Famous Quitters," February 1990, p. 33.

[28] See footnote 25.

[29] Califano, Joseph A., Jr., *Governing America*, Simon & Schuster, 1981, p. 185.

[30] Statement of the American Medical Association to the Environmental Protection Agency Science Advisory Board, Indoor Air Quality and Total Human Exposure Committee, December 4, 1990.

[31] Heart Corps, "Famous Quitters," February 1990, p. 30.

[32] United States Environmental Protection Agency, Office of Research and Development, Office of Air and Radiation, "Respiratory Health Effects of Passive Smoking: Lung Cancer and Other Disorders," 12/92.

[33] See footnote 29.

[34] Heart Corps, "Famous Quitters," February 1990, p. 31.

[35] "Eddie Kendricks, 52; Sang Falsetto with Temptations," Chicago Sun-Times, 10/7/92, p. 79.

[36] Heart Corps, "Famous Quitters," February 1990, p. 32.

[37] Contemporary Theatre, Film, and Television, Gale Research, Inc., Volume 10, pp. 267-268 (1993).

[38] Tobacco Hall of Shame 1991, Roswell Park Cancer Institute, Buffalo, New York.

[39] Heart Corps, "Famous Quitters," February 1990, p. 30.

[40] *Id.* at p. 33.

[41] Contemporary Theatre, Film, and Television, Gale Research Company, Volume 4, pp. 302-304 (1987).

[42] Heart Corps, "Famous Quitters," February 1990, p. 30.

[43] *Id.* at p. 32.

[44] "How I Quit Smoking," compiled by Lynn Minton.

[45] Penguin Encyclopedia of Popular Music – 1989.

[46] Contemporary Theatre, Film, and Television, Gale Research, Inc., Volume 6, p. 315 (1989).

[47] Heart Corps, "Famous Quitters," February 1990, p. 31.

[48] *Id.*

[49] Contemporary Theatre, Film, and Television, Gale Research, Inc., Volume 7, pp. 324-326 (1989).

[50] "How I Quit Smoking," compiled by Lynn Minton.

[51] "In Love Again," *People,* 12/14/95, p. 54.

[52] Contemporary Theatre, Film, and Television, Gale Research, Inc., Volume 7, pp. 322-323 (1986).

[53] "How I Quit Smoking," compiled by Lynn Minton.

[54] Tobacco Hall of Shame 1991, Roswell Park Cancer Institute, Buffalo, New York.

[55] "The Jazz Singer - The enduring magic of Sarah Vaughn," Connoisseur Magazine, March 1989, pp. 146-149.

[56] World Book 1991.

[57] Shepherd, Donald and Slatzer, Robert, *The Life and Times of John Wayne*, Doubleday and Co., p. 260, 1985.

[58] Jennings, Dan, Saturday Evening Post, 10/27/62, pp. 28-33.

[59] "Singer Mary Wells dies at 49; Motown star recorded 'My Guy'", The Buffalo News, 7/27/92.

[60] "40 Years Gone, Hank Sr. Lives On in Spirit," Chicago Sun-Times, 1/14/93, p. 4.

[61] Heart Corps, "Famous Quitters," February 1990, p. 32.

[62] "Tobacco Road," William Ecenbarger, Philadelphia Inquirer Magazine, 11/17/91, p. 34; 1991 World Book.

[63] World Book 1991.

[64] *Id.*

[65] *Time*, February 5, 1973, p. 69.

[66] "Former First Lady Pat Nixon Dead at 81," Chicago Sun-Times, June 23, 1993, p. 26.

[67] See footnote 18.

[68] *Id.*

[69] *Id.*

[70] Heart Corps, "Famous Quitters," February 1990, p. 31.

[71] "Marlboro Man" Wayne McLaren, 51, Lung Cancer Victim," Chicago Sun-Times, 7/25/92, p. 37.

[72] *Id.*

[73] *Id.*

[74] "After Cancer, no longer a model smoker," USA Today, 9/25/95, Sec. D, p. 4.

[75] *Id.*

[76] *Id.*

[77] *Id.*

[78] "Former Cigarette Glamour Model Sues Tobacco Company," *Tobacco on Trial*, 9/30/95, pp. 1, 2; "So You Think You Want to Smoke," Ecenbarger, William, *Readers Digest*, 9/94, pp. 61-62.

[79] King, Larry, *Tell Me More*, p. 263.

[80] *Id.*

[81] *Id.*

[82] *Id.* at p. 264.

[83] World Book 1991.

84 Tobacco Hall of Shame 1991, Roswell Park Cancer Institute, Buffalo, New York.
85 Lehrer, Jim, *A Bus of My Own*, G.P. Putnam Sons, 1992, pp. 171-172. "What a Heart Attack Taught Me," Lehrer, Jim, Condensed from "A Bus of My Own," Reader's Digest, September 1992, 102-103.
86 *Id.*

IV

SOUND SMOKING ADVICE

For more than 35 years, millions of Americans have looked daily to "Ann Landers," Esther "Eppie" Lederer, and "Dear Abby," Abigail Van Buren, twin sisters more than 75 years young, for advice for personal problems and concerns including health matters. A sample of these letters and replies are included to demonstrate the personal and family tragedies of the smoking holocaust. They are designed to give the objective perspective of persons who are not smoking sympathizers, anti-smoking activists or tobacco industry spin control artists. Perhaps some lessons can be learned from this barrage of heart-rendering tragedies that invariably end in death or serious illness.

1. WE CAN WAIT

The following Dear Abby February 7, 1993[1] column in the Chicago Tribune reflects the impact smoking has not only on the victims, but on the aggrieved family members:

> DEAR ABBY: Recently my husband was in the hospital with severe breathing problems caused by many years of heavy smoking. The oxygen level in his blood was so low, none of the nurses and doctors could believe he was still walking around.
>
> It was touch and go for a while, but he finally made it, thank God. Several days later, I read this article in our local newspaper's letters-to-the-editor column. I hope you think it's worth sharing with your readers.
>
> Edna Giffen, Zanesville, Ohio

DEAR EDNA: Thanks for sending the piece as it appeared in the Zanesville Times Recorder. I hope my readers realize it is an exercise in sarcasm, written tongue-in-cheek.

* * *

"To the Editor:

"Smoking should be allowed everywhere. The use of tobacco products should be encouraged, even for children! Smoking is very beneficial to our society:

"It brings families together (usually in hospitals' intensive care units or at funerals). It helps support the dry cleaning industry (necessitates cleaning clothes more frequently). The pharmaceutical companies profit (medication for asthma, emphysema and chemotherapy for lung cancer).

"It creates a healthy challenge to our cosmetic industry to create new ways to cover up ugly, tobacco-wrinkled skin. Smoking keeps thousands of doctors, nurses and hospital workers employed indefinitely.

"Secondhand smoke keeps children less jumpy and rowdy (they are sick more often, and can't breathe as well). Forget condom machines in the schools, put in cigarette machines! So let's forget all this nonsense about banning smoking. Buy a pack today! I hope to see you in my office soon."

Dr. David C. Zangmeister, Dresden, Ohio

* * *

The letter reminds me of a warning sign outside a Chicago-area cemetery, "Drive Carefully, We Can Wait."

2. FOOD FOR THOUGHT

One of the most disturbing events that can ruin a day is having smoke drifting into one's face during a meal at a restaurant. Many restaurants are banning smoking entirely. Others have designated nonsmoking sections of varying sizes. How many times have you asked for a table in the nonsmoking section and been placed next to a table in the smoking section? Being on the border can be compounded if the restaurant has a poor ventilating system. By the way, restaurants generally do not charge extra for the carcinogens and toxins in secondary tobacco smoke. Hopefully, in attempting to reach former Surgeon General Koop's goal of a smokefree society by the year 2000, all public enterprises including restaurants will become smoke-free. Los Angeles in July 1993 and New York City in December 1994 as well as numerous other cities have taken the step of requiring all restaurants to be smoke-free.

The following letter and answer in Dear Abby's November 10, 1992 column in The (Lake County, Illinois) News-Sun[2] captures part of the smoking-in-restaurants problem:

> DEAR ABBY: What is the proper etiquette when smokers and non-smokers are dining out together?
>
> Recently, eight of us decided to eat out. It was the birthday of one and the others were treating him to a birthday party. The restaurant did not take reservations.
>
> As we entered the restaurant, we were asked if we wanted to sit in the smoking or non-smoking section. I said, "Non-smoking," but was quickly (and loudly) corrected by one of the smokers.
>
> There were three smokers and five non-smokers in our party. The three smokers chain-smoked during the entire meal.
>
> Since the meal took about two hours, I don't think it would have been unreasonable for the smokers to have abstained for that short period of time – or they could have excused themselves for a few minutes if they wanted a cigarette.
>
> Also, since the non-smokers were in the majority, I think our party should have been seated in the non-smoking section.
>
> What is your opinion?
>
> NON-SMOKER

* * *

> DEAR NON-SMOKER: In recent years, non-smokers have become so militant about having their space polluted with cigarette smoke, smokers have been made to feel like king-sized outcasts.
>
> With three smokers in your party who were so desperate for a cigarette they chain-smoked through the entire meal, your party did not belong in the non-smoking section.
>
> However, I would have based my decision on whether or not the guest of honor was a smoker, and accommodated that person.

3. WOMEN BEWARE

Occasionally a columnist will briefly answer many letters from readers at once. In her October 28, 1992 Chicago Tribune column, Abigail Van Buren[3] answered questions as to the number-one killer of women as follows:

> DEAR READERS: The No. 1 killer of women is *not* breast cancer – it's lung cancer. Smoking is associated with more deaths and illness than drugs, alcohol, automobile accidents and AIDS combined.

As long as the tobacco industry gears a portion of its advertising to women to help make up for the nearly half million annual premature American deaths from tobacco smoke and secondary tobacco smoke, lung cancer will probably remain the number one killer among women. Educating women as to the dangers of tobacco smoke should be a high priority of every organization or health care provider that has concerns for the health and well-being of women.

4. SLOW MOTION SUICIDE

Approximately 419,000 American smokers die prematurely each year from the carcinogens and toxins in tobacco smoke. Many have been aware of the major health risks of smoking since even before the United States Surgeon General issued his landmark report in 1964 entitled "Smoking and Health." My father said he would give up some years of his life in return for the enjoyment of smoking. Not only did he sacrifice a number of years, but smoking led to a much poorer quality during the last decade of his tobacco smoke-ravaged life largely confined to a nursing home with emphysema and residuals of a stroke. Ann Landers in her September 22, 1992 Chicago Tribune column[4] captured the self-destruction inclination of smokers when she published the following letter and her response:

> DEAR ANN LANDERS: I took note of a recent letter in your column from a woman who said she was sick at heart because her mother had been murdered by cigarettes. Please permit me to say it was not murder. It was *suicide*, and there's a world of difference.
>
> Montreal Reader

DEAR MONTREAL: You bet there is, but sad to say, the results are the same. With what we know about tobacco these days, anyone who continues to smoke is killing himself, as surely as if he put a gun to his head and pulled the trigger.

Former Department of Health, Education and Welfare Secretary Joseph A. Califano, Jr., in 1979 described smoking as "slow motion suicide." Like my father, most of the 419,000 smokers who die prematurely each year from tobacco smoke have committed slow motion suicide.

5. BAN TOBACCO PRODUCTS

It has been suggested by some that tobacco should be made illegal. Food and Drug Administration Commissioner Dr. David Kessler in February 1994 raised the question as to whether nicotine-containing cigarettes should be regulated as drugs. If so, tobacco could very well be banned before the end of the century.

I am raising the possibility in the chapter on the courts of making it a felony to grow, distribute or sell tobacco now that it has been determined as of January 1993 to be a Class A human carcinogen by the Environmental Protection Agency. Ann Landers addresses this issue in her October 9, 1992 column in the Chicago Tribune[5] with the following letter:

DEAR ANN LANDERS: In my opinion, there is only one solution to the problems associated with smoking, and that is to make tobacco an illegal substance. The growing of tobacco must be banned and concurrently the manufacture of cigarettes and other tobacco-related products prohibited.

I am 71 years old and have done my share of smoking. I started when I was 14 and didn't quit until I was 44. I am well aware that the manufacturers of tobacco products have a rich and powerful lobby. But is it morally right to continue such an operation when the results are so devastating?

I often wonder how the people who work in the tobacco industry deal with their consciences when they see what the product is doing to the health and welfare of millions of people. We all are well aware that the sickness, death and property damage caused by smoking is appalling.

Please, Ann, ask your readers to support the banning of tobacco products. As long as cigarettes are readily available, there will be smokers. And new smokers are getting hooked at such an early age it's tragic.

Harry in Newport News, VA

DEAR HARRY: I share your sentiments about tobacco, but what you suggest would not succeed. We had a similar experiment and it was a miserably failure. It was called Prohibition. Remember?

In my opinion, the way to go is education and a higher tax on cigarettes.

Hopefully, what happened in Prohibition would not occur for several reasons. Unlike Prohibition where a large percentage of Americans drank alcoholic beverages, only 26% of American adults and less than 20% of all Americans smoke. Moreover, a reasonable amount of consumption of alcoholic beverages does not normally harm others; however, secondary tobacco smoke kills thousands of innocent victims each year and renders many more seriously ill.

Education is important, but its benefits are often offset by slick advertising. A higher tax on cigarettes ($2 to $3 per pack) is one of the important solutions to the smoking problem and will be addressed in detail later.

6. KILLING KIDS

The tobacco industry must make up for the losses of nearly a half million Americans who die prematurely each year and many more who become seriously ill by recruiting children, women, minorities and foreign customers. Don't kid yourself! Joe Camel is designed to create a recognition image just like Mickey Mouse. The following letter which appeared in the Dear Abby column in the April 2, 1992 Chicago Tribune[6] says it all about tobacco advertising geared towards kids:

DEAR ABBY: This letter is in response to "Former Smoker." You said, "Please don't blame the tobacco companies; we live in a country where people have the right to choose."

Abby, surely you are aware that the tobacco industry entices replacement smokers from our youth. Please note the following:

Tobacco advertising is aimed at kids. The tobacco industry needs 5,000 children to begin smoking every day to maintain its current market. Statistics show us that 60 percent of smokers begin by age 14, and 90 percent begin by age 19.

Children do not have the cognitive ability that adults have and are easy prey for the tobacco industry. Nicotine, the addictive substance in cigarettes, may be more difficult to quit using than heroin.

Our kids get hooked at an early age; then many spend the rest of their lives trying to stop using tobacco. Yes, we make our own choices, but it takes more than one school health-education class to counteract the tobacco industry's multibillion dollar blitz. We believe that every child has the right to be protected from exposure to advertising that promotes smoking as part of the good life, or connects smoking with sports or other health-giving activities.

> Connie Acott, Project Director,
> Tobacco-free Schools,
> Colorado State University

DEAR CONNIE: Thank you for some startling facts. I hope my young readers see your letter and take it seriously. It could add years to their lives.

In effect, the tobacco industry has adopted a making-money-by-addicting-kids policy. Joe Camel appears to be featured as the number one kid killer. I do not believe that there has been any prior similar concerted effort to destroy the health of our children.

7. LABOR OF DEATH

The tobacco industry lobbyists are quick to point out that the industry provides jobs for many Americans which would be lost if smoking decreases. Ann Landers in her "Gem of the Day" item in the January 28, 1993 Chicago Tribune[7] has the perfect response to the job argument:

GEM OF THE DAY: The tobacco industry reports that it provides jobs for 57,000 Americans - and this does not include physicians, X-ray technicians, nurses, hospital employees, firefighters, dry cleaners, respiratory specialists, pharmacists, morticians and gravediggers.

Come to think of it Adolf Hitler created millions of jobs in Nazi Germany in the 1930s to turn their economy around. Perhaps that is a reason why wonder the British Royal College of Physicians of London in 1971 referred to the toll caused by smoking as "the present holocaust."

8. PREMATURELY EXTINGUISHING THE FLAME

I expressed my condolences to a physician friend on the passing of his father, also a physician. Although his father stopped smoking 25 years earlier, the cause of his death was the smoking related lung cancer. When I told the son of my book plans, he urged me to proceed quickly and he would purchase the first copy. His anger toward the tobacco industry overflowed as well as his desire to save others from the fate of his father. Smoking at no matter what age has the potential to destroy. The Dear Abby July 18, 1992 Chicago Tribune column[8] reprinted the following letter which captures the feelings of grieving family members:

> DEAR ABBY: (July 7, 1989) I am writing this letter in the waiting room of the intensive care unit of the Boulder (Colo.) Community Hospital. My mother is on a respirator due to severe lung damage. She has asthma and smoked cigarettes for 50 years. Now she has emphysema and pneumonia.
>
> Before she was hooked up to the respirator, she begged me to help her. Now I can only comfort her and pray for her. For years, the family asked her to quit smoking, but it was something she couldn't – or didn't want to – do. My mother is a strong woman, but her addiction to cigarettes got the best of her, even after seeing my father go through surgery for lung cancer eight months ago.
>
> (Aug. 6, 1989) I was interrupted when I started to write the above letter and am now able to finish it.
>
> My mother passed away on July 18. She was only 65 years old. It's too late to save her now, but it may not be too late for some of your readers.
>
> Smokers, please think about the pain and suffering you can cause yourself and your family by continuing to smoke.
>
> I don't have a mother now, and my children, ages 12 and 18, don't have a grandma anymore. Please, please quit smoking now, if not for yourself, then for those who love you.
>
> Susan Ortez, Denver
>
> DEAR SUSAN: My heart goes out to you and your family. If your letter inspires only one person to quit smoking, it will be well worth the space in this column. Thanks for writing.

The principal choice of smokers boils down to whether they prefer smoking with a premature death and lower quality of life or living with a higher quality of life and seeing their loved ones longer.

9. SMOKING AND CEMETERIES - A SAD OBITUARY

The real Marlboro Country is one's local cemetery. Many of the nearly half million annual obituaries caused by tobacco smoke and secondary tobacco smoke should read similarly to the following one referred to in Dear Abby's February 22, 1993 Chicago Tribune column:[9]

DEAR ABBY: A few months ago, you had a letter in your column from "Long Islander," who wrote, "The first thing I look for in my newspaper is the obituary column, and when the cause of death is cancer, I always wonder if the deceased had been a heavy smoker." Enclosed is an obituary from the Star-Free Press in Ventura, Calif., dated Jan. 5, 1993. It says:

"Yolanda Angelari Mitchell, 60, died New Year's Day at Community Memorial Hospital from emphysema, after a lifetime of cigarette smoking."

I wonder if Yolanda Mitchell had seen the letter from "Long Islander" and requested to be identified in her obituary as "a heavy smoker."

We will never know, will we?"

Richard N. Keller, Ventura, Calif.

DEAR RICHARD KELLER: Yes, we will. Yolanda's obituary stated that she was survived by a sister, Madaline Newhart of Ventura, and a son and daughter-in-law, Donnie and Jonie Mitchell.

I telephoned Madaline and introduced myself as "Dear Abby." At first she didn't believe me (nobody does); then I offered my condolences on the loss of her sister. She graciously accepted and said that she and her sister had been reading my column for years in the Ventura Star-Free Press.

I told her that her sister's obituary was the first I had seen that mentioned the deceased had been a "lifetime smoker."

"Yolanda wanted to have that included in the write-up," she said, "and her son, Donnie, agreed that it was a good idea, too."

She went on to say: "I'm in treatment myself for emphysema. I was also a heavy cigarette smoker. I'm five years older than Yolanda, and when we were kids, everybody thought it was smart to smoke. Nobody realized what a dangerous habit it could be.

"Yolanda had all sorts of respiratory problems, and her doctor ordered her to quit smoking, but she was too far into the habit and couldn't quit," Madaline added. "Thank God Donnie doesn't smoke and neither does his wife. They've got a couple of really cute kids they would like to see grow up."

I asked Madaline if she had any objections to my publishing this. She replied, "Go right ahead, honey ... it might make kids realize that smoking can be a killer."

So, thank you, Madaline Newhart. And thank you, Donnie Mitchell.

It would be helpful if more obituaries or writeups of cancer, heart, and emphysema victims indicated whether the deceased was a heavy smoker. It would serve as an important reminder to readers that the poisonous tobacco road will lead to a premature visit to their local cemetery - Marlboro Country.

A subsequent letter appeared in the March 8, 1993 Chicago Tribune:[10]

DEAR ABBY: I was surprised to see that you agreed with "Long Islander," who wanted obituaries to state whether persons who had died of lung cancer had been habitual smokers.

In the first place, an obituary is hardly the place to chastise the deceased for self-destructive habits. Secondly, if we are going to use death notices as object lessons, what about other unhealthy vices?

Shouldn't obituaries read: "Harry gave himself a heart attack because he salted everything he ate, and he never met a fried food he didn't like"? Or, "Jane's death from skin cancer was brought on my her 30-year quest for the perfect tan"?

Abby, I'm sure you wouldn't approve of using such remarks in an obituary, yet you seem to encourage using the fact that a person had been a habitual smoker in that person's obituary because it supports your personal anti-smoking campaign.

In case you're wondering, I have never used tobacco in any form, but I can understand why smokers resent being singled out for public abuse.

In your column, you keep reminding people to show compassion and understanding for alcoholics and drug addicts, but nicotine addicts (for you) are fair game. Why?

Perhaps those who have a public forum – such as yourself – should tone down the criticism, and concentrate on advocating a generally healthy lifestyle.

A Moderate Texan in Freeport

DEAR MODERATE TEXAN: Please forgive me if I sound like a fanatic, but over the years I've heard many a smoker say, "I'm sorry I got into this terrible habit." But I've yet to hear anyone say, "Gee, I'm glad I'm a smoker."

The British have a way with their dry humor of cutting to the core quickly. The same must be done with tobacco smoke. The carcinogens and toxins in poisonous tobacco smoke not only kill nearly a half million Americans prematurely each year, but are responsible for killing about another 2.5 million human beings around the world. Over the next decade about 4.2 million Americans and more than 30 million human beings worldwide will die prematurely from tobacco smoke, many from American tobacco exports. Newspapers around the world will have to expand the space allocated to obituaries to handle the smoking onslaught. Historians may look back and designate the carcinogens and toxins in poisonous tobacco smoke and secondary tobacco smoke as the dark plague of the twentieth and twenty-first centuries.

The following letter printed in the Chicago Tribune's May 11, 1993 Dear Abby column[11] should be seen in obituary columns around the country about 419,000 times a year:

> DEAR ABBY: You recently published a letter from a reader who requested that her obituary include the fact that she had been a heavy smoker. Perhaps that started a new trend, because I read the following obituary in The New York Times on Feb. 25, 1993:
>
> "Jane Doe, R.N. died after a long illness ...Daughter of... sister of...cousin of...A brilliant person, iconoclast and achiever. She smoked two packs of cigarettes daily for 40 years. In addition to her family and friends, the tobacco industry will miss her. Graveside service Feb. 28 at 1 p.m."

More obituary writers should include the smoking habits of the deceased in their writeups. Such knowledge will serve not only as a somber warning to surviving family members of the lethal nature of tobacco, but also as a warning to all readers.

10. A Habit of Many Diseases

Ann Landers in her March 18, 1993 column[12] points out the link between smoking and a fatal illness, sudden infant death syndrome. A similar letter could have been written about lung cancer, leukemia, emphysema, heart disease, strokes, cataracts, gum disease, and many other childhood and adult diseases and illnesses. Physicians at the Rush Medical Center in Chicago and the Sloan Kettering Cancer Institute in New York called smoking by a parent in the presence of a child a form of child abuse, a subject discussed in the following letter to Ann Landers:

> DEAR ANN LANDERS: A friend of mine who was a heavy smoker recently lost her baby to SIDS (sudden infant death syndrome). I am enclosing an article that recently appeared in USA Today about the link between women who smoke and this cruelest of all baby killers. People need to be aware of the connection.
>
> I see people smoking as they drive, with the windows rolled up. There are often children in the back seat. To me, this is child abuse. I've seen women holding babies in their arms with cigarettes dangling from their mouths while ashes and smoke get in the child's face.

I'm a single man, and I won't date a woman who smokes. Maybe if you print this article, it will wake up some of these foolish people.

Brunswick, GA

DEAR BRUNSWICK: Thanks for your comments and the clipping. Here are the highlights:

A new study has revealed that babies whose mothers smoked during pregnancy or soon after giving birth are much more likely to die of SIDS than infants whose moms never smoked cigarettes.

Scientists have established a link between prenatal smoking and SIDS in the past few years, but this is the first study to show that an infant's exposure to smoke *after* birth can be linked to death from SIDS.

According to the study in Pediatrics, babies exposed to smoking only in utero were twice as likely to die of SIDS as the infants of non-smoking women. Babies exposed both in the womb and after birth were three times as likely to become SIDS victims.

Well, dear readers, this is a strong message for all pregnant women and new mothers. I hope they get it.

If a pregnant woman or mother of a young child read the March 18, 1993 Ann Landers letter and the underlying medical studies, it would be difficult to ascertain how she could continue smoking or permit her husband to smoke. Any mother who so continues would appear to be guilty of child abuse and child neglect.

As Ann Landers response to the following letter appearing in the September 23, 1993 Chicago Tribune[13] regarding parental smoking in the presence of an asthmatic child indicates, such irresponsible behavior is clearly a form of child abuse:

DEAR ANN LANDERS: My problem is my ex-husband. He is a smoker. I personally do not care if he croaks from all his smoking. But the problem is that our 7-year-old son, "David," has asthma and "Mark" continues to smoke around him.

I have sent Mark tons of information about the effects of secondhand smoke on asthmatics, but the ignorant fool still smokes around David during weekend visitations. What can I do to stop him from smoking around my son? Don't tell me to talk to him. He tuned me out years ago.

Sylacauga, Ala.

DEAR ALABAMA: Enlist the help of the child's pediatrician. Asthma is a serious condition, and Mark may be endangering David's life by smoking in his presence. This could be cause for losing visitation rights.

11. REDUCED QUALITY OF LIFE

Smoking not only reduces longevity, but also reduces the quality of life during the final years or phase. The following letter appearing in the May 13, 1993 Dear Abby Chicago Tribune column[14] underscores the reduction of quality-of-life residual of smoking:

DEAR ABBY: I just read the letter from the man who says he's glad he smokes. He sounds just like my dad. He always insisted that he didn't inhale, so it didn't matter.

He is now 84, and has had chronic emphysema for the past 10 years. I don't know how many times we've had to rush him to the hospital because of the lung problems. He now sits in his chair with the oxygen machine running 16 hours a day.

Its no wonder people are proposing taxing cigarettes at $2 a pack; Medicare has to pick up the tab for millions of people like my beloved dad.

I'm signing my name, but please don't use it; I don't want to embarrass my father.

His Daughter, Glendale, Ore.

It would be interesting to ascertain what percentage of people hooked up to oxygen machines smoke or previously smoked. Hospitals, nursing homes, and oxygen machines are some of the external accoutrements of the residual of years of smoking. Preventable major operations, difficulty breathing, pain and coughing are some of the internal suffering incurred by years of smoking. No matter how you cut it, smoking greatly reduces the quality of one's life during the final years. Perhaps the $2 per pack proposed federal tax increase on cigarettes is too low. As until recently in Canada, a pack of cigarettes should cost at least $7.00. It would serve as a deterrent that would save lives and suffering.

The following letter from a physician about her father-in-law appearing in the May 3, 1993 Chicago Tribune's Dear Abby column[15] should be read and reread by any smoker who has any concern about his or her family and quality of life:

DEAR ABBY: I can't get your "proud smokers" column off my mind. My father-in-law also used to say, "I know that smoking isn't good for me, but I'd rather enjoy my time on earth and die a little earlier than deprive myself of the things I enjoy."

I was in medical school at the time. Unfortunately, Dad didn't get very much more enjoyment because he had to have bypass surgery. Then he needed his arteries stripped so his brain could get proper blood supply. Then they stripped his femoral arteries, not once, but twice – all the while he continued to "enjoy himself" as he smoked one cigarette after another.

Soon his leg became gangrenous because there wasn't enough artery to save, so they amputated his leg almost to his hip. By that time, I was a resident in pathology, and Dad's other leg began to lose circulation, and his bypasses were clogging.

Had enough? Well, so did he. Fortunately, he died before they did any further amputations.

Through all of this, Dad never deprived himself of the pleasure of smoking, but he deprived his family of having him around to celebrate his 60th birthday. You may use my name.

Lisa K. Helfend, M.D., San Rafael, Calif.

Dear Lisa: Thank you for a powerful letter and giving me permission to use your name. Perhaps this will send a message to those who need it.

12. LEVEL WITH THE KIDS

Ways must be found to combat the tobacco industry's campaign to replace many of the nearly half million Americans who die prematurely each year from smoking with minors under age 18. The Joe Camel character has a recognition factor as great as Mickey Mouse. Joe Camel being enticing to young children creates a favorable image for smoking in the later childhood years. About 60% of smokers begin prior to age 14. Ann Landers in her April 6, 1993 Chicago Tribune column[16] published the following letter from the American Medical Association focusing on a way to counteract the tobacco industry's Joe Camel advertising barrage:

DEAR READERS: Here's a letter from the American Medical Association on one of my favorite subjects. I am delighted to share it with you.

DEAR ANN LANDERS: In an effort to increase awareness among young children about the dangers of smoking, U.S. Surgeon General Antonia Novello and the American Medical Association are sponsoring a nationwide contest called Say No, Old Joe.

The tobacco industry is spending millions to encourage smoking. It is succeeding. Every day, 3,000 children light up their first cigarette. The most heinous of the industry's efforts is the use of a marketing tool called "Old Joe Camel," who portrays cigarette smoking as a "cool thing to do."

The AMA and Dr. Novello want to encourage students to help stop tobacco use among their peers by fighting back. They are asking students in kindergarten through 8th grade to draw a poster or write a letter, poem or essay, one page or less, telling Old Joe Camel why he should stop smoking. We hope that teachers will use it as a springboard to discuss the dangers of smoking with their students.

More than 175,000 students entered the contest. Hopefully this and similar contests will be repeated each year. It is an example of the powerful influence education can have on the health of children.

13. CHEWING TOBACCO HARMS

There is a growing myth that chewing tobacco, unlike cigarette smoke, cannot cause any harm and is a macho thing to do since it is used by many professional athletes. The following Ann Landers Chicago Tribune column published July 18, 1993[17] dispels this myth:

DEAR ANN LANDERS: Something terrible is going on in our country, and nobody is paying the least bit of attention. I am talking about the increase in the use of chewing tobacco and snuff by young people.

The use of chewing tobacco by professional athletes, especially baseball players, is an important factor in this ever-growing trend. Young people get the idea that it is safe because baseball players they look up to are seen on TV with a plug of tobacco in their mouths, spitting juice all over the place. What the TV *doesn't* show are the ugly brown stains on their teeth or the facial deformities that result from cancer of the mouth.

According to the Centers for Disease Control, nearly 5.5 million adults used chewing tobacco and snuff in 1991, which is the most recent data available. The highest percentage of users was among men age 18 to 24.

In December, Surgeon General Antonia Novello warned that the United States faces an epidemic of oral cancer in the coming decade because of the widespread use of smokeless tobacco. About 23 percent of the people who chew tobacco also smoke. This means they are getting a double dose of a product we know can produce cancer as well as gum and mouth disease.

Please, Ann, take this up in your column. Millions of young people read you and listen to what you have to say.

A.H., Salem, Ore.

14. DON'T BLOW YOUR MONEY ON TOBACCO

There must be something better to do with one's money than to spend it on a product that is likely to kill you or render you seriously ill or make non-smoking friends ill from its carcinogens and toxins. The following Ann Lander's April 18, 1993 Chicago Tribune column[18] points out the enjoyment a person can experience through diverting funds subsidizing the tobacco industry into other areas:

DEAR READERS: What follows appeared in the spring 1993 issue of the Illinois Farm Bureau Almanac. It was sent by a reader from Toulon, Ill.

Since today's teenagers are cigarette manufacturers' "market of tomorrow," I decided to run this editorial in the column. Here it is:

Cigarettes:
Can You Afford Them?

Sarah was 15 when she began having a cigarette or two with her girl-friends in the school parking lot or at a weekend party. After a few months of bumming cigarettes, she started buying her own and was smoking more than a pack a day within six months.

The American Cancer Society says Sarah is an average smoker – puffing on 23 cigarettes a day. If Sarah were to place all the cigarettes she smoked in a year end-to-end, their length would be more than 7-1/2 football fields.

If Sarah buys a pack of cigarettes a day for $2, she will spend $14 per week and $728 per year. If she maintains her habit during her sophomore, junior and senior years, she'll spend $2,184.

If Sarah saved the money and spent it on something other than cigarettes, here's what she could buy in one year:

• A Sony portable sound system with AM/FM radio, compact disc player, dual reverse cassette player, detachable speakers and remote control: $480 (240 packs of cigarettes).

• A velvet blazer and matching pleated chiffon skirt by Esprit: $194 (97 packs of cigarettes).

• A pair of Levi's 501 button-fly stonewashed jeans: $29.98 (15 packs of cigarettes).

- Def Leppard's "Adrenalize" compact disc: $11.99 (six packs of cigarettes).

- Two movie tickets plus popcorn: $14 (seven packs of cigarettes).

That's 365 packs of cigarettes. Is it worth it? It's up to you to decide.

15. STOP CHILD AND SPOUSE ABUSE

It is incomprehensible how a spouse can jeopardize the health of another spouse or a child living in the same household. Well-known Chicago area columnist Jack Mabley published a letter in his August 2, 1993 column in the Daily Herald[19] which states:

"My wife reads your column in the Daily Herald on a regular basis," an Arlington Heights man writes me. "Maybe if you printed this – which is true – it would have an impact on her...or for that matter, on many others. If we just save one life, it's worth it."

Here is what he hopes his wife will read: "After 38 years of married life, I'm aware there is really a significant other in my wife's life.

"Her affair has become all consuming, and she wishes to do nothing to end it...in fact, while I try to understand her needs and answer them, I'm willing to admit that I'm helpless. Maybe, even, the end is in sight.

"I could cope if it was a question of looks, position, money, love or passion...but, how in the world do I cope and compete with a cigarette?

"In a day and age where the evils of smoking are so well known, and the effects of secondhand smoke are well documented...I'm willing to admit, when or if it comes to a choice between Pall Malls and me, I'd lose.

"There seems to be absolutely no desire on her part to quit. What do I do?

"It's hard to hug someone covered with stale cigarette odors; it's difficult to say 'I understand' in a cloud of smoke. It's impossible to say 'I love you' while coughing.

"I am not interested in a divorce. Is the only solution death? If so, one or both of us.

"What a waste. There has to be some hope...can you offer any?"

I was reminded about a story of an acquaintance of mine, a very heavy smoker in his fifties who stopped after a major heart attack. He had a regular fitness program, but did not look well. He mentioned that he had seen some of my letters and commentaries in one of the Chicago papers on the dangers of smoking and showed them to his wife. It turned out that his wife was still smoking heavily including when they were in an automobile.

I urged him to try to get her to stop smoking since he was clearly being subjected to high doses of secondary tobacco smoke after a near fatal heart attack. She is clearly guilty of spouse abuse. Hopefully, she will stop smoking for the sake of saving his life. Otherwise, my acquaintance will not be around much longer.

ENDNOTES

[1] Taken from a DEAR ABBY column by Abigail Van Buren. © Dist. by UNIVERSAL PRESS SYNDICATE. Reprinted with permission. All rights reserved.

[2] Taken from a DEAR ABBY column by Abigail Van Buren. © Dist. by UNIVERSAL PRESS SYNDICATE. Reprinted with permission. All rights reserved.

[3] Taken from a DEAR ABBY column by Abigail Van Buren. © Dist. by UNIVERSAL PRESS SYNDICATE. Reprinted with permission. All rights reserved.

[4] Permission granted by Ann Landers and Creators Syndicate.

[5] Permission granted by Ann Landers and Creators Syndicate.

[6] Taken from a DEAR ABBY column by Abigail Van Buren. © Dist. by UNIVERSAL PRESS SYNDICATE. Reprinted with permission. All rights reserved.

[7] Permission granted by Ann Landers and Creators Syndicate.

[8] Taken from a DEAR ABBY column by Abigail Van Buren. © Dist. by UNIVERSAL PRESS SYNDICATE. Reprinted with permission. All rights reserved.

[9] Taken from a DEAR ABBY column by Abigail Van Buren. © Dist. by UNIVERSAL PRESS SYNDICATE. Reprinted with permission. All rights reserved.

[10] Taken from a DEAR ABBY column by Abigail Van Buren. © Dist. by UNIVERSAL PRESS SYNDICATE. Reprinted with permission. All rights reserved.

[11] Taken from a DEAR ABBY column by Abigail Van Buren. © Dist. by UNIVERSAL PRESS SYNDICATE. Reprinted with permission. All rights reserved.

[12] Permission granted by Ann Landers and Creators Syndicate.

[13] Permission granted by Ann Landers and Creators Syndicate.

[14] Taken from a DEAR ABBY column by Abigail Van Buren. © Dist. by UNIVERSAL PRESS SYNDICATE. Reprinted with permission. All rights reserved.

[15] Taken from a DEAR ABBY column by Abigail Van Buren. © Dist. by UNIVERSAL PRESS SYNDICATE. Reprinted with permission. All rights reserved.

[16] Permission granted by Ann Landers and Creators Syndicate.

[17] Permission granted by Ann Landers and Creators Syndicate.

[18] Permission granted by Ann Landers and Creators Syndicate.

[19] Reprinted from the August 2, 1993 issue by permission of the Daily Herald, Arlington Heights, Illinois.

One Cartoon = 1,000 Anti-Tobacco Words

1. The Medicine Men

One thought provoking cartoon is worth a thousand words. Gary Trudeau's Doonesbury cartoon which appeared in the May 16, 1993 comic section of the Chicago Tribune[1] effectively refutes every tobacco industry medical spin control tactic alleging or implying that smoking is not dangerous to one's health. Frequently and astonishingly one hears allegations by the tobacco industry that the medical and scientific evidence is inconclusive about the impact of tobacco smoke and secondary tobacco smoke on health. Trudeau's cartoon focusing on a 1885 Dartmouth Medical College Professor of Physiology's medical textbook indicated that over 100 years ago the medical world knew the dangers of all forms of smoking. This insightful cartoon which follows helps unmask the misleading and deceitful statements of the tobacco industry which have followed for more than a century:

DOONESBURY

Garry Trudeau

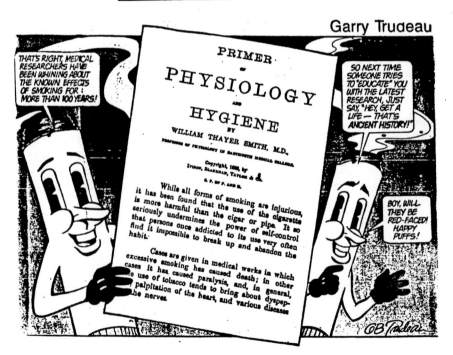

The cartoon also reaffirmed the statement by King James I in 1604 that tobacco is loathsome to the eyes, nose and lungs. I am reminded by an old cigarette commercial attempting to downplay some negative medical reports regarding cigarettes boasting that they were not medicine men, but tobacco men. Gary Trudeau has reminded us that for more than 100 years the medicine men have warned against the deadly results of smoking.

2. PASSIVE SMOKE KILLS

More than 200 million nonsmoking Americans are being subjected by 46 million smokers to the carcinogens and toxins of secondary tobacco smoke or passive smoke. One way the tobacco industry has portrayed the machoism and joys of smoking is by mounting the Marlboro Man on his horse heading over to Marlboro Country. By now many Americans believe that Marlboro Country may be one's local cemetery which accommodates nearly a half million Americans who die prematurely each year from tobacco smoke and secondary tobacco smoke while many more become seriously ill. The Environmental Protection Agency issued a report on January 7, 1993 finding secondary tobacco smoke or passive tobacco smoke to be a Class A human carcinogen in the same class as radon, benzene, and asbestos. At least one Marlboro Man, Wayne McClaren, was ravaged and recently died from tobacco smoke just like the cowboy on the respirator pictured in this Mike Peters cartoon which appeared in the January 16, 1993 Chicago Tribune:[2]

The horse is fuming and so are many of the spouses, children, and friends of those who succumb to passive tobacco smoke each year. Studies have shown that animals are impacted in a manner similar to human beings. The saying "treating one like a dog" would be an appropriate way to describe how tobacco companies impact on human beings.

3. THE BIG LIE

The tobacco industry has misled the American public regarding the dangers of tobacco smoke and secondary tobacco smoke for many years. Armed with a huge bankroll, they have hired some of the best attorneys and lobbyists money can buy. Tobacco industry and PAC money has been blatantly targeted to attempt to buy off politicians at the expense of the health of Americans. Hitler was a proponent of the "big lie" which led to 20 million deaths in World War II. The tobacco industry has perpetrated another "big lie" which will lead to the premature death of over four million Americans and 30 million human beings worldwide this decade and the serious illness of many more. The July 1, 1993 cartoon in the Chicago Tribune by Don Wright of the Palm Beach Post[3] vividly shows that the tobacco industry claim that secondary tobacco smoke is no problem is a lot of hot air:

Through spir   trol and propaganda, tobacco companies hope that the warnings abc   .he enormous risk to both smokers and nonsmokers of tobacco smoke .nd secondary tobacco smoke will go in one ear and out the other. If the .obacco industry is successful, more needless preventable deaths and serious illnesses will occur. The victims, their families, and our health care system will pay the price.

4. SMOKING IS THE PATH TO EXTINCTION

The carcinogens and toxins in tobacco smoke and secondary tobacco smoke are responsible for nearly a half million American deaths a year and about three million worldwide. Extrapolating over the next century, tobacco smoke and secondary tobacco smoke will be responsible for over 40 million American deaths and over 300 million deaths worldwide. This Gary Larson cartoon featured in "The Far Side"[4] depicts a possible reason why dinosaurs became extinct:

THE FAR SIDE   By GARY LARSON

The real reason dinosaurs became extinct

Hopefully our civilization which is subjected to an environment of poisonous tobacco smoke will not meet the same fate.

The Gary Larson cartoon will not be featured in tobacco company advertising campaigns to attract children, women, and minorities to the smoking ranks. Nor will this similar "Jurassic Park" cartoon by Dick Locher in the July 6, 1993 Chicago Tribune[5] be featured in tobacco company efforts to attract new smokers to make up for the nearly half-million who die prematurely each year from tobacco smoke or the effects of secondary tobacco smoke:

5. U.S. IS AN EXPORTER OF DISEASE, DISABILITY AND DEATH

Since 1964 the United States Surgeon General has warned of the dangers of tobacco smoke and since 1986 of the dangers of secondary tobacco smoke. Congress has ordered that health warnings be placed on all domestic tobacco products. However, The U. S. Department of Agriculture has subsidized tobacco growers and encouraged the export of American cigarettes throughout the world. Former Surgeon General Koop during Nova's April 12, 1994 Public Broadcast report looking at smoking in China labelled the United States as an exporter of disease, disability, and death.

America's tobacco exports increased more than five-fold over the last six years. More than three million human beings around the world die prematurely each year from tobacco smoke and secondary tobacco smoke, about one-sixth being Americans. It is ironic and tragic that one arm of the Government warns its citizens of the dangers of tobacco while another arm encourages the growth and exportation of poisonous tobacco products around the world. The Joe Camel cartoon by Chip Bok appearing in the March 19, 1992 Chicago Sun-Times[6] captures this blatant inconsistency:

The cartoon has a "20 Class A Cigarettes" label. The cartoonist from drafts of Environmental Protection Agency reports on secondary tobacco smoke probably anticipated that tobacco smoke and secondary tobacco smoke would be classified as a Class A carcinogen like asbestos, radon and benzene. The label "poison" would also have gotten the message across.

6. JOE "KID KILLER" CAMEL

The Joe Camel type ads appear to be designed to create a cigarette product recognition for young children in which the tobacco companies hope to parlay into lifetime addicted smokers by the time these youngsters reach age 14. The tobacco industry appears to be counting on kids to help replenish the nearly half million Americans who die prematurely from tobacco smoke and secondary tobacco smoke each year and the many more who become seriously ill.

The outward physical impact of tobacco smoke and secondary tobacco smoke should raise serious questions with more children or adults regarding the safety of tobacco products. During the period the Chicago and North Western Railroad had a smoking car, I occasionally was required to walk through the car when I was late for the train in order to get a seat. Even after a five-minute walk from the train to my home, my wife could always tell from the tobacco odor on my clothes when I walked through the smoking car.

Many heavy smokers will have bloodshot eyes, yellow-stained teeth, browned fingers and clothes sporadically patterned with cigarette burns. Add watery eyes, an irritated nose, and a sore throat with a smoker's cough and you have a sad picture as to how it feels to be a smoker. Moreover, the eyes, nose, and throat problems are being imposed on more than 200 million American nonsmokers.

Steve Benson's March 22, 1992 Chicago Sun-Times cartoon[7] "Hey Kids! Color the Camel" is an accurate portrayal of what smoking does to one's body:

Every person under 18 who is concerned about his or her appearance should be required to look at the Benson cartoon for a few minutes and then before starting smoking or lighting up their next cigarette look at himself or herself in the mirror.

As the American Medical Association and former surgeon General Antonio Novella have pointed out, it is no secret that children are one of the main sources for replenishing the premature loss of more than 400,000 American lives each year from smoking. The Joe Camel type ad has been an enormously successful device around the world in portraying a fun-positive smoking image to children. The Milt Priggie March 21, 1992 Chicago Tribune cartoon[8] vividly portrays this crime against humanity:

The carcinogens and toxins in cigarette smoke are intended to treat all 46 million American smokers and more than 200 million American non-smokers equally. The poisonous ingredients of tobacco smoke put at risk the lives and health of all smokers or those who come in contact with secondary tobacco smoke whether macho cowboys like the Marlboro man or children like the Joe Camel kid. Jack Higgins captured the impact of cigarette smoke in the following deadly cartoon appearing in the March 11, 1992 Chicago Sun-Times:[9]

The impact of cigarette smoke on the Marlboro Man's horse and Joe Camel might be summarized in one word - deadly. And that is the real impact of the carcinogens and toxins of poisonous tobacco smoke on the human body. They are deadly.

7. Making Kids the Death Target

Most kids love to draw. The tobacco industry through Joe Camel type ads is enticing children to reach for a lethal product - cigarettes. Drawing cigarettes might be more of a health risk than real bullets for the children of our country. Approximately 22,000 Americans die from handguns each year, but nearly a half million die from tobacco smoke and secondary tobacco smoke. Dick Locher in the following cartoon appearing in the April 13, 1993 Chicago Tribune[10] vividly shows the tobacco industry getting ready to aim its poisonous product at a prime target, the youth of our country:

8. Increase the Cigarette Tax

Since late 1990 there has been talk of health care reform which would entail providing health care for the 32 to 37 million Americans who do not currently have health insurance. The cost of genuine health care reform would be substantial. A portion of the cost can be obtained through a substantial tax on substances which add billions of dollars to health care costs such as tobacco or alcohol, including wine and beer, which are also known as sin taxes. The experiences in Canada and California have shown that a cigarette tax increase results in a marked decrease in smoking, especially among teens. President Bill Clinton in his September 22, 1993 health care proposal to Congress suggested a seventy-five cent per pack cigarette tax. The House Health Subcommittee of the Ways and Means Committee voted on March 22, 1994 to increase the Federal tax on cigarettes by $1.25 a pack, but the measure died later in 1994 along with health care reform. As the following Doonesbury cartoon appearing in the March 8, 1993 Chicago Tribune[11] points out, tobacco industry lobbyists have and will continue to fight such sin tax increases:

DOONESBURY

It would be a sin not to place heavy taxes on tobacco products and alcoholic beverages, including wine and beer, to pay for health care reform and for the improvement of health of all Americans. In addition, a sizeable gun and ammunition tax as proposed by Senator Daniel Moynihan would help pay for the costly health care from the residuals of gunshot wounds.

9. LET THE KIDS TELL IT THE WAY IT IS

One of the most effective ways of combating the tobacco industry's exploitation of children, minorities and women is to have representatives of these groups take on the industry through rational and creative appeals.

The American Medical Association and former Surgeon General Antonio Novello sponsored an anti-smoking contest for children from grades 2 through 8 to submit a poem, letter, essay or poster telling "Old Joe Camel" why he should stop smoking. More than 175,000 entries were received. The following poster submitted by the winner of the sixth to eighth grade category, Adrian Carson of the Roosevelt Middle School in Decatur, Illinois, graphically portrays the reasons why children should not smoke:[12]

Carson's poster should be sent to every member of Congress and every state legislator. The poster should be prominently displayed in all classrooms and in every school health textbook. It should be distributed to all school children and their parents. A copy should be given to President Clinton, Hillary Clinton, and every member of the Federal government who has any interest in health care reform. Perhaps this will increase the support for a $2.00 to $3.00 tax per pack of cigarettes rather than the mere seventy-five cent increase proposed by the President in September 1993 and a $1.25 proposed increase by the House Health Subcommittee of the Ways and Means Committee in March 1994.

These cartoons are all worth 1,000 words in the war against tobacco. Perhaps they have and will have some impact in saving the lives of American children and adults from poisonous tobacco smoke and secondary tobacco smoke.

ENDNOTES

[1] Doonesbury © G.B. Trudeau. Reprinted with permission of UNIVERSAL PRESS SYNDICATE. All rights reserved.

[2] Mike Peters cartoon. Reprinted by permission: Tribune Media Services.

[3] Copyright, Don Wright, The Palm Beach Post.

[4] The Far Side cartoon by Gary Larson is reprinted by permission of Chronicle Features, San Francisco, CA. All rights reserved.

[5] Dick Locher cartoon. Reprinted by permission: Tribune Media Services.

[6] Chip Bok cartoon. Reprinted by permission of Chip Bok and Creators Syndicate.

[7] Steve Benson cartoon. Reprinted by permission: Tribune Media Services.

[8] Milt Priggie cartoon. Reprinted by permission of Milt Priggie.
[9] Jack Higgins cartoon. Reprinted by permission of Jack Higgins.
[10] Dick Locher cartoon. Reprinted by permission: Tribune Media Services.
[11] Doonesbury © G.B. Trudeau. Reprinted with permission of UNIVERSAL PRESS SYNDICATE. All rights reserved.
[12] Adrian Carson poster. Reprinted by permission of Adrian Carson.

VI

Courting the Tobacco Industry

A. Pre-1994

Until recently it would appear fair to say that the judicial system of the United States has inadvertently served as an enabler of an industry that has played havoc with the health of Americans.

Of the more than 800 claims filed against the tobacco industry since 1954 , less than 50 have gone to trial. The industry has lost only three times and two losses were overturned on appeal.[1]

One would think that our sophisticated judicial system fueled with over 800,000 lawyers would have readily provided relief for the nearly half million premature fatal victims and their families from tobacco smoke and secondary tobacco smoke and the many more who become seriously ill each year. It is unfortunate in our society that the only industry which produces a consumer product that is likely to kill and render human beings seriously ill when used as intended has been so successful in combating challenges within our judicial framework.

The reasons are multifold. Since the early 1950s smokers have been warned of the dangers of tobacco smoke by responsible medical experts. Five-year old asthmatic children are aware of the dangers. As a young child, I was aware that tobacco smoke irritated my eyes and nose and caused visible health problems for my heavy smoking parents such as excessive coughing and spitting out phlegm.

After the late Surgeon General Dr. Luther Terry documented the harmful effects of smoking in the first Surgeon General's report on smoking and health in 1964, Congress responded with legislation the following year. Warnings were placed on each pack of cigarettes and on all cigarette advertising which are rotated quarterly.

Also, it has only been since March 1980 that scientific evidence proved secondary tobacco smoke to be harmful.[2] The Environmental Protection Agency in December 1992 finally confirmed the dangers of secondary tobacco smoke by finding it to be a Class A human carcinogen, a category shared with asbestos, benzene, and radon.[3] This finding may encourage courts to impose strict liability on the tobacco industry. Courts may no longer be the guaranteed safe haven for the tobacco industry to hide behind when it produces and sells poisonous products as they were prior to the 1992 Environmental Protection Agency report. It appears that approximately eighty percent of jurors and judges do not smoke and most of these nonsmokers have seen family members and/or close friends ravaged by poisonous tobacco smoke. At some point the inate wishes of these jurors and judges to rectify wrongs may finally come into play against the sharp tactics and talent of tobacco industry strategists and lawyers.

Finally, the tobacco industry has utilized sharp legal talent in dragging out cases and increasing costs so that most potential plaintiffs and their lawyers cannot afford protracted litigation. Unlike more than ninety percent of cases that are settled, tobacco companies rarely, if ever, enter into monetary settlements. In dragging out cases and building up legal fees, tobacco company lawyers have ocasionally drawn the wrath of respected jurists such as New Jersey Federal District Court Judge H. Lee Sarokin who succinctly stated in 1992 that "the tobacco industry may be the king of concealment and disinformation." *Haines v. Liggett Group, Inc.,* 140 F.R.D. 681, 683 (D. N.J. 1992). Interviews with former summer law clerks or interns with law firms defending tobacco companies who worked on these tobacco litigation cases could very well determine whether the law firms representing tobacco company defendants and their attorneys have been engaged in the types of practices alluded to by Judge Sarokin such as concealment of material evidence or even the possible manufacture or fabrication of evidence.

The frequently heard argument that one has a right to smoke just as one has a right to drink alcohol has a hollow ring. A reasonable amount of alcohol consumption does not normally harm others; however, the carcinogens and toxins of poisonous secondary tobacco smoke kill thousands of innocent victims each year, render many more seriously ill, and endanger the health of more than 200 million nonsmoking Americans. Although the

First Amendment guarantees individuals many rights, there are limits as pointed out by Justice Oliver Wendell Holmes in *United States* v. *Schenck,* 249 U.S. 47, 52 (1919), when he stated that "free speech would not protect a man in falsely shouting 'fire' in a theatre and causing a panic." Clearly, the First Amendment does not afford smokers the right to expose more than 30 million children and nonsmoking spouses to potentially harmful or even fatal secondary tobacco smoke. Nor should any other unwilling person be exposed to secondary tobacco smoke in public facilities or in the workplace.

The recent United States Supreme Court decisions and a Mississippi state court decision appear to have at least stemmed the legal tide which has long favored the tobacco industry and have afforded some encouragement to potential plaintiffs and their counsels.

The United States Supreme Court's June 24, 1992 7-2 decision in *Cipollone* v. *Liggett Group,* 112 S. Ct. 2608 (1992), recognized the right of victims of smoking-related death and illness to sue tobacco companies in state court. Despite warning labels advising of risks, there are certain classes of plaintiffs who would still appear to have a potential valid cause of action against tobacco companies even without the imposition of a strict liability theory. They would include children rendered ill from tobacco smoke prior to birth, children harmed by secondary tobacco smoke in the household after birth, and individuals who cannot read or read English and are thus unable to read the warnings on tobacco product packages. Finally, there would appear to be a class of plaintiffs whose addiction started before the cigarette warnings were initiated in 1965. Of course, those filing a lawsuit would have to meet the difficult burden of proving that tobacco smoke was the cause of their illness and not job related or caused by other environmental factors.

The Supreme Court ruled on June 18, 1993 that placing a nonsmoking prisoner in the cell with a smoking prisoner could constitute cruel and unusual punishment in violation of the Eighth Amendment of the Constitution. *Helling* v. *McKinney,* 113 S.Ct. 2475 (1993). Although the decision did not refer to the Environmental Protection agency's January 7, 1993 report that secondary tobacco smoke is a Class A human carcinogen, the Court recognized the dangers to a non-smoking prisoner being placed in a cell with a five-pack a day smoker.

The *Helling* decision reminded me of the previously noted 1961 Northwestern University ethics class discussion conducted by Professor Paul Schilpp. Professor Schilpp, who had left Germany in the 1930s, raised the question of an appropriate penalty for Lieutenant Adolf Eichman who was on trial for the World War II atrocities he had committed against the

Jews and others. Almost the entire class favored the death penalty, but Professor Schilpp argued it was too lenient. The professor suggested locking Eichman in a cell 24 hours a day with narrated films of his atrocities until he was driven out of his mind. Perhaps if Professor Schilpp had been aware of the dangers of secondary tobacco smoke, he would have suggested putting Eichman in a cell with a smoker. Such punishment would be cruel and unusual by any standard. The Supreme Court in *Helling* appears to ackowledge that placing a nonsmoking prisoner in a cell with a smoking prisoner could constitute cruel and unusual punishment. It would appear that courts will be making similar holdings in child custody and smoking in the workplace cases.

Judge Eugene Bogan on May 11, 1993 became the first American jurist to rule that cigarettes are inherently dangerous for human consumption. *Wilks v. American Tobacco Co.*, Washington County Circuit Court, Mississippi, No. 91-12-3555. Judge Bogan stated that "cigarettes are defective because when used as intended, they cause cancer, emphysema, heart disease and other illnesses." The courageous judge called cigarettes "the most lethal product which may be legally sold in this country." He added that under the strict liabiliity doctrine "cigarette manufacturers must be held liable for the deaths and disease arising from the use of their products." As usual, the tobacco company prevailed at trial.

Administrative tribunals have awarded employees workmen's compensation benefits whose health problems were caused or aggravated by smoking on the work premises in a number of states including California, Oregon, New York, Wisconsin and Massachusetts. Pursuant to section 504 of the Rehabilitation Act of 1973, 29 U.S.C. §794, and the Americans with Disabilities Act of 1990, 42 U.S.C. §12,101 et seq., the United States Merit Systems Protection Board and several courts have found that a nonsmoker was a disabled or handicapped person who is eligible to ask for reasonable accommodation under section 504 of the Rehabilitation Act. Courts in at least 12 states consider smoking when deciding child custody cases.[4] In many cases courts have prohibited a parent from smoking near his or her child and in several cases smoking has been a determinative factor over which parent is awarded custody.[5]

Almost every adult in the United States can recall a family member or friend who has experienced a serious illness and/or died prematurely from smoking. About 26 percent of American smoke, down greatly from the 50 percent who smoked in the early 1950s. The percentage of judges and jurors who smoke should be below the 26 percent figure. As each month and year passes, more medical and scientific data is added to the overwhelming evidence that the carcinogens and toxins in tobacco smoke and secondary tobacco smoke is one of the leading killers and disablers in the United States. Faced with this overwhelming evidence, it would follow that judges and juries will do what is legally and morally correct - what the Supreme Court did in *Cipollone* in giving an individual the right to sue tobacco companies in state courts, what the high court did in *Helling* in finding that placing a nonsmoker in a cell with a smoker could constitute cruel and unusual punishment, and what Mississippi State Court Judge Bogan did in *Wilks* finding that cigarettes are inherently dangerous for human consumption.

Fortunately tobacco lobbyists and PAC money may not be as effective in protecting tobacco interests with judges as it apparently has been with some legislative bodies. Nevertheless the Federal legislative route and administrative route have at times been more expeditious and productive in protecting the rights of the nation's smoking victims than the courts. Some signs point to much of the same in the future. Congress has banned direct cigarette advertising on radio and television and some have proposed an extension of the ban to all tobacco products. Efforts to attempt to limit the sale of cigarettes to minors could be strengthened by Congress passing tougher legislation to withhold federal grant funds to states whose enforcement efforts are lax. Many state and local governmental entities have passed measures banning smoking in public facilities including restaurants and malls. Actions by Federal administrative agencies and Congress to ban smoking in the workplace and in all public places would complement state and local measures. Likewise, large Federal tobacco taxes will complement state tobacco taxes and serve to reduce the amount of smoking and public exposure to poisonous tobacco smoke and secondary tobacco smoke.

Unburdened by expensive discovery procedures, strict rules of evidence which at times enable tobacco companies to conceal the truth, and stringent burdens of proof, the legislative and administrative processes have been more expeditious ways of dealing with serious health and safety problems especially when the perpetrators have placed profits ahead of all health and safety concerns.

The tobacco industry and pro-tobacco Congressmen have ignored and our courts do not deal with a basic moral tenet of western civilization - the Seventh Commandment which says "Thou Shalt Not Kill." Judges and jurors should focus more on this fundamental moral issue when addresssing future actions against the tobacco companies.

The wheels of justice often spin too slowly or not at all in our judicial system. Nearly a half million Americans die prematurely from tobacco smoke and secondary tobacco smoke and many more become seriously ill each year. Yet our judicial system is apparently incapable of stopping what the British Royal College of Medicine in 1971 referred to as "the present holocaust," the annual death toll caused by cigarette smoking. Perhaps that is why Shakespeare said when King Henry VI was plotting to be king, "The first thing we do, let's kill all the lawyers. " King Henry VI, Act IV, Section 2. If Judge Sarokin is correct in his belief that "the tobacco industry may be the king of concealment and disinformation," perhaps the tobacco company lawyers deserve such bashing.

It would appear that some changes must be made in our judicial system in order to effectively curtail the use of the courts to perpetuate "the present holocaust." In order to get around the procedural, discovery, and evidentiary safeguards that insulate the tobacco industry from most legal attacks, perhaps the legislative branch of government could be of assistance. States could make the growth, manufacture, sale or distribution of tobacco products a felony - i.e. , the manufacture, sale, or distribution of a dangerous consumer product which when used as intended is likely to cause death or serious illness. Violators would include both tobacco company employees and officers. Such step would take the tobacco companies outside the civil arena and place them where they belong, just like Lieutenant Eichman, in the criminal arena. Leading nearly a half million Americans a year to preventable death is an unconscionable crime of such magnitude it can no longer go unpunished. Matters such as damages could still be litigated civilly. Tobacco companies should no longer be permitted to hide behind our legal system when manufacturing, selling, and distributing a dangerous consumer product which when used as intended is likely to cause death or serious illness.

B. POST-1993

A new wave of tobacco litigation finally emerged in 1994 highlighted by the class action lawsuit. The unique aspect of the tobacco class action lawsuit is that resources expended by law firms representing plaintiffs are spent on behalf of thousands of class members rather than on behalf of one person. This strategy deprives tobacco companies of being able to pursue the normal tactic of forcing plaintiffs to spend huge amounts of money and eventually being forced to withdraw the lawsuits because of lack of funds.

The most significant class action was put together by nearly 60 prominent law firms in March 1994 in the Eastern District of Louisiana against seven United States cigarette manufacturers. *Castano v. American Tobacco Company*, U.S.D.C. E.D. La. 94-1044. The action was based on the testimony of Food and Drug Administration Commissioner Dr. David Kessler before the Congressional Subcommittee on Health and Environment that tobacco companies intentionally sell cigarettes containing an addictive level of nicotine.

Judge Okla B. Jones II in *Castano* on February 17, 1995 cleared the way for the first nationwide class action against the tobacco industry on behalf of 40 million current smokers and 50 million smokers who have quit smoking.[6] The judge found that the tobacco companies could be sued for punitive damages on accusations of addicting millions of cigarette smokers and concealing the addictive nature of tobacco.[7] The tobacco industry was successful in convincing an appellate court that a large national class was unmanageable. *Castano* v. *American Tobacco Company*, '84 F. 3d 734 (5th Cir. 1996).

The discovery phase of the post-*Castano* numerous state court class actions should uncover evidence that may conclusively establish that the tobacco industry had knowledge of the addictive nature of cigarettes but placed industry profits ahead of human lives. The post-*Castano* cases should demonstrate the overwhelming need for increased regulation of an amoral industry not caring if it produces and exports a lethal consumer product that when used as intended kills millions of human beings and renders many more seriously ill.

In a related action, a Florida state court judge certified a class action on December 13, 1994 brought by 30 airline flight attendants who alleged they were harmed by exposure to secondhand tobacco smoke. *Broin* v. *Philip Morris* et al.[8] The 30 flight attendants filed on behalf of a class of about 60,000 flight attendants who have contracted lung cancer, emphysema and other diseases as a result of their exposure to secondary tobacco smoke in airplane cabins.[9]

A class action complaint was filed in a Florida state court against eleven tobacco product manufacturers, the Tobacco Institute, and the Council for Tobacco Research in May 1994.[10] It was alleged that tobacco companies knew nicotine was addictive and suppressed medical and scientific evidence of nicotine's addictiveness. It was also alleged that the tobacco companies' advertising campaigns were deceitful and encouraged minors to smoke. In October 1994 a Florida state court judge certified a class defined as

> All United States citizens and residents, and their survivors, who have suffered, presently suffer or who have died from diseases and medical conditions caused by their addiction to cigarettes that contain nicotine.

The Florida Supreme Court denied the tobacco company class certification appeal on October 3, 1996.

Recently a new kind of tobacco lawsuit emerged - medical cost third party liability suits. As of September 30, 1996, 17 states have filed lawsuits seeking reimbursement from tobacco companies for cigarette-related medical costs[11] for treating thousands of smokers with illnesses such as lung cancer and heart disease.[12] The State of Florida is seeking to recover $1.4 billion paid over the past five years in Medicaid bills for smokers.[13] An attorney for the State of Mississippi argues that the state is an innocent third party who is paying the bills for smoking - for the related illnesses such as heart disease and cancer.[14]

The only federal court case addressing the issue as to whether a ban on cigarette billboard advertising is constitutional upheld the ban.[15] A Baltimore ordinance was designed to bar cigarette advertising on billboards in the parts of the city most frequented by children and was designed to prevent the illegal purchase of cigarettes by minors. The Federal District Court held that since it is reasonable to assume advertising increases smoking among the general public, it would have a similar effect on children. This District Court held that enacting an ordinance to promote compliance with a state law prohibiting the sale of cigarettes to minors was a "substantial" government interest, the ordinance directly advanced Baltimore's interest in promoting compliance with the state law prohibition against the sale of cigarettes to minors, and the ordinance was not pre-empted by Federal or state law. The Court of Appeals for the Fourth Circuit affirmed the District Court decision holding that the ordinance directly advanced the city's stated public interest in reducing minors' smoking, was not more extensive than necessary to serve that interest, and thus was a permissible regulation of commercial speech. The Supreme Court was not encouraging when it handed down a decision in *44 Liquormart, Inc. v. Rhode Island,* 116 S.Ct. 1495 (1996), overturning restrictions of outdoor advertising of alcoholic beverages to help combat underage drinking and remanded the Baltimore cigarette billboard advertising case.. *Penn Advertising of Baltimore, Inc.,* v. *Schmoke,* 116 S.Ct. 2575 (1996).

The Supreme Court let stand a state court ruling in *R.J. Reynolds Tobacco Company,* v. *Mangini, cert. den.* 115 S.Ct. 577 (1994), a case alleging that the R. J. Reynolds' Joe Camel advertising campaign targeted minors and therefore constituted an unfair business practice which was not preempted by Federal law. The action by the Supreme Court on November 28, 1994 cleared the way for a California lawsuit accusing R.J. Reynolds Tobacco Company of targeting children with its Joe Camel campaign.

Through the gathering of resources by the class action lawsuit route and by the resources of states being utilized to stop the drain of limited medical resources by seeking reimbursement from the tobacco companies, the possibility of several significant legal inroads may be emerging against an amoral dangerous industry that appears to be a plague against the health of all Americans - the tobacco industry supported by its armada of ruthless lawyers who believe that profits are more important than human life and health. Like most Americans, the vast majority of judges and jurors who do not smoke are aware of the dangers of poisonous tobacco smoke and secondary tobacco smoke. After providing decades of protective legal cover to the tobacco industry, it appears that the American legal system may be finally assisting in the exposure of the merchants of death.

An example of this newly emerging judicial concern about the human and other costs of smoking emerged in an April 21, 1995 decision by the Florida Supreme Court upholding the City of North Miami's regulation requiring job applicants to sign an affidavit that they have not used tobacco products for a year.[16] North Miami, which pays 100% of its employees' insurance costs, showed that employees who smoke cost it $4,611 more per year than nonsmokers. The Florida Supreme Court said that there is no right to smoke that is protected under the state constitutional clause granting freedom from government intrusion.

It appears that the courts are finally coming "a long way baby." Judges are human beings who will normally understand the dire health and economic consequences of the carcinogens and toxins of poisonous tobacco smoke and secondary tobacco smoke. The law firms such as Shook, Hardy & Bacon of Kansas City, Missouri, who have been described as hired guns or the cigarette industry,[17] may find both plaintiffs' counsels and courts less intimidated by their tactics. And ultimately, the courts may get to the overriding issue in tobacco company litigation - the truth - that is, whether the carcinogens and toxins of tobacco smoke and secondary tobacco smoke cause serious illnesses such as lung cancer, heart disease, and emphysema. The courts should come to the same conclusion as every five-year old asthmatic child, every reputable objective scientist, and every forthright physician with no ties to the tobacco industry - tobacco is a lethal consumer product that when used as intended is likely to cause death or serious illness.

The tobacco industry's withholding of relevant health information to the nation's 46 million smokers and 200 million nonsmokers over the last half century should be rectified and compensated through our judicial system. When the whole truth of the tobacco industry coverup comes out, the pendulum should shift and tobacco companies may no longer be able to hide behind the protective rules of our judicial system. Our judicial process will no longer serve as a facilitator for hiding the truth and denying justice.

ENDNOTES

[1] "A Tobacco Case's Legal Buccaneers," *New York Times*, 2/6/95, section C, p. 3; "A Fortress Up in Smoke," American Bar Association Journal, 10/96, p.30

[2] "Small-Airways Dysfunction in Nonsmokers Chronically Exposed to Tobacco Smoke," James R. White, Ph.D. and Herman F. Froeb, M.D., New England Journal of Medicine, Vol. 302, No. 13, March 27, 1980, pp. 720-723; *Id.* editorial "(Passive) Smokers Versus (Voluntary) Smokers" at pp. 742-743.

[3] United States Environmental Protection Agency, Office of Research and Development, Office of Air and Radiation," Respiratory Health Effects and Passive Smoking: Lung Cancer and Other Disorders," 12/92 (released 1/7/93).

[4] "Fla. High Court OKs Smoke Ban," The National Law Journal, 5/8/95, p. A 6.

[5] *Id.*

[6] "Smokers can sue for damages," The Atlanta Journal/Constitution, 2/18/95, p. A-1.

[7] *Id.*

[8] Tobacco on Trial, 1995, No. 1, p. 8; "Smoking suit cleared for takeoff," Chicago Tribune, 12/13/94, sec. 3, p. 1, 641 So.2d 888(Fla. App. 3 Dist. 1994), review denied, 654 So.2d 919 (Fla. Sup. Ct. 3/27/95);

[9] December 12, 1994 court order, Dade County Circuit Court 11th Judicial Circuit, following remand at 641 So. 2d 888 (Fla. 1994).

[10] *Engle* v. *R.J. Reynolds Tobacco Co.,* et al.; "Florida court spurns Big Tobacco appeal," Chicago Sun-Times, 10/4/96, p.40.

[11] "States Team Up Against Tobacco Industry," Chicago Sun-Times, 3/9/95, p. 25; "Illinois joins the pack suing tobacco firms," Chicago Tribune, 9/18/96, sec. 1, pp.1,24; "Utah sues tobacco firms over health costs," Chicago Sun-Times, 10/1/96, p.14.

[12] "Florida Launches Legal Assault on Tobacco Industry," Chicago Sun-Times, 2/22/95, p. 22.

[13] *Id.*

[14] "Mississippi seeks tobacco reparations," USA Today, 12/19/94, Sec. D, p. 1.

[15] *Penn Advertising of Baltimore, Inc.* v. *Mayor & City Council of Baltimore*, 862 F. Supp. 1402 (D. Md. 1994), aff'd 63 F.3d 1318 (4th Cir. 1995).

[16] *Kurtz* v *City of North Miami*, 625 So.2d 899(Fla. App.3 Dist. 1993), rev. gr., 640 So.2d 1106(Fla. 1994), 653 So.2d 1025 (Fla. 1995), *cert. den.*, 116 S.Ct. 701(1996).

[17] "Did Big Tobacco's Barrister Set Up a Smokescreen?-Shook Hardy may catch heat for alleged misuse of study results," Business Week, 9/5/94, pp. 68-70.

Saving 419,000 Lives and Up to $100 Billion a Year Through Preventive Health Care

O ccasionally there appears to come out of nowhere a possible solution or partial solution of an extremely complex problem. After the November 3, 1991 senatorial election in Pennsylvania where Harris Wofford upset Dick Thornburgh, it appeared that the health care-cost problem might be the number one domestic concern for many Americans. Health care cost Americans an estimated $756 billion a year in 1991.[1] Anywhere from 32 to 37 million Americans are not covered by any health insurance.[2] It has been estimated that an additional 60 million are underinsured.[3] Led by President Bill Clinton there were increasing cries for major changes in our health care system or for national health insurance to help solve the nation's health care problems. A primary problem facing this country is the method of payment of any proposed health care changes and the funds to finance these increased health care costs. The billions of dollars in savings realized through one aspect of preventive health care – those obtained through a strong smoking reduction program – could be used to finance these health care changes.

A significant part of any health care proposal should include preventive medicine – taking steps to reduce preventable illnesses and thus the cost of treating these preventable illnesses. Such steps should include a strong Government-led program to reduce smoking. This man-made tobacco

plague should not continue unabated. Smoking prematurely takes an estimated 419,000 American lives each year from cancer, heart disease, emphysema, and other diseases resulting in millions of hospitalizations each
year from smoking-related illnesses, and costs the taxpayers a substantial
portion of the estimated $756 billion 1991 annual health care fiscal pack-
age thought to be about $65 billion a year.[4] The Advisory Council on
Social Security reported in December 1991 that tobacco is the cause of one
of six American deaths each year and that smoking costs the taxpayers $22
billion a year in health costs plus $65 billion a year in economic costs.[5]
Annually 30% of American cancer deaths, including 85% of all lung cancer deaths, are attributable to smoking.[6] Between 30-35% of fatal heart attacks are caused by smoking.[7] And smoking is the primary etiologic factor
behind 80-90% of emphysema and chronic bronchitis cases.[8] Cigarette
smoke, including secondary tobacco smoke affecting more than 200 million nonsmokers, is the cause of more preventable deaths each year than
AIDS, auto accidents, cocaine, heroin, alcohol, fire and suicide combined.[9]
Moreover, symptoms of tobacco smoke bothering nonsmokers are eye irritation, coughing, nasal discharge, stuffiness, throat irritation, and
headaches.[10] Individuals wearing contact lenses or afflicted with allergies
may suffer the most from secondary tobacco smoke. The curative rather
than preventative health care approach wastes billions of dollars annually.

The late Surgeon General Dr. Luther Terry documented the harmful
health effects of smoking in the first Surgeon General report on smoking
and health in 1964.[11] Former Surgeon General Koop documented the
harmful effects of secondary tobacco smoke in 1986 in a report entitled
"The Health Consequences of Involuntary Smoking."[12] Congress in 1984
required all cigarette manufacturers and advertisers to have one of the following four warnings on each pack of cigarettes or advertisements to be
rotated quarterly:[13]

> SURGEON GENERAL'S WARNING: Smoking Causes Lung Cancer,
>   Heart Disease, and Emphysema;
>
> SURGEON GENERAL'S WARNING: Quitting Smoking Now
>   Greatly Reduces Serious Health Risks;

SURGEON GENERAL'S WARNING: Pregnant Women Who
   Smoke Risk Fetal Injury and Premature Birth;

SURGEON GENERAL'S WARNING: Cigarette Smoke Contains
   Carbon Monoxide

The American Cancer Society,[14] the American Lung Association,[15] the American Heart Association,[16] and the American Medical Association[17] have repeatedly warned of the severe dangers of smoking and secondary tobacco smoke. Cigarette smoke is like a handgun with deadly, silent fire. As former HEW Secretary Califano warned, smoking is "slow motion suicide."[18]

Cocaine and heroin advertising is prohibited. Although tobacco, or agent "golden leaf" which can serve as a human lung defoliant, kills many more Americans each year than heroin and cocaine combined, we still permit cigarette advertising with the exception of direct radio and television ads. We should take tobacco as seriously as heroin and cocaine.

"Marlboro Country" may be the local cemetery with enough plots to accommodate the more than 400,000 Americans who prematurely perish each year from tobacco. The tobacco companies have become merchants of over 400,000 premature deaths each year. As the late Senator Robert F. Kennedy told the First World Conference on Smoking and Health in New York City on September 11, 1967:[19]

> Each year cigarettes kill more Americans than were killed in World War I, the Korean War, and Vietnam combined; nearly as many as died in battle in World War II. Each year cigarettes kill five times more Americans than do traffic accidents. Lung cancer alone kills as many as die on the road. The cigarette industry is peddling a deadly weapon. It is dealing in people's lives for financial gain.

Recently a health physicist knowledgeable in indoor air pollution examined portions of two buildings containing federal offices where smoking was not permitted in a large city downtown area.[20] When asked what would happen if smoking were to be initiated in these facilities, the expert said the areas would be turned into "gas chambers" in one building because of the age, shape and serious ventilating system problems and in the other building because of serious air flow obstructions based on remodeling. The expert noted that these buildings were not atypical. Aside from the obvious health problems for smokers, it is not surprising that nonsmokers working in "gas chamber" conditions nearly a quarter of their lives (40 hours out of 168 hours each week) would develop serious health problems. The "gas chamber" observation is consistent with a recent court decision holding that a nonsmoking prisoner's exposure to secondary tobacco smoke from a smoking cellmate could constitute cruel and unusual punishment in violation of the Eighth Amendment of the Constitution.[21] In 1971, the British Royal College of Medicine, in its second Report, "Smoking and Health Now," referred to the annual toll caused by cigarette smoking as "the present holocaust."[22]

Smoking is an often overlooked form of child and spouse abuse; studies have established a correlation between parental smoking and children's illnesses and one spouse smoking with increased nonsmoking spouse illnesses. Merely living with a smoking spouse boosts the nonsmoking spouse's risk of contracting lung cancer by 30%.[23] Dr. Allan Luskin of Rush Medical Center, a major medical center in Chicago, recently said, "it is my opinion that parents or caregivers who smoke in the presence of a child are guilty of child abuse."[24] He further pointed out that "smoke not only increases the risk of a child getting asthma in the first place, it makes asthma worse when it is there."[25] Dr. William Cahan, of Memorial Sloan-Kettering Cancer Center in New York, also calls children's exposure to secondhand smoke child abuse.[26]

Is there any difference between manslaughter – the killing of a human being by another without malice – and the tobacco industry facilitating the premature death of over 400,000 Americans a year? We punish the former while we glamourize and subsidize an industry that furthers the killing of over 400,000 Americans a year.

A powerful lesson could be learned from our Canadian neighbors.[27] The Canadian health care system was in serious financial difficulty. A Canadian study of its health care system revealed that a substantial portion of its health care costs were attributable to the adverse health effects of smoking. In order to pay for the enormous portion of its health care costs due to smoking, the Canadian government raised the price of a pack of cigarettes up to $7.50 of which more than two-thirds went for taxes. For every ten per cent rise in the Canadian price of cigarettes, also known as lethal cancer sticks, there was a 4% drop in the number of cigarettes sold in Canada.[28] A $3.00 a package excise tax based on an American adult per capita annual consumption of 3,500 cigarettes and estimated about 46 million adult smokers (age 18 and over) would raise approximately $25 billion in annual revenues.[29] Moreover, the Advisory Council on Social Security noted the large increase in the cost of cigarettes in Canada has resulted in a 37% decline in teenage smoking.[30] Recently, largely because of cheaper American cigarette imports, a black market has developed in Canada and the Canadian government has been forced to reduce the tax on cigarettes.[31]

California appears to have learned from the Canadian lesson. California Proposition 99, passed in 1990, provided for a 25 cent per package tax increase (from 10 cents to 35 cents a pack) with funds earmarked for anti-smoking advertising.[32] During the first year Proposition 99 was in effect, cigarette consumption dropped more in California than any other state – 14% compared to a nationwide average 3% drop.[33]

A Centers for Disease Control study released in November 1991 revealed that 28.1% of adult Americans smoked as of 1988, down from 28.8% the year before, 30% in 1985, and 40% in 1964.[34] An estimated 25.7% of adults in 1991 were current smokers.[35]

Unfortunately teenagers, women, and minorities appear to have been targeted with advertising and promotion campaigns designed to replenish the 419,000 who die annually from diseases caused by smoking.[36] If a strong Government program spurred by heavy taxation of cigarettes can reduce the number of adult smokers in half to about 13% in the next five years, this country could save up to $100 billion a year in smoking-related health costs or about 15% of our 1991 estimated annual $756 billion health care expenditure which has been projected to reach $1.1 trillion by the year 2000.[37] Heavy taxation similar to Canada's taxation of cigarettes will generate added revenues to help pay for whatever health care changes the taxpayers, Congress and the President deem necessary.

President Clinton proposed a 75 cent per pack cigarette tax increase as part of his health care reform package in the fall of 1993.[38] A Congressional subcommittee voted for a $1.25 increase in March 1994.[39] Some advocate a $2 - $3 per pack cigarette tax increase. If a large cigarette tax increase is enacted, the United States will have gone a long way to solve a long-term problem without breaking the budget – through the prevention of health care problems by reducing smoking and forcing the remaining smokers to pay for their self-inflicted illnesses through heavy taxation. And in so doing, perhaps the remaining smokers can help pay for the 32 to 37 million Americans who do not have health insurance.

What about the powerful tobacco interests who may do almost anything to block such changes? In 1992 New Jersey Federal District Court Judge H. Lee Sarokin after reviewing tobacco company documents said that "the tobacco industry may be the king of concealment and disinformation" and that the documents may contain evidence of fraud.[40] Hopefully the concerned American health interests can drown out the health-insensitive self-centered motivated cries of the tobacco lobby. So far the health interests have not been very successful. Tobacco company advertising dollars as well as the advertising dollars of their non-tobacco producing subsidiaries so control the media that smoking-related health stories – like smoking is a cause of cervical cancer[41]-appear to be frequently suppressed.

The tobacco lobby has as its champions of consumer death some of the most senior members of Congress. Between 1985 and 1990 about two thirds of House members and half of the Senators received tobacco PAC contributions.[42] Certain Congressmen and tobacco company executives may go down in history as the persons responsible for more premature deaths than anyone in the twentieth century other than Adolf Hitler.

And to those sympathetic to the tobacco lobby, it is noted that the American Medical Association in a December 4, 1990 statement to the Environmental Protection Agency recommended that environmental tobacco smoke be classified as a human carcinogen. In the last paragraph of its statement, the American Medical Association said the following about the tobacco industry:[43]

> We know of no other industry which would be allowed to produce a product which kills so many. It is now clear that *tobacco is lethal, not only to those who use it as intended by the manufacturer but to those who have not assumed those risks.* (Emphasis added)

A huge amount of taxpayer dollars each year subsidizes "the killing fields and factories" of the tobacco industry. These dangers of tobacco smoke were recognized by the Advisory Council on Social Security in December 1991 when it recommended to limit cigarette vending machine sales, ban advertising, stop subsidies to tobacco farmers except those who stop growing tobacco, and double the cigarette tax.[44]

If we heed this American Medical Association warning, then perhaps this country will set in place the cornerstone, rather than 419,000 annual premature tombstones, of a kinder and gentler health care policy – reduction and elimination of smoking – whether promulgated by conservatives or liberals or Republicans or Democrats. In doing so, up to $100 billion a year in health care costs including $30 billion from a large excise tax for treatment of preventable cigarette-related illnesses, could be saved and utilized for whatever health-related programs the taxpayers, the President and Congress deem advisable. Then perhaps former Surgeon General Koop's goal of a "smoke-free society by the year 2000" could be realized.[45]

ENDNOTES

[1] "Pressure on for health care reform,"*Chicago Tribune*, 12/15/91, sec. 1, p. 1.
[2] *Id.*

[3] CNN Newscast – Week of December 9, 1991.

[4] White, Larry, *Merchants of Death*, Beech Tree Books, 1988, p. 21; The Journal of the American Medical Association (JAMA), review of book (p. 3202) "An Ounce of Prevention: Strategies for Solving Tobacco, Alcohol, and Drug Problems" by Don Calahan, 12/11/91, Vol. 266, No. 22; HHS Secretary Dr. Louis Sullivan letter to Chicago Tribune, *Chicago Tribune*, 4/26/91.

[5] Advisory Council on Social Security Report, 12/91.

[6] The Journal of the American Medical Association (JAMA), 12/11/91, Vol. 266, No. 22, p. 3220.

[7] *Id.*

[8] *Id.*

[9] Warner, Kenneth E., *Selling Smoke: Cigarette Advertising and Public Health*, American Public Health Association, 1986, p. 98.

[10] Whelan, Elizabeth M., *A Smoking Gun: How the Tobacco Industry Gets Away With Murder*, George F. Stickley Co., 1984, p. 193.

[11] U.S. Public Health Service – *Smoking and Health: Report of the Advisory Committee to the Surgeon General of the U.S. Public Health Service*, PHS Pub. No. 1103, U.S. Dept. of Health, Education and Welfare, Public Health Service, Centers for Disease Control, 1964.

[12] *The Health Consequences of Involuntary Smoking, A Report of the Surgeon General*, United States Department of Health and Human Services, Public Health Service, Centers for Disease Control, 1986.

[13] P.L. 98-474, 15 U.S.C. §1331, Comprehensive Smoking Education Act.

[14] "The Smoke Around You – The Risks of Involuntary Smoking," American Cancer Society, 8/89.

[15] "Facts About Second-Hand Smoke," American Lung Association, 11/90.

[16] "Smoking and Heart Disease," American Heart Association, 1986; Cf. *New York State Journal of Medicine*, 12/83, Vol. 83, No. 13, pp. 1267-1268.

[17] *The Journal of the American Medical Association*, 12/11/91 issue.

[18] Califano, Joseph A. Jr., *Governing America*, Simon & Schuster, 1981, p. 185.

[19] *New York State Journal of Medicine*, 12/83, Vol. 83, No. 13, p. 1249.

[20] The examination was conducted by James L. Repace, a health physicist and senior analyst in the air policy office of the Environmental Protection Agency, who has published more than 30 papers in the scientific, medical, and engineering literature related to indoor air pollution from environmental tobacco smoke and who has testified on several occasions before Congressional committees.

[21] *McKinney* v. *Anderson*, 924 F. 2d 1500 (9th Cir. 1991), aff'd 113 S. Ct. 2475 (1993).

[22] Taylor, Peter, The Smoke Ring – Tobacco, Money & Multi-National Politics, Pantheon Books, 1984, p. xiv.

[23] EPA, Office of Air Radiation, Indoor Air Facts No. 5 – Environmental Tobacco Smoke, 6/89, p. 2; Fontham, Elizabeth T.H., and 11 other physicians, "Lung Cancer in Nonsmoking Women: A Multicenter Case-Control Study," Cancer Epidemiology Biomakers & Prevention, 11/91, Vol. 1, pp. 35-43.

[24] "Asthma – Deadly but Treatable," *Time*, 6/22/92, p. 62.

[25] *Id.*

[26] "Smoking Issue is Heating Up Custody Suits," Wall Street Journal, 8/17/92, p. B-1.

[27] Advisory Council on Social Security Report, 12/91; Transcript of Osgood File, CBS Radio Network, 5/16/91; "An Industry Under Siege," *MacLean's*, 3/19/90, pp. 34-36.

[28] Osgood File, *Id.*

[29] Whelan, *supra*, at forward, pp. 142, 212; Warner, *supra*, at p. 81; Congressional Quarterly's Editorial Research Reports, 9/21/90, p. 549.

[30] Advisory Council on Social Security Report, 12/91.

[31] "Canada Cuts Cigarette Taxes to Fight Smuggling," New York Times, 2/9/94, p. A3; "Canadian Tobacco Taxes Pared to Fight Smuggling," Wall Street Journal, 2/9/94, p. B 12.

[32] Americans for Nonsmokers' Rights Update, Vol. 10, No. 2, Summer 1991, p. 1.

[33] *Id*; See also *Milwaukee Journal,* 12/9/91 p. 3, citing the Journal of the American Public Health Association, 11/92.

34 Morbidity and Mortality Weekly Report (MMWR), Centers for Disease Control, Vol. 40, No. 44, pp. 756-757 (11/8/91).

35 Morbidity and Mortality Weekly Report, Centers for Disease Control and Prevention, 4/2/93, Vol. 42, No. 12, pp. 230-233.

36 *The Journal of the American Medical Association* (JAMA), "Tobacco Foes Attack Ads that Target Women, Minorities, Teens and the Poor," 9/26/90, pp. 1505-1506; JAMA, "Brand Logo Recognition by Children Aged 3 to 6 Years – Mickey Mouse and Old Joe the Camel," "RJR Nabisco's Cartoon Camel Promotes Camel Cigarettes to Children," "Does Tobacco Advertising Target Young People to Start Smoking?", "Tobacco Marketing – Profiteering from Children," Vol. 266, No. 22, pp. 3145, 3185-3186; Newsweek – "I'd Toddle a Mile for a Camel – New Studies suggest cigarette ads target children," 12/13/91, p. 70; *New York State Journal of Medicine*, "Mixed messages for women – A social history of smoking and advertising," Vol. 85, No. 7, pp. 335-340, "Getting women hooked: defending the indefensible," p. 341, "Cigarette smoking and ill health among black Americans," pp. 344-349, 7/85.

37 See footnote 1.

38 "Clinton to Seek 75-Cent Increase in Cigarette Tax," Wall Street Journal, 10/20/93, p. A 2.

39 "The Butt Stops Here," *Time*, 4/18/94, p. 58.

40 *Haines v. Liggett Group, Inc.*, 140 F.R.D. 681, 683 (D. N.J. 1992).

41 *Reducing the Health Consequences of Smoking: 25 Years of Progress, A Report of the Surgeon General*, U.S. Department of Health and Human Services, 1989, p. 58; Slattery, M., et al., "Cigarette Smoking and Exposure to Passive Smoke Are Risk Factors for Cervical Cancer," JAMA (1989), pp. 1593-1598.

42 Memorandum to Political Consultants and Candidates of both Parties at Every Level regarding Tobacco Issues in Political Campaigns by The Advocacy Institute, 9/20/90.

43 Statement of the American Medical Association to the EPA Science Advisory Board, Indoor Air Quality and Total Human Exposure Committee, 12/4/90, p. 8.

44 Advisory Council on Social Security Report, 12/91.

45 Koop, Dr. C. Everett, *Memoirs of America's Family Doctor* – Koop, Random House, 1991, pp. 179-180.

SMOKING IS A FORM OF
CHILD AND SPOUSE ABUSE

Child abuse is defined, in part, as physical abuse "leading to possible injury to the child."[1] Spouse abuse would appear to be similarly defined. Although calling smoking in the home a form of child or spouse abuse may sound overly dramatic, a growing body of research has established that secondary tobacco smoke in the home results in serious health problems and increases health risks for millions of children and nonsmoking spouses. Speaking bluntly, secondary tobacco smoke in the home constitutes an often overlooked form of child and spouse abuse resulting in the illness or death of one's children and/or nonsmoking spouse.

The tobacco companies are aiding and abetting such mayhem. Moreover, the tobacco industry apears to be creating an atmosphere conducive to such abuse through Joe Camel type ads.

Studies have established a correlation between parental smoking and children's illnesses and one spouse smoking with increased nonsmoking spouse's risk of contracting lung cancer by 30%.[2] Dr. Allan Luskin of Rush Medical Center, a major medical center in Chicago, recently said "it is my opinion that parents or caregivers who smoke in the presence of a child are guilty of child abuse."[3] He further pointed out that "smoke not only increases the risk of a child getting asthma in the first place, but it makes asthma worse when it is there."[4] Dr. William Cahan of Memorial Sloan-Kettering Cancer Center in New York also calls children's exposure to secondhand smoke child abuse.[5] Courts in 12 states consider smoking when deciding child custody cases.[6] In many cases courts have prohibited a parent from smoking near his or her child and in a few cases it has been a determinative factor over which parent is awarded custody.[7]

There is little doubt that exposing anyone to the 43 known carcinogens in tobacco smoke increases the health risk to anyone, including a spouse and children.[8] These carcinogens or cancer causing agents include tar, benzene, and formaldehyde.[9] In addition, cigarette smoke contains toxic agents that include carbon monoxide, hydrogen cyanide, and nicotine.[10] Cigarette smoke weakens children's lungs and airways making them more vulnerable to poisons, pollutants and germs.[11]

Children who are exposed to routine cigarette smoke are more likely to suffer from at least 50 different illnesses according to a review of 143 scientific studies published in January 1992 by the Child Studies Research Group at the University of Manchester, England.[12] These illnesses include sudden death syndrome, middle ear infection and adolescent meningitis.[13] Infants whose parents smoke are more likely to have severe bronchitis or pneumonia, asthma, leukemia and other childhood cancers and greater susceptibility to emphysema as adults.[14]

Infants whose mothers smoked during pregnancy have significantly less lung capacity than children of nonsmokers according to a study conducted by the Harvard University Medical School published in May 1992.[15] The lead author, John P. Hanrahan, pointed out that smoking during pregnancy exposes the baby to many toxic substances which retard fetal growth. For example, Dr. Hanrahan, pointed out that if a baby's airways are narrowed just 10 percent, airflow is reduced to two-thirds of normal. According to Dr. Douglas Holaclaw, Professor of Pediatrics at the University of Philadelphia, babies whose mothers smoke during pregnancy generally are born about eight ounces or about 10 percent lighter than babies of nonsmokers.[16] Infants whose mothers smoked during pregnancy are more likely to be premature, to die during the last two months of pregnancy or the first month after birth, to suffer from cerebral palsy, or to have learning and behavioral problems.[17]

Congress in 1984 recognized the danger of cigarette smoke to babies whose mothers smoked during pregnancy when it required all cigarette manufacturers and advertisers to have one of the four warnings on each pack of cigarettes or advertisements to be rotated quarterly including the following warning:[18]

SURGEON GENERAL'S WARNING: Pregnant Women Who Smoke
Risk Fetal Injury and Premature Birth

Louis W. Sullivan, M.D., former Secretary of Health and Human Services, noted that 2,537,000 cases of child abuse and neglect had been reported in 1990 and 1,500,000 of them were substantiated.[19] There were 2,694,000 reported cases of child abuse and neglect in 1991.[20] None of these reported child abuse cases involved smoking in the household.

Precise statistics involving the number of abused spouses are not readily available.[21] Studies have indicated that between 50 and 60 percent of families reported that the husband and wife engaged in some form of violent physical behavior, approximately 21% of 47.5 million married couples in the United States in 1976 beat their spouses anywhere from six times a year to daily, that there are at least 15 million battered wives in the United States today, and that 10 percent or 4.7 million are badly battered wives.[22] None of the reported spouse abuse cases included instances of smoking in the household.

About 45.8 million or 25.3% of adult Americans smoked as of 1990.[23] In 1988, about 42% (approximately 8,000,000) of all American children five years of age and under lived in a household with a smoker according to the National Center of Health Statistics.[24] These children were almost twice as likely to be in fair or poor health than those children who have not regularly inhaled secondary tobacco smoke.[25] Researchers at the University of North Carolina determined that children of smokers scored lower on tests measuring reasoning ability and vocabulary than did children of nonsmokers even after excluding factors such as gender, race, parents' education, mother's test scores and smoking during pregnancy.[26] Another study reported that while exposure to passive tobacco smoke is not uncommon in infants only three weeks old, 61% of babies not indicating exposure to secondhand tobacco smoke at three weeks of age tested positive for environmental tobacco smoke exposure from both household and nonhousehold sources by the time they reached their first birthday.[27]

The Environmental Protection Agency released a report in draft form in June, 1992, finalized in December 1992, linking environmental tobacco smoke to a range of childhood illnesses and termed it a "known human carcinogen."[28] The report stated that exposure to secondary tobacco smoke accounts for between 150,000 to 300,000 respiratory infections in babies each year.[29] The report concludes that passive tobacco smoke not only aggravates up to a million existing cases of childhood asthma each year, but triggers 8,000 to 26,000 new cases annually.[30]

Although the studies did not provide secondhand tobacco smoke exposure figures for children over five, they would have to be at least as great as the number of children five and under who are exposed to tobacco smoke in their homes. When coupled with the nonsmoking spouses of these eight million chiildren five and under and those nonsmoking spouses of children over five, at a minimum smoking parents appear to be endangering the health of at least 30 million American children and nonsmoking spouses. This would constitute more cases than all the reported instances of child abuse and spouse abuse about which so much has been written. Clearly, endangerment and the destruction of children's and spouse's health from the secondary tobacco smoke of the smoking spouse is just as serious as the reported cases of child and spouse abuse. As former HHS Secretary Sullivan advised parents, "I can't think of a more compelling reason for parents to quit smoking than ensuring their children's chance for a healthy life."[31]

After examining two buildings in a large midwest city, a well-known health physicist knowledgeable in indoor air pollution recently testified that the work areas would be turned in "gas chambers" if smoking were to be initiated in these facilities and these facilities were not atypical.[32] The "gas chamber" observation is consistent with Federal Court of Appeals and Supreme Court decisions that a nonsmoking prisoner's exposure to secondary tobacco smoke from a smoking cellmate could constitute cruel and unusual punishment in violation of the Eighth Amendment of the Constitution.[33] Forcing children and nonsmoking spouses to live in a "gas chamber" environment such as a home or ride in an automobile exposed to the carcinogens and toxins of poisonous tobacco smoke constitutes a form of cruel and unusual punishment known as child or spouse abuse.

The American Medical Association in a December 4, 1990 statement to the Environmental Protection Agency recommended that environmental tobacco smoke be classified as a human carcinogen. In the last paragraph of its statement, the American Medical Association said the following about the tobacco industry:[34]

> We know of no other industry which would be allowed to produce a product which kills so many. It is now clear that *tobacco is lethal, not only to those who use it as intended by the manufacturer but to those who have not assumed those risks.* (Emphasis added)

At least 30 million American children and nonsmoking spouses have not assumed those risks. Any spouse who subjects a family member to a lethal substance such as tobacco smoke has committed a cruel and health damaging form of child and/or spouse abuse.

It does not appear that any child or spouse advocacy or protection group has given serious thought to categorizing smoking in a household as a form of child or spouse abuse. Whether such categorization might jeopardize some contributions from donors such as tobacco companies or dilute efforts to prevent cases of violent abuse is unclear. However, one fact is clear. Secondary tobacco smoke in the home is jeopardizing the health and lives of at least 30 million American children and spouses.

Groups advocating the prevention of child abuse and spouse abuse should take notice of the harmful effects of tobacco just as King James I did in 1604 when he said in his *Counterblast to Tobacco* that tobacco was hateful to the nose, harmful to the brain, and dangerous to the lungs. These groups formed to prevent child and spouse abuse should utilize their resources and networks to eradicate the harming and killing of one's children and spouse from secondary tobacco smoke in the home. If these groups succeed, we may have a kinder and gentler America built around the family.

Failure means a crueler, meaner and sicker America - a license for the tobacco industry to continue exposing at least 30 million unaware children and spouses to the harmful carcinogens and poisons of secondary tobacco smoke.

Tobacco is the only consumer product that when used exactly as the manufacturer intends causes death and disease. Risking and endangering the health of millions of innocent children and spouses is a silent but deadly form of child and spouse abuse. Anyone who cares about the American family should recognize this fact and do everything posssible to eradicate smoking in American households.

The elimination of smoking in American homes will do more for the health of the American family than the elimination of violence on our television and movie screens, another worthy goal, and would help restore the foundation of our system of values – the caring and helping of others, especially family members and close friends. The tobacco industry has gone a long way towards destroying this value system by facilitating family members jeopardizing or destroying the health of other family members.

ENDNOTES

1 Child Abuse and Neglect: An Informed Approach to a Shared Concern, Clearinghouse on Child Abuse and Neglect, U.S. Department of Health and Human Services, Administration for Children, Youth and Families, Children's Bureau, National Center on Child Abuse and Neglect, 3/86, p. 1.

2 Environmental Protection Agency, Indoor Air Facts No. 5 – Environmental Tobacco Smoke, 6/89, p. 2; Cf. "Environmental Tobacco Smoke and Cardiovascular Disease," A Position paper from the Council on Cardiopulmonary and Critical Care, American Heart Association, *Circulation*, Vol. 86, No. 2, 8/92. See also Fontham, Elizabeth, T.H. and 11 other physicians, "Lung Cancer in Nonsmoking Women: A Multicenter Case – Control Study," Cancer Epidemiology Biomakers & Prevention, 11/91, Vol. 1, pp. 35-43; cf. "Secondhand Smoke Might Harm Rover," *Chicago Sun-Times*, 5/18/92, health section, p. 4 (a recent study revealed that even dogs are 50% more likely to develop lung cancer when

they live with owners who smoke. American Journal of Epidemiology, 1992 – John Reif, Colorado State University).

[3] "Asthma – Deadly but Treatable," *Time*, 6/22/92, p. 62.

[4] *Id.*

[5] "Smoking Issue is Heating Up Custody Suits," Wall Street Journal, 8/17/92, p. B-1.

[6] "Fla. High Court OK's Smoke Ban," The National Law Journal, 5/8/95, p. A-6.

[7] *Id.*

[8] Environmental Protection Agency, Indoor Air Facts No. 5, *infra*, see note 1.

[9] "Environmental Tobacco Smoke in the Workplace – Lung Cancer and Other Health Effects," NIOSH Current Intelligence Bulletin 54, 6/91, p. 3.

[10] *Id.*

[11] "Healthy Kids 4-10," American Academy of Pediatrics, Fall 1991, p. 26.

[12] "Kids get sick from second-hand smoke," Gary-Post Tribune, 1/7/92, p. A5, referring to an article in the journal for the Association of Nonsmokers Rights entitled "Children and Passive Smoking," by Anne Charlton, 12/91.

[13] *Id.*

[14] "Secondhand Smoke" Pamphlet, Association for Nonsmokers – Minnesota, 8/91.

[15] "Baby's lungs damaged by smoking mom," *Chicago Sun- Times*, 5/12/92, p. 12, based on article "The Effect of Maternal Smoking During Pregnancy on Early Infant Lung Function," Hanrahan, John P., lead author, American Review of Respiratory Disease published by the American Lung Association, vol. 145, pp. 1129-1135 (1992).

[16] "Baby's lungs damaged by smoking mom," *Id.*

[17] "Secondhand Smoke" Pamphlet, *supra*, see note 14.

[18] Public Law 98-474, 15 U.S.C. §1331, Comprehensive Smoking Education Act.

[19] Remarks by Dr. Sullivan on April 28, 1992 to the National Center on Child Abuse and Neglect – Region V Conference in Chicago.

[20] Current Trends in Child Abuse Reporting and Fatalities. The Results of the 1991 Annual Fifty State Survey prepared by the National Center on Child Abuse Prevention Research, p. 2.

[21] Langley, Roger and Levy, Richard C., *Wife Beating: The Silent Crisis*, E.P. Dutton, 1977, pp. 2-3.

[22] *Id.* at pp. 2-4.

[23] Advance Data No. 202, U.S. Department of Health and Human Services, Public Health Service, Centers for Disease Control, National Center for Health Statistics, 6/18/91, pp. 7-8.

[24] *Id.* at p. 5.

[25] *Id.*

[26] "Parental Cigarette Smoking and Cognitive Performance of Children," Health Psychology, Vol. 10, No. 4, pp. 282-288 (1991).

[27] "Passive Smoke During the First Year of Life," *American Journal of Public Health*, Vol. 81, No. 7, 7/91, pp. 850-853.

[28] United States Environmental Protection Agency, Office of Research and Development, Office of Air and Radiation, "Respiratory Health Effects of Passive Smoking: Lung Cancer and Other Disorders," 12/92; "Poison at Home and at Work," *Newsweek*, 6/29/92, p. 55.

[29] *Id.*

[30] *Id.*

[31] "Secondhand Smoke" Pamphlet, *supra*, see note 14.

[32] The examination was conducted by James L. Repace, a health physicist and senior analyst in the air policy office of the Environmental Protection Agency who has published over 30 papers in the scientific, medical and engineering literature related to indoor air pollution from environmental tobacco smoke and who has testified on several occasions before Congressional committees.

[33] *McKinney* v. *Anderson*, 924 F. 2d 1500 (9th Cir. 1991), aff'd 113 S. Ct. 2475 (1993).

[34] Statement of the American Medical Association to the EPA Science Advisory Board, Indoor Air Quality and Total Human Exposure Committee, 12/4/90, p. 8.

BAN TOBACCO ADVERTISING

In early 1991 a California man came out with yet another new brand of cigarettes.[1] Presumably it had a comparable number of carcinogens and toxins as the other brands on the market. What distinguished this new brand from the others was its descriptive name - "Death" - packaged with a picture of a skull. For the approximately 419,000 American smokers who prematurely die from tobacco smoke each year, and many more who become seriously ill, whatever brand they smoked could have been named "death." The manufacturer of "Death" cigarettes sold 25,000 packs in Los Angeles in the spring of 1991. The real challenge for the manufacturer of cigarettes which will likely result in death is how to market and convince people to purchase a consumer product that could very well result in their death.

The American tobacco industry along with their advertising firms merit a solid "A" in convincing millions of Americans to buy a product that when used as intended causes death and/or serious illness. The industry has to find ways to replace the 419,000 American smokers who die prematurely each year from the carcinogens and toxins in poisonous tobacco smoke and the many more who become seriously ill. Their replacement victims are primarily children, women, and minorities, the majority of whom start smoking by age 14.

The means by which the tobacco industry addicts children, women and minorities is clever advertising largely protected by the First Amendment. Radio and television ads were effective means until banned in 1970. Magazine, newspaper, and billboard advertising remain. Joe Camel glamorizes smoking for youngsters as young as three by encouraging them to consider embarking on this addictive and deadly habit a little later in

life. The Virginia Slims type ad misleads women into believing that smoking and slimness which reflect good health are linked. Just look at a random sample of the nation's 46 million smokers. They appear no slimmer or
heavier than the nation's 200 million nonsmokers.

This century the tobacco industry has undertaken a misleading advertising campaign which shifts according to the medical, scientific, and legal
winds. The medical warnings have been there since King James I warning
in 1604. However, since at least the 1920s there have been scientific bases
for the alarm.

During the early years athletes, radio and television dignitaries, and
movie stars glamorized smoking. Fortunately such ads as the we are "not
medicine men," but tobacco men failed to carry the day. After an alarming
report linking smoking to lung cancer in the early 1950s, there was more of
an effort to focus on television ads. When radio and television ads were
banned in the 1970s, the tobacco industry and their advertising firms became more creative. The Marlboro Man glamorized manhood, Joe Camel
became a positive smoking image for kids, and Virginia Slims became a
sexy and weight control symbol for women. Billboards featuring Joe
Camel became as recognizable for three-year olds as Mickey Mouse.

When evaluating the appropriateness of banning advertising a product,
one must necessarily focus on its harmful features. However, in fairness to
the tobacco industry, there are some serious arguments that have and could
be made for continuing cigarette advertising. Cigarette advertising is a big
business. United States cigarette manufacturers spent $3.27 billion on
cigarette advertising and promotion in 1988.[2] Clearly, a ban on cigarette
advertising would result in the loss of some jobs. Secondly, assuming a
correlation between tobacco company advertising expenditures and the
number of smokers, a ban on all tobacco advertising, including billboards,
will result in fewer smokers and fewer smoking-related illnesses. This may
mean a loss of income to health-related businesses such as hospitals and
nursing homes since smoking-related illnesses are a major source of secondary medical care in the United States.

However, the major argument that has again surfaced by the Federal
Trade Commission staff wanting to ban the R.J. Reynolds Joe Camel ad
campaign in August 1993 was the First Amendment right of freedom of
commercial speech. There are limits to the First Amendment when it
comes to public health and safety. Supreme Court Justice Oliver Wendell
Holmes pointed out in 1919 that "free speech would not protect a man in
falsely shouting 'fire' in a theatre and causing a panic."[3] Clearly, the First
Amendment does not afford smokers the right to expose more than 200
million nonsmokers, including more than 30 million children and non-

smoking spouses, to potentially harmful or even fatal poisonous secondary tobacco smoke. Nor should any other person be exposed to secondary tobacco smoke in the workplace or in public facilities. Likewise, the advertisers of lethal products should be prevented from facilitating the spread of death and illness from the carcinogens and toxins of poisonous tobacco smoke. Curbing cigarette ad campaigns designed to attract children, women and minorities to a lifetime of nicotine addiction is a valid exercise of the type of public health and safety not protected by the First Amendment.

Nearly a half million Americans die prematurely each year from smoking cigarettes and many more must stop smoking because of serious illness. In order for the American domestic tobacco market to continue to flourish, the tobacco companies must replenish the huge annual domestic human loss. Children, the majority of whom begin this addictive habit by age 14, women, and minorities have become attractive and major replacement resources.

Misleading advertising has been the means to reach the end of replacing the lost smokers each year. For example, Joe Camel ads have created a high positive recognition factor among three to six year olds priming them for the leap into addictive smoking by age 13 as do the "Camel Cash" and "Marlboro Gear" gift enticements. There is no question among reputable scientists and physicians that smoking kills. Joe Camel ads glamorizing a lethal consumer product at the expense of children's health are misleading and the first step towards this deadly habit.

Some of the old television ads were works of art. The ads slickly mislead by implying that the claims were true when at best the tobacco companies did not know if they were true.

Old Dennis James bragged about Old Gold being made by tobacco men and "not medicine men." He then went on to say that "if you want a treat instead of a treatment, get Old Gold cigarettes."[4] I wonder how many smokers of Old Gold got lung cancer, with its accompanying radiation and chemotherapy treatments, thanks to Mr. James.

Kools ran an ad claiming to be "America's most refreshing cigarette" urging smokers to "switch from hots to snow-fresh Kools." Kools were advertised "as clear as a breath of fresh air." The ad was silent about the carcinogens and toxins from poisonous tobacco smoke that pollute the air. The Kools "breath of fresh air" television ad reminds me of how my heavy smoking late father-in-law quit. He was with his family puffing a cigarette in Rocky Mountain National Park. He suddenly put out the cigarette and said, "what am I doing ruining this wonderful clear air?" Needless to say, he was not recruited by Philip Morris to be the Marlboro Man in Marlboro Country.

Marlboro ran several television commercials advising that "you get a lot to light with a Marlboro, filter, flavor, pack or box." A common box for Marlboro smokers was a coffin which too often was sent with the smoker to Marlboro Country, the local cemetery.

Winston ran a television ad "Winston Tastes Good Like a Cigarette Should" showing Winston cigarettes being served with a meal on Capitol Airlines. Fortunately cigarettes cannot be smoked today on most domestic flights and are normally not distributed on any flight. Capitol Airlines and most of its smokers have gone under. Hopefully cigarettes will be banned on all international flights in the near future.

The Pete Lorillard Company moved from the "Tobacco Men, Not Medicine Men" ad to the scientific area showing Old Gold reduced tar and nicotine. A number of studies, including one published in the August 17, 1993 American Lung Association Journal, revealed that the brand of cigarettes one smokes has little effect on the amount of tar and nicotine one gets. By running the ad, the tobacco company was implicitly admitting cigarettes were harmful. The ad even showed a research scientist capped by the allegation that Old Gold was "naturally reduced in tar and nicotine content."

Salem did the glamour television ad featuring a beautiful young woman who informed the viewer that "Salem refreshes taste as springtime refreshes you" and was "menthol fresh." The beautiful young lady neglected to mention that tobacco smoke causes premature wrinkling and aging, hardly glamorous.

For many years Americans apparently have been impressed by entertainers and athletes endorsing products. The tobacco industry took advantage of this tendency when endorsing their products. Bob Cummings of the television series "Father Knows Best" informed the viewing audience of the three Hawaiian traditions - a lei, a kiss, and a lei of Winston which showed that Winston was just as popular in Hawaii as on the mainland. What Uncle Bob failed to do was inform the viewers that for many Americans smoking was the kiss of death preceding their being laid to permanent rest.

Jim "Catfish" Hunter of American League baseball fame and the Pittsburgh Steelers Superbowl quarterback Terry Bradshaw took time off from their busy schedules to make television commercials for Red Man Chewing Tobacco. Many kids followed their idols path and started down the fatal chewing tobacco road. The use of chewing tobacco is a deadly habit engaged in by 12 million Americans with the average user starting at age 9 1/2.[5] Oral cancer including cancers of the throat, mouth, tongue, and lip is 50 times more common among longtime chewing tobacco users than among nonusers. According to a Public Health Service survey, one out of six males between 12 and 25 used smokeless tobacco in 1992. Although in terms of athletic achievement, Catfish Hunter and Terry Bradshaw were hall of famers, when one examines their adverse impact on the young people in our country through plugging Red Man Chewing Tobacco ads, they may more appropriately be referred to as hall of shamers.

The exploitation of women by the tobacco industry was brought to light in the Virginia Slims commercial noting that men were masters, women were slaves, and "You've come a long way baby." The television ad states that in the old days men were masters and women were slaves, but in 1920 you won them all. The ad featured a "slim cigarette for women only tailored for a woman's hand." It concluded "You've got your own cigarette, baby. You've come a long, long way."[6] Women have come a long way with gaining the long overdue right to vote in 1920, but with increasing acceptance by society of women smoking their lung cancer rate has also soared. Lung cancer death rates among women who smoke increased six times from the 1960s to the 1980s.[7] The glamour of smoking portrayed in cigarette advertising has resulted in millions of American women dying prematurely and aging prematurely demonstrated most vividly by facial wrinkles.

Those who hid behind the shield of the First Amendment as support for killing kids from the carcinogens and toxins of poisonous tobacco smoke should be reminded that the Supreme Court has set limits when it comes to public health and safety. As Supreme Court Justice Oliver Wendell Holmes pointed out in 1919, "free speech would not protect a man in falsely shouting 'fire' in a theatre and causing a panic." Likewise, tobacco advertising designed to condition children as young as age three to consider embarking on the addictive and deadly smoking habit by age 13 and smokeless tobacco habit before age 10 should not be protected by the First Amendment.

A review of Supreme Court decisions raises a serious question as to whether the highest court would uphold a total ban on cigarette advertising. The Supreme Court in 1972 upheld a Congressional ban on tobacco advertising on radio and television. *National Association of Broadcasters v. Kleindienst*, 405 U.S. 1000 (1972), (summarily) *aff'd sub nom Capitol Broadcasting Co. v. Mitchell*, 333 F. Supp. 582 (D. D.C. 1971).

The Supreme Court held for the first time in 1975 that commercial advertising was entitled to First Amendment protection. *Bigelow v. Virginia*, 421 U.S. 809, 826 (1975). The Court has given commercial speech less protection than social or political discussing. In *Posadas de Puerto Rico v. Tourism Company of Puerto Rico,* 478 U.S. 328 (1986), the Supreme Court upheld a prohibition on advertising of legal gambling casinos to the residents of Puerto Rico. Chief Justice William Rehnquist observed that since the legislature could have prohibited gambling, it could take the lesser step of banning advertising. The Court in *Posadas* noted that since government unquestionably has the right to ban the sale of hazardous products, it has considerable discretion in reducing demand for harmful products such as cigarettes through restrictions on advertising.

The Supreme Court as precedent for its holding in *Posadas* cited cases upholding restrictions on the advertisement of alcoholic beverages[8] and cigarettes.[9] It appeared that the Court was leaving to government entities the decision whether to ban the advertising of hazardous goods including cigarettes. See also *Penn Advertising of Baltimore, Inc. v. Mayor & City Council of Baltimore,* 862 F. Supp. 1402 (D. Md. 1994), aff'd 63 F. 2d 18 (4th Cir. 1995), where lower federal courts upheld the constitutionality of a Baltimore city ordinance banning outdoor cigarette billboard advertising. However, the Supreme Court was not encouraging when it rendered a decision in *44 Liquormart, Inc. v. Rhode Island,* 116 S.Ct. 1495(1996), overturning restrictions of outdoor advertising of alcoholic beverages to help combat underage drinking and remanded the Baltimore cigarette billboard advertising case, 116 S.Ct. 2595(1996).

As the Supreme Court apparently indicated on November 28, 1994, the First Amendment is not a license for tobacco companies to entice kids through Joe Camel type ads to embark on a habit that will shorten their lives. The Court let stand a lower court ruling authorizing a civil trial for charges that R.J. Reynolds Tobacco Co. ads allegedly targeted children with its Joe Camel ad campaign in violation California's consumer protection law. *R.J. Reynolds Tobacco Co. v. Mangini,* 115 S.Ct. 577 (1994).

It has been pointed out that there are four basic goals of cigarette advertisers - advertising aimed at enticing children and young adults to experiment with cigarettes and initiate tobacco habits, advertising designed to reduce current smokers' resolve to quit or to consider quitting, advertising aimed to increase current smokers' daily consumption of cigarettes, and advertising geared to encouraging former smokers to revise their habits.[10]

The Joe Camel ads are the perfect example of how the cigarette industry gears its appeals to children, many as young as age three. Children generally do not have the maturity to make rational and informed judgments about their health and especially smoking. Since the majority of smokers start this addictive habit by age 13, the tobacco company appeal through glamour, machisimo, and independent decision making has the effect of bypassing much of the adverse health information regarding smoking.

When Joe Camel and Mickey Mouse enjoy the same recognition factor for three to six year olds, one knows that the tobacco industry is succeeding in perpetuating the use of its poisonous product. Hopefully, no court will hold the First Amendment protects this type of activity. If it does, it would be like giving the gun industry the right to flood the billboards with Joey "the rifle" ads, the cocaine and heroin cartels with Tommie "crack" ads, and the beer and liquor industry with "Bobbie" beer and booze ads designed to attract minors as new customers.

Not only is cigarette advertising harmful in that it sometimes persuades persons to start a health-destroying habit or not quit that habit, but there is a strong statistical correlation that cigarette advertising in magazines is associated with diminished coverage of the hazards of smoking.[11] This is especially true for magazines directed to women. Dr. Kenneth Warner, who was the senior scientific editor of the 1989 U.S. Surgeon General's Report on Smoking and Health, found that as "the percentage of advertising revenue from cigarettes rises, the probability of discovering the hazards of smoking fell."[12] So not only are cigarette ads misleading, the tobacco companies through advertising dollars appear to be placing pressure on publications not to run stories which may negatively impact on smoking.

When I have pointed out the high tobacco advertising low-smoking news story correlation to some of the nation's leading weekly news publications, they became very defensive and sometimes responded with personal rather than the typical form letters. When I questioned Newsweek on January 13, 1993 about its failure to provide any coverage regarding the Environmental Protection Agency's landmark report the previous week concluding that secondary tobacco smoke causes lung cancer and greatly increases the risk of respiratory illness in children[13] and whether tobacco advertising revenues were a factor in the lack of coverage, I received the following personal note from Newsweek dated April 6, 1993:

> We know that many of our readers object to the publication of cigarette advertisements, and we can appreciate their concern. We feel, however, that if we were to accept some ads and reject others, we would be, in effect, endorsing those products whose ads we do accept. Therefore it has always been our policy to accept advertising from the makers of all legal products, as long as it conforms to the standards of good taste and ethical practice established by the Better Business Burea [sic] and our own Advertising Acceptance Committee.
>
> We hope you realize, though, that our editorial department is completely independent of our advertising department, and we maintain this separation

so that our editorial staff can remain absolutely free of any conceivable pressure from our advertisers. Thus, our running ads from tobacco companies has never prevented us from conscientiously reporting on the health hazards and social problems related to smoking. We keep our readers informed about new findings establishing the connection between smoking and, for example, heart disease, ulcers and lung cancer....

Naturally, we hope you will reconsider your decision to cancel.

Apparently Newsweek failed to examine the amount of space devoted to cigarette advertising versus the amount devoted to articles and news items concerning the dangers of smoking. At a minimum, Newsweek devoted 20 times more space to cigarette advertising. Moreover, the publication does not appear to recognize the difference between permitting the advertising of a consumer product which is legal, but harmful, and a product which is illegal. Neither should be advertised. Many magazines such as the Readers' Digest have found a way to recognize this distinction. Finally Newsweek inaccurately indicated that I wished to end my subscription. I never threatened to do so since I enjoy certain facets of the publication and would like to continually monitor their cigarette advertising versus smoking news stories. Perhaps Newsweek should invite one of their prestigious columnists to write a column on why cigarette advertising should be banned.

I received a more conciliatory personal letter from U.S. News and World Report on February 23, 1993, which stated:

Let me assure you that our coverage of the Environmental Protection Agency Report has no correlation with cigarette advertisements. In addition, your views about the tobacco advertisements in the magazine have been sent to our Advertising Department in New York.

Critical or complimentary, it is helpful to hear from readers. I hope that you will continue to follow U.S. News, and that you will find we are still offering the candid and objective journalism you value.

By the way, how many letters did you see through 1993 regarding smoking in Time, Newsweek, or U.S. News and World Report?[14] I do not recall seeing any through 1993, but I do remember seeing many full-page cigarette ads. I recall reading a number of health features in these publications, but rarely do they speak of smoking as a health problem even though the carcinogens and toxins of poisonous tobacco smoke are responsible for nearly a half million premature American deaths a year and many more serious illnesses.

Not all news publications permit tobacco industry advertising because of a desire or need for revenues. For example, the *Seattle Times* was reported to have curtailed its tobacco advertising at the end of 1993. However, it appears for the most part weekly news publications, women's publications and some others have found tobacco company advertising revenues to be more important than the health of their readers. I was astounded when observing full-page R.J. Reynolds Co. ads in the April 7, 1995 Chicago Tribune and Chicago Sun-Times admitting that Salems smell up one's hair, clothes, car and home, but does it "less". In other words, R.J. Reynolds has admitted smoking "stinks." As far as tobacco companies are concerned, no news is good news with their advertising dollars tending to promote no news.

The bottom line is that banning cigarettes and tobacco advertising will stop misleading children and adults regarding the impact of smoking on one's health and will encourage publications that carry health articles to have the financial freedom to inform the public regarding the dangers of smoking. It is time that the tobacco industry came out in the open from behind the coattails of the First Amendment. The tobacco men should go to the background and the medicine men should emerge. Then, thousands of human lives may be saved. The tobacco industry's slick spin control and buzz words which permeate the advertising media will not be missed.

ENDNOTES

[1] Newsweek, 5/13/91, p. 51.

[2] "Cigarette Advertising and Magazine Coverage of the Hazards of Smoking," The New England Journal of Medicine, Vol. 326, 1/30/92, No. 5, pp. 305-309, at p. 305.

[3] *United States v. Schenck*, 249 U.S. 47, 52 (1919).

[4] TV-1088, Museum of Broadcast Communications Archives, Chicago.

[5] Feinstein, John, "A Baseball Tradition – Chewing Tobacco – That Can be Deadly," Washington Post, Health, 10/19/93, pp. 12-15.

[6] See footnote 4.

[7] "Cancer Deaths Jumps in Women Who Smoke," New York Times, 9/12/95, p. B-6.

[8] *Posadas de Puerto Rico v. Tourism Company of Puerto Rico*, 478 U.S. 328 (1986).

[9] *Id.*

[10] Warner, Kenneth E., Ph.D., "Selling Smoke: Cigarette Advertising and Public Health," American Public Health Association, 1986.

[11] "Cigarette Advertising and Magazine Coverage of the Hazards of Smoking," The New England Journal of Medicine, Vol. 326, No. 5, 1/30/92, pp. 305-306.

[12] *Id.*

[13] United States Environmental Protection Agency, Office of Research and Development, Office of Air and Radiation, "Respiratory Health Effects of Passive Smoking: Lung Cancer and Other Disorders," 12/92.

[14] U.S. News and World Report ran a cover story on April 18, 1994 entitled "Should Cigarettes Be Outlawed?" The news magazine published several letters pertaining to the story on May 2, 1994.

A Program to Prevent Minors Smoking and Using Tobacco

To Combat Tobacco Industry's Efforts to Addict Minors to Poisonous Tobacco Smoke

The tobacco companies must find replacements for the approximately 419,000 Americans who die prematurely each year from smoking and the use of smokeless tobacco. They have found the primary replacement source – our children! About 3,000 teens light their first cigarette each day with the average starting age being 12 and 90% of smokeless tobacco users start by their teenage years.[1] The tobacco industry has succeeded in getting underage kids addicted to tobacco far beyond their wildest expectations. A recent study shows that most new smokers are teenagers.[2]

About 60% of youngsters who smoke start prior to age 14. A survey by the federal Office on Smoking and Health found that the average age where a smokeless tobacco user started the habit is 9 1/2.[3] The National Cancer Institute reports that oral cancer - including cancers of the lip, tongue, mouth and throat - is as much as 50 times more common among longtime snuff users than nonusers.[4]

About 3.7 million teens or 16% of all teenagers smoke. Another 6.8 million or 29% have experimented.[5] Approximately 60% of the 16-18 year old group smoked or had tried smoking.[6] About 70% of American under-18 smokers had bought cigarettes for themselves, 85% bought cigarettes at small stores or gasoline stations, and 14% bought them at vending machines.[7]

The addiction of teens and pre-teens to tobacco has been spurred since 1988 by Joe Camel type ads. Camels share of the under 18 cigarette market has soared since the Joe Camel cartoon was introduced in 1988 from 0.5% in 1988 to 32.8% in 1991.[8] "Old Joe," the cartoon camel used to advertise Camel cigarettes, is as familiar to six-year olds as Mickey Mouse. Over 90% of six-year olds know Old Joe and link him with his product, the same rate they have for Disney's childhood icon.[9] Children are conditioned as early as age three through Joe Camel that smoking is fine.[10] The tobacco industry sells over $1.25 billion in tobacco products each year to children under 18 - over one billion packs of cigarettes and 26 million cannisters of chewing tobacco.[11] Although the tobacco industry spin controllers deny trying to appeal to kids, their arguments are about as convincing as their contending that tobacco smoke and secondary tobacco smoke is not harmful to one's health.

There appears to be a correlation between the age one starts smoking and his or her ability to quit. Approximately 90% of current smokers began smoking prior to age 21.[12] Children are beginning to use tobacco at an earlier age with the average first use being 11 to 14.[13] Almost three quarters of high school daily smokers still smoke seven to nine years later although in high school only 5% thought they would be smoking five years later.[14]

The ease of children's accessibility to tobacco products is alarming. In more than 40 states the sale of tobacco to underage children is illegal. However, studies throughout the country have shown that underage children can purchase cigarettes 70-80% of the time over the counter and over 90% of the time through vending machines.[15] It has been reported that children can purchase cigarettes from vending machines in "adult only" places such as bars 77% of the time.[16]

An American Medical Association physician estimated that 80% of the nearly 3,000 American children who begin smoking each day will never be able to free themselves of the habit and one-third will die prematurely from a smoking related disease.[17] The question that must be asked is how can we stop or reduce the addiction of our youth to tobacco and protect our children from the premature cancers, heart disease, emphysema, and other illnesses that follow.

The answers are not easy, but there are approaches which if utilized could have a marked impact on underage smoking and preventing youth from starting. They include:

1. Parents stopping;

2. Educational institutions banning smoking by faculty and support staff;

3. Combatting appeals of smoking such as weight control, assertion of independence, and machoism;

4. Parents playing an active role such as by kissing children good night which also serves as a breath checker;

5. Banning tobacco advertising;

6. Enforcing existing laws and promulgating new regulations and laws against underage smoking, such as banning cigarette vending machines;

7. Publicize votes of pro-tobacco Congressmen who accept tobacco PAC and industry money; and

8. Placing a huge tax on cigarettes to offset low generic prices designed, in part, to attract teens.

1. PARENTS SHOULD STOP SMOKING

It is a basic human nature trait that people do not like being lectured to or told what to do. This is especially true with teenagers.

One of the more effective ways of persuading a person to undertake or cease a course of action is to lead by example. It has been reported that the chances of an adolescent smoking is nominal if neither parent smokes, higher if one parent smokes, and even higher if both parents smoke.[18] If the parent(s) can stop smoking, it will send a powerful signal to their child that there may be something to the bombardment of health warnings they have heard in school and in the media. The parents will not be hypocrites. They will be leading by example.

2. EDUCATION

A substantial amount of time and effort has been devoted by parents, physicians, antismoking organizations, and educators trying to combat underage smoking. As a result of the Joe Camel type advertising campaigns of the tobacco industry, the success in this area has been less than desired.

Something which apparently has not been tried on a large scale has been taking children to visit those portions of nursing homes and hospitals, including Veterans Administration hospitals housing patients who have been ravaged by the carcinogens and toxins of poisonous tobacco smoke. One live view would be worth thousands of words. It would be like seeing first hand the survivors of concentration camps at the end of World War II rather than mere photographs of these skeletal human beings. The field trips to nursing homes and hospitals could be part of a health education course focusing on the dangers of drugs, alcohol, and tobacco.

The course curriculum could be supplemented by additional materials such as comments by celebrities which appear in Chapter III of this book, the advice columns in Chapter IV, and the one cartoon equals 1,000 anti-tobacco words in Chapter V. Experiences of former smokers and deceased smokers could help supplement the lectures and present different perspectives of the dangers of smoking.

A game for two to six players ages 12 to adult emphasizing the dangers of smoking called "Smokers Wild" could be utilized.[19] The players have various roles to play including The Undertaker (Doug Graves), the Doctor (Mel Practice), the Taxman (Owen More), and the Tobacco Planter (Roland Myone). In a lighter vein the game focuses on the problems and dangers of smoking. The game can be utilized effectively as a classroom teaching device.

Films which are available through a number of health organizations and many antismoking organizations, bringing in physicians equipped with chest X-rays and diagrams, and panels of ex-smokers are additional ways to broaden education. In addition, schools should be active participants in such national events as the annual Great American Smokeout Day each November.

Former Surgeon General M. Joycelyn Elders, M.D., issued a report in 1994 entitled "Preventing Tobacco Use Among Young People: A Report of the Surgeon General."[20] The 314-page report examines the health effects of early smoking and smokeless tobacco use, the reasons why young men and women begin using tobacco, the extent to which they use it, and efforts to prevent tobacco use by young people.[21] An executive summary of the Report was distributed at a national town meeting to prevent tobacco use by young people on March 24, 1994 entitled "Youth and Elders Against Tobacco Use."[22] Both the Report and Executive Summary set forth the major conclusions as follows:[23]

1. Nearly all first use of tobacco occurs before high school graduation; this finding suggests that if adolescents can be kept tobacco-free, most will never start using tobacco.

2. Most adolescent smokers are addicted to nicotine and report that they want to quit but are unable to do so; they experience relapse rates and withdrawal symptoms similar to those reported by adults.

3. Tobacco is often the first drug used by those young people who use alcohol, marijuana, and other drugs.

4. Adolescents with lower levels of school achievement, with fewer skills to resist pervasive influences to use tobacco, with friends who use tobacco, and with lower self-images are more likely than their peers to use tobacco.

5. Cigarette advertising appears to increase young people's risk of smoking by affecting their perceptions of the pervasiveness, image and function of smoking.

6. Communitywide efforts that include tobacco tax increases, enforcement of minors' access laws, youth-oriented mass media campaigns, and school-based tobacco-use prevention programs are successful in reducing adolescent use of tobacco.

School administrators and school boards should be advised of the importance of the need to promote a smoking education program. Smoking on the premises by students as well as the faculty which theoretically sets an example should be banned. However, the ultimate success of such program may depend on whether the Principal, Superintendent, and/or School Board members are smokers or nonsmokers.

Legislation can assist schools in their efforts to combat smoking. Congress recently approved and President Clinton signed into law a bill prohibiting smoking in schools and in Head Start and community health centers.[24] The House of Representatives approved a measure that all schools that receive federal drug-prevention funds teach the dangers of smoking.[25] State legislation such as Illinois Public Act 89-0181 signed into law July 19, 1995, providing for the elimination of smoking on elementary and secondary school property would be extremely helpful in curbing the tobacco industry's exploitation of our nation's youth by jeopardizing their health.

3. COMBAT APPEALS OF SMOKING

The ultimate success or failure of curbing underage smoking may boil down to the three special appeals of smoking to young people - weight control, assertion of independence and adulthood, and machoism.

There is some evidence that at the initial stages of smoking cessation, some former smokers gain weight. Proper diet and exercise under medical supervision can be effective in combating this tendency. However, the long-term benefit of not having at least 43 carcinogens and toxins from poisonous secondary tobacco smoke continuously entering one's body would appear to more than offset a possible weight gain.

There is a great desire of young people to be independent faster than their chronological age dictates. The best example is that almost every teen I know wants to drive a car by himself or herself the day he or she reaches age 16. And how many cases have you heard of serious auto accidents in that first week or month of teenage driving? Cigarette companies through clever and exploitive advertising frequently prey on this same lack of experience, judgment, and maturity to lead teens down the path of a lifetime of nicotine addiction and avoidable health problems.

A $2 - $3 tax on a pack of cigarettes would make it prohibitively expensive for many teens to start smoking and continue smoking. If a teen were to smoke a pack a day, the additional $3 per pack tax would cost the teen an additional $1,095 a year. If a pack currently costs $2, the teen's annual smoking bill would be $1,825. Most teens would prefer to buy a car, stereo, or spend the money on other items. Incurring $1,000 to $2,000 a year in smoking expenses is hardly an assertion of independence and will more likely result in a greater financial dependence on the parents. Moreover, the teens would knowingly be taking added health risks which hardly leads to independence.

Teen visits to nursing home and hospital patients, especially family members and friends, suffering from smoking related lung cancer, heart disease, and emphysema might make smoking seem less glamorous and machismo. Teens will be able to smell the bad smoking breath, hear the labored breathing and endless coughing, and see the yellow fingernails of smoking patients first hand.

Banning smoking in all public places, including teen hangouts, and pressuring the television industry and Hollywood to eliminate smoking from films and programs might also contribute to making smoking less glamorous and machismo. If enough employers prohibited smoking in the workplace, this might also make smoking less desirable.

4. PARENTS PLAYING SUPPORTIVE ROLE

Many teen smokers are afraid of their parents discovering their habit. My wife and I were recently with parents genuinely fond of their teenagers who kiss their children good night, but in the process are able to ascertain through smelling their breath whether their children had been drinking alcohol or smoking. Parent awareness must be an early step in dealing with an underage smoking problem.

There are steps parents can undertake to try to dissuade pre-teen and teenage children from engaging in the unhealthy smoking and chewing tobacco habits. A professor of pediatrics at the University of North Carolina pointed out that "hearing that their breath will taste bad and no one will want to kiss them has more meaning" than merely telling a teen not to smoke.[26] Parents can also point out that smokers' clothes smell, their teeth and nails become yellow and stained, their skin sags and wrinkles, they have less energy, employers often prefer to hire nonsmokers, smokers hands tremble slightly, and more than three out of four teenagers say they would rather date a nonsmoker.[27] In addition, the addiction and difficulty quitting should be explained as well as the harm to one's body.[28] Parents can set good examples by not allowing anyone to smoke in the home, requesting a table in the nonsmoking section of a restaurant, refusing to allow children to wear T-shirts with cigarette emblems or slogans, and by prohibiting the use of candy cigarettes. With one of six deaths in the country related to tobacco use, parents should consider telling a child if the death or serious illness of a friend or relative were due to tobacco.

5. BAN ADVERTISING

Youngsters learn about cigarettes and other tobacco products through advertising. Tobacco companies have tons of money to spend on advertising. In 1970 cigarette advertising was banned on radio and television. The courts have upheld the ban. The ban should be extended to magazines, newspapers, store windows, billboards, and all other forms of advertising which has been primarily geared through Joe Camel type ads to attract youngsters to the addictive tobacco habit. Efforts to eliminate ads should also be undertaken on the state and local government level.

Smoking and tobacco kill. Advertising is the means by which tobacco companies spread and attract their poisonous product. Tobacco is the only consumer product that when used as intended causes death and disease.

Recently a former advertising agency employee working on a tobacco company account confided in me that it was understood that the tobacco company client's advertising campaign was to be geared to attract pre-teens and teens to the particular brand. I was surprised when he said that employees were given the option to decline to work on the tobacco company account if they had moral qualms about promoting youth smoking.

There are more than 200 million nonsmokers in this country or about 80% of the American population. They could be a powerful force in impacting on cigarette advertising if they chose to boycott products of tobacco companies such as Philip Morris' Kraft and Oscar Mayer foods and RJR Nabisco's crackers and cookies as well as current and former suppliers of chemicals, papers, and filters such as Kimberly-Clark and Dow Chemical. The more than 200 million nonsmokers could also divest themselves of the tobacco company and suppliers stock holdings and encourage institutions of higher education, government, bank trust departments, and union pension funds to do the same.

6. ENFORCE LAWS BANNING UNDERAGE SMOKING AND NEW LAWS

It is no secret that American teenagers appear to have easy access to cigarettes even though it is illegal to sell tobacco products to minors in most states. In August 1992, I noticed an unattended vending machine in a hotel men's room in North Carolina where a five-year old boy could have purchased a pack of cigarettes. In 1990, children under age 18 bought cigarettes from vending machines on the average of 450,000 times each day.[29]

The United States Department of Health and Human Services' Office of Inspector General issued a report in May 1990 entitled "Youth Access to Cigarettes" finding that 45 states had laws prohibiting the sale of cigarettes to minors.[30] President Bush in July 1992 signed P.L. 102-321 which required states to ban the sale and distribution of tobacco products to anyone under age 19 by October 1, 1994. P.L. 102-321 required the states to enforce their laws "in a manner that can reasonably be expected to reduce the extent to which tobacco products are available to underage youth" or risk a reduction in Federal funds for mental health, alcohol, and other drug abuse programs.

The HHS Office of Inspector General reported in December 1992 that all but three states had banned the sale of tobacco to minors under age 18;[31] however, only Florida and Vermont were enforcing their laws restricting the sale to minors statewide and four states are funding local initiatives to reduce youth access.[32]

The Secretary of Health and Human Services proposed a "Model Sale of Tobacco Products to Minors Control Act: A Model Law Recommended for Adoption by States or Localities to Prevent the Sale of Tobacco Products to Minors." The model law called for:

1. Licensing of vendors and revocation of their license if they sell to minors;

2. A graduated schedule of penalties so that vendors and employees are punished proportionate to their violation of the law;

3. Penalties for failing to post signs;

4. Designating State or local law or health officials for enforcement;

5. Civil in addition to criminal penalties to avoid overloading the criminal justice system;

6. An age of legal purchase of at least 19;

7. Banning or greatly restricting access to vending machines, and

8. Minimizing the burden of compliance on retail outlets.

Although the model did not call for such measure, some have advocated the banning and sale of cigarettes in the United States as perhaps the ultimate way of reducing underage smoking.

As long as minors have easy access to tobacco products at convenient stores, grocery stores, gas stations and vending machines, the war against underage smoking will not be won. However, cooperation between federal, state, and local law enforcement officials is essential if progress is going to be made.

Parents and the rest of the nation's over 200 million nonsmokers should be aware of efforts by tobacco state legislators such as Congressman Thomas L. Bliley of Virginia, appropriately a funeral director by profession, to propose legislation that would make it easier for children to smoke. Representative Bliley was responsible for a proposed change or repeal of federal legislation that would result in the states losing federal grants for failure to enforce minimum age laws for tobacco sales.

President Clinton on August 10, 1995 endorsed proposed regulations that the Food and Drug Administration administer governing the sale and distribution of nicotine-containing cigarettes and smokeless tobacco products to children and adolescents in order to address the serious public health problems caused by the use and addiction to these products. 60 Fed. Reg. 41314 (8/11/95). They were published in final form on August 28, 1996. 61 Fed. Reg. 44395 (8/28/96).

These proposed regulations would accomplish the following:

1. Prohibit cigarette sales from vending machines and self-service displays;

2. Allow only over the counter sales to customers 18 and over who show proof of their age;

3. Ban the sale of individual cigarettes or packs of fewer than 20 sometimes referred to as "kiddie packs";

4. Prohibit distribution of free cigarette samples;

5. Forbid outdoor tobacco ads within 1,000 feet of schools and playgrounds;

6. Forbid brand name advertising at sporting events and on products not related to tobacco use such as caps, t-shirts, or gym bags.

7. Limit cigarette advertising in magazines with significant numbers of young readers and limit all outdoor advertising to black-and-white text with no photographs;

8. Require the tobacco companies to spend $150 million annually in a campaign to deter young persons from smoking.

President Clinton indicated on August 10, 1995 that he concurred with Food and Drug Administration findings that the nicotine in cigarettes should be declared to be an addictive drug and that his goal is to cut youth smoking by 50% within seven years.[33] These proposed measures would constitute the most aggressive government restrictions on the tobacco industry's dissemination of tobacco products to minors which over a period of time would prevent millions of premature American deaths from poisonous tobacco smoke. These regulations will prevent a form of kid killing, an amoral business tactic which the tobacco industry appears to have found to be quite profitable. Fortunately, for the sake of Americans and all humanity, both President Clinton and FDA Commissioner Dr. Kessler are much more concerned about the health and welfare of American youth than are tobacco company officials and their political allies in the halls of Congress and state legislatures.

7. VOTE OUT REPRESENTATIVES WHO ACCEPT PAC MONEY

Almost half of the members of Congress accept money from the tobacco industry and PACs. A number of state officials receive similar poisoned money from the merchants of death. These officials are more susceptible to voting against cigarette tax increases which result in the reduction of underage smoking, laws to strengthen the enforcement of legislation making it illegal to sell tobacco products to minors, and other legislation such as making smoking illegal in public places such as restaurants and malls which serve to discourage smoking by minors.

The following senators in office as of February 1, 1993 who received the most money from the tobacco industry and PACs for the period January 1, 1991 through June 30, 1992 were:[34]

1.	Ford, Wendell (D-Ky.)	$59,198
2.	Dole, Robert (R-Kans.)	36,400
3.	Nickles, Don (R-Okla.)	29,000
4.	Bond, Christopher (R-Mo)	25,250
5.	Dodd, Christopher (D-Conn.)	23,700
6.	Coats, Dan (R-Ind.)	23,500
7.	Fowler, Wyche (D-Ga.)	22,500
8.	D'Amato, Alfonse (R-N.Y.)	20,500
9.	Packwood, Bob (R-Ore.)	19,300
10.	Hollings, Ernest (D-S.C.)	16,498

The following members of the House of Representatives in office as of February 1, 1993 who received the most money from the tobacco industry and PACs for the period January 1, 1991 through June 30, 1992 were:[35]

1.	Gephardt, Richard (D-Mo.)	$26,198
2.	Bliley, Thomas (R-Va.)	23,158
3.	Rose, Charlie (D-N.C.)	19,000
4.	Boucher, Rick (D-Va.)	18,150
5.	Rostenkowski, Dan (D- Ill)	17,000
6.	Lancaster, H. Martin (D-N.C.)	14,198
7.	Dingell, John (D-Mich.)	14,000
8.	Towns, Edolphus (D- N.Y.)	13,745
9.	Fazio, Vic (D-Calif.)	13,000
10.	Taylor, Charles (R-N.C.)	12,700

As Democratic Representative Chester Atkins of Massachusetts stated:[36]

> The cigarette companies are always there with open wallets, and it does make a difference in people's judgment. There's no question about it. It has a substantial impact.

Parents of teenagers and pre-teens as well as the remainder of the more than 200 million nonsmoking Americans should keep a close eye on these legislators and others to make sure that they are not bought off by the tobacco PACs and companies by passing legislation that would endanger the health of American youth or thwarting the passage of such legislation that would benefit the health of this country's young people. The phrase "vote the bums (crooks) out of office" might be appropriate in certain circumstances. These legislators may be aiding and abetting the destruction of our children's health by accepting tobacco money.

It is hard to understand how tobacco lobbyists could undertake activities designed to undermine the health of our nation's youth. It made sense when a close friend of a tobacco lobbyist said that many lobbyists can only stomach this "kid killing" work for three to four years. Then they had to seek a more humane work activity.

8. CONCLUSION

The war against underage smoking can be won. It will take the cooperation of parents, creative educational efforts, enforcement of underage smoking laws, the banning of advertising including Joe Camel ads, much higher cigarette taxes, elimination of smoking in public places and the work place, and an awareness of the attempts of the tobacco companies and PACs to buy the influence of local, state and federal legislators. America's youth will live healthier lives and America's health care costs will be reduced because of the need to treat fewer premature cancer, heart and emphysema patients whose illness was either caused or worsened by smoking.

President Clinton had the right idea when he proposed a seventy-five cent per pack cigarette tax increase in his September 1993 health care reform proposal. However, the President ignored the advice of those concerned about health by limiting the proposal to seventy-five cents rather than $2 to $3 per pack. There should be no compromise when the issue is the lives of human beings. Both California and Canada's cigarette tax increases resulted in the significant reduction in teen smoking. A health care reform package that contains a large cigarette tax would be most beneficial to America's youth. It may make smoking too expensive and force our youth to refrain from or stop a habit that prematurely killed many of their grandparents, is prematurely killing many of their parents, and eventually will cut short their lives.

And, most importantly, the regulations proposed by the Food and Drug Administration and supported by President Clinton in August 1995 and finalized a year later designed to limit the sale and distribution of nicotine-containing cigarettes and smokeless tobacco products to children and adolescents in order to address the serious public health problems caused by the use and addiction to these products should be strictly enforced.

ENDNOTES

[1] "CDC urges nationwide ban on cigarette sales to most teens," Chicago Tribune, Evening Edition, 7/16/92, p. 7; Chicago Tribune Evening Edition, 5/18/93, p. 7.

[2] "New smokers mostly all teen-agers – study," Daily Herald, 12/3/93.

[3] "A Baseball Tradition – Chewing Tobacco – That Can be Deadly," Health Section, Washington Post, 10/19/93, pp. 12-15, at 15.

[4] "Snuff it out" and "Facts to Know About Smokeless Tobacco," RDH (Registered Dental Hygienist), Vol. 15, No. 2, 2/95, pp. 45-50, at 50.

[5] "Smoking: A Teen Trap," Chicago Evening Tribune, 11/5/93, p. 7.

[6] Id.

[7] Id.

[8] D. Franza, J. et al., "RJR Nabisco's Cartoon Camel Promotes Camel Cigarettes in Children," Journal of the American Medical Association (JAMA), 1991: 266: 3154-3158.

[9] Id.

[10] Fischer, P., et al., "Brand Logo Recognition by Children Aged 3 to 6 Years," JAMA 1991, Vol. 266, pp. 3145-3148.

[11] D. Franza, J., et al., "Who Profits from Tobacco Sales to Children?", JAMA, 1990: Vol. 263, pp. 2784-2787.

[12] National Institute on Drug Abuse, Drug Use Among American High School Students, College Students and Other Young Adults, 1987.

[13] National Institute on Drug Abuse, Drug Use, Drinking and Smoking: National Survey Results from High School, College, and Young Adult Populations, 1989.

[14] Id.

[15] Altman, D. et al., "Reducing the Illegal Sales of Cigarettes to Minors," JAMA, 1989: Vol. 261, pp. 80-83.

[16] National Automatic Merchandising Association as reported by the Americans for Nonsmokers' Rights, Berkeley, California.

[17] Letter from Thomas P. Houston, M.D., Director of the American Medical Association Department of Preventive Medicine and Public Health, Chicago Tribune, 9/15/92, sec. 1, p. 20.

[18] Chicago Tribune, Evening Health, 10/21/93, p. 7.

[19] "Smokers Wild" is distributed by Gamma Two Games, Ltd., 1306 Seymour Street, Vancouver, British Columbia, Canada V6B 3P3.

[20] U.S. Department of Health and Human Services. *Preventing Tobacco Use Among Young People: A Report of the Surgeon General*, Atlanta, Georgia: U.S. Department of Health and Human Services, Public Health Service, Centers for Disease Control and Prevention, National Center for Chronic Disease Prevention and Health Promotion, Office on Smoking and Health, 1994.

[21] Id.

[22] Executive Summary of footnote 20.

[23] See footnote 20 at pages 5-6 and footnote 22 at pages 5-6.

[24] "New Laws on Smoking Unlikely This Year," New York Times, 4/18/94, sec. A, p. 7.

[25] Id.

[26] Healthy Kids 4-10 Years. The Magazine from the American Academy of Pediatrics, Fall 1991, pp. 22, 24-25.

[27] Id. at pp. 24-25.

[28] Id.

[29] "Kids Say Don't Smoke," by Andrew Tobias and SmokeFree Educational Services, Inc., 1991.

[30] Youth Access to Tobacco, Office of Inspector General, Department of Health and Human Services, 12/92, p. i.

[31] Id.

[32] Id. at pp. i-ii.

[33] "Clinton Proposed Widespread Curbs on Young Smokers," New York Times, 8/11/95, pp. A1.

[34] Figures from Advocacy Institute in Washington, D.C., 10/26/92.

[35] Id.

[36] Representative Atkins quoted in "Tobacco Lobby Pervades Congress," *Boston Globe*, 9/24/89.

BAN SMOKING IN PUBLIC PLACES

Most Americans spend a substantial portion of each day in public places such as worksites, day care centers, schools and universities, military and educational living quarters, restaurants, public buildings, malls and athletic arenas and stadiums. Many children and adults are exposed to high levels of poisonous secondary tobacco smoke up to eight hours a day in these facilities.

Think of those unpleasant experiences in restaurants where smoke was blowing in your face for two to three hours at a time. And how about the baseball or football game where the person next to you was blowing smoke in your face for more than three hours while you were supposed to be enjoying the fresh air and sunshine. And have you ever worked at a position where a co-worker was spreading the carcinogens and toxins of secondary tobacco smoke 40 hours a week into your eyes, nose, and lungs.

It is a crime for a person to physically assault another person. It should be illegal for a person to chemically assault a person in a public facility with the carcinogens and toxins of poisonous secondary tobacco smoke. Smoking in a public facility should be at least a misdemeanor punishable by a large fine. Clearly, it is a much more serious offense against human beings than illegal parking or parking at a meter whose time has expired.

The spark that recently stimulated a great concern about the adverse health impact of secondhand tobacco smoke was the report released by the Environmental Protection Agency on January 7, 1993 containing strong evidence that secondary tobacco smoke poses a serious cancer threat to adults and a major health threat to children. The report warns that each year environmental tobacco smoke causes 3,000 lung cancer deaths, contributes from 150,000 to 300,000 respiratory infections in babies, triggers 8,000 to 26,000 new asthma cases in previously unaffected children, and exacerbates symptoms in 200,000 to a million asthmatic children.[1]

The Environmental Protection Agency (EPA) announced guidelines on smoking in public buildings on July 21, 1993 to help curb illness from secondhand tobacco smoke reinforcing the EPA's stand six months earlier when the agency declared that secondhand tobacco smoke caused cancer and respiratory disease and should be regulated.[2] The EPA's voluntary guidelines urged that all restaurants, schools, day-care centers, and other places where children spend time prohibit smoking or establish practices to insure that air from smoking areas is not recirculated to the rooms occupied by children.[3] The guidelines urged parents not to smoke in their homes and nonsmokers should be protected from secondhand smoke in public areas and in the workplace.[4]

The extent of America's exposure to environmental tobacco smoke is not easy to fully comprehend. The EPA in its June 1989 pamphlet "Indoor Air Facts No. 5" entitled "Environmental Tobacco Smoke" succinctly explained why environmental tobacco smoke is so abundant and harmful.

The EPA pointed out that "ETS comes from secondhand smoke exhaled by smokers and sidestream smoke emitted from the burning end of cigarettes, cigars, and pipes." Environmental tobacco smoke is a "mixture of irritating gases and carcinogenic tar particles." The EPA report goes on to point out that these gases and carcinogenic tar particles are a known cause of lung cancer, respiratory symptoms, and have been linked to heart disease.

As of June 1989, the EPA pointed out that there were 50 million American smokers annually smoking 600 billion cigarettes, four billion cigars, and the equivalent of 11 billion pipefuls of tobacco annually. Since people spend approximately 90 percent of their time indoors, about 467,000 tons of tobacco are burned indoors each year. Over a 16-hour day, the average smoker smokes about two cigarettes per hour taking about ten minutes per cigarette. The EPA points out that it only takes a few smokers in a given space to release a more-or-less steady stream of environmental tobacco smoke into the indoor air.

The EPA points out that because the organic material in tobacco does not burn completely, cigarette smoke contains more than 4,700 chemical compounds including carbon monoxide, nicotine, carcinogenic tars, sulfur dioxide, ammonia, nitrogen oxides, vinyl chloride, hydrogen cyanide, formaldehyde, radio-nuclides, benzene, and arsenic. There are 43 carcinogenic compounds in tobacco cells. In addition, some substances are mutagenic which means they can cause permanent, and often harmful, changes in genetic materials of cells.

Smoking in the home, according to the EPA, includes serious respiratory changes in children with asthmatic children particularly at risk. The risk of cancer and heart disease is much greater.

The EPA concluded in June 1989 that environmental tobacco smoke can be totally removed from the indoor air only by removing the main source - cigarette smoking.[5] The agency points out that separating smokers and nonsmokers in the same room as in some restaurants may reduce, but will not eliminate nonsmokers' exposure to harmful tobacco smoke since they are on the same ventilation system.[6] The EPA points out that research indicates that total removal of tobacco smoke through ventilation is both technically and economically impractical.[7]

Surprisingly, a 1987 Gallup opinion poll found that 55% of all persons interviewed, including both nonsmokers and smokers, favored a total ban on smoking in public places.[8] A 1994 New York Times/CBS News poll revealed that 67% of the persons interviewed favored such ban, up from 61% in a November 1991 Gallup poll.[9]

The tobacco company spin control spokespersons have attempted to poke flaws in the methodology of the EPA studies. However, I have not heard of one reputable scientist or physician supporting the tobacco industry position or maintaining that smoking and secondary tobacco smoke are not harmful to human beings. As recently reported in the Journal of the American Medical Association, smoking by physicians declined from 18.8% in the mid-1970s to 3.3% in 1990 and 1991.[10] Apparently the tobacco industry is attempting to persuade the American public that it is all right to smoke unless the government can show "beyond a reasonable doubt," the standard for criminal guilt, that tobacco smoke and secondary tobacco smoke are harmful to the smokers and the nonsmokers. Such a high standard is not utilized for recall of potentially dangerous children's toys, a potentially dangerous car defect, where contaminated food is found, when a few bottles of a medication such as Tylenol has been contaminated, or when a few bottles of Perrier has been found to contain benzene, one of the compounds contained in secondary tobacco smoke. Unlike other industries, the tobacco industry has been given a free ride to poison American children and adults with the 43 carcinogens and toxins in secondary tobacco smoke and thus endanger the health and lives of more than 200 million American nonsmokers.

It is imperative to the health of our nation that we eradicate our workplaces, restaurants, public buildings, malls, athletic facilities, schools, daycare centers, and public transportation vehicles from the harmful tobacco smoke by banning smoking in all these facilities. Steps have been taken at the local, state and federal levels to eliminate smoking in public facilities, but more needs to be done. For example, as of March 1992 over 500 communities in the United States have enacted ordinances restricting smoking in workplaces, restaurants and other public places, 19 completely eliminated smoking in workplaces, and 25 eliminated smoking in all restaurants.[11] Since environmental tobacco smoke meets the criteria of the Occupational Safety and Health Administration for classifying substances potentially occupational carcinogens, both the EPA and the National Institute of Occupational Safety and Health recommend that smoking be eliminated in all workplaces, or be restricted to private rooms that have a separate ventilation system which is exhausted directly outside.[12]

The private sector, whether because of concerns for its employees or because of fear of lawsuits, has voluntarily established total smoking bans in 34% of workplaces as of March 1992 compared with 2% in 1986. Another 34% restrict smoking in all common areas.[13] Caring parents, concerned employers, and responsible elected officials are coming to the same conclusion - smoking in public facilities should be banned. The only groups opposing these bans besides the smokers are the tobacco industry and those related businesses who believe that profits are more important than human lives.

1. RESTAURANTS

One of the largest employers in the United States is the restaurant industry, including the fast-food chains. Both customers, including young children, and the millions of restaurant workers are at risk from the carcinogens and toxins from poisonous secondary tobacco smoke. Moreover, evidence is mounting that smoke-free restaurant ordinances do not have an adverse impact on overall restaurant sales.[14] The ultimate goal should be banning smoking from restaurants in order to reach former Surgeon General Koop's goal of a smoke-free society by the year 2000.

There is little question that waiters, bartenders, and other food service workers face a significantly elevated risk of lung cancer from breathing customers' smoke.[15] Dr. Michael Siegel, whose research was conducted during his residency at the University of California at Berkeley, reviewed studies of indoor air quality in restaurants, bars, offices and homes containing at least one smoker as well as several epidemiology studies of mortality among food service workers published between 1977 and 1993.[16]

Dr. Siegel found that levels of secondhand smoke in restaurants were 1.6 to 2 times higher than in offices and 1.5 times higher than in homes with at least one smoker.[17] The level of secondhand smoke in bars which tend to have more smokers and poorer ventilation than restaurants was 3.9 to 6.1 times higher than offices and about 4.5 times higher than in homes containing a smoker.[18] Dr. Siegel estimates that restaurant workers face a 50% greater risk of developing lung cancer than the general population.[19] This conclusion is consistent with the EPA report released in January 1993 estimating that about 3,000 nonsmokers die annually of lung cancer caused by secondhand smoke. Moreover, Dr. Siegel points out that while being seated for an hour or two in a restaurant nonsmoking section may help customers, nonsmoking sections do not help employees who work eight-hour shifts since tobacco smoke tends to diffuse to fill all areas, a basic law of physics.[20]

In a related study, Dr. Siegel found that California waitresses and waiters are twice as likely to die of lung cancer as people in other occupations because they inhale their customers' secondhand cigarette smoke.[21] Waitresses have the highest mortality rate of any predominantly female occupation in California.

By industry estimates as many as 25% of fast food customers are under 18, 10% are under age 10, and as many as 40% of the employees in fast food restaurants are under 18.[22] The overwhelming majority of fast food restaurants permit smoking on the premises.

A group of 15 state Attorney Generals in May 1993 formed a working group to study tobacco-related issues, with a focus on passive smoke and children.[23] The study was sparked by the EPA January 1993 report concluding passive tobacco smoke is carcinogenic. The report concluded that nonsmokers who inhale passive smoke face increased risks of lung cancer, respiratory track infections, asthma attacks and coughing, with children at particular risk. Since millions of American children spend time eating and playing in designated areas in fast food restaurants and working behind counters, the 15 Attorney Generals have developed a series of recommendations to the fast food industry to facilitate the development of smoke free restaurant environments.[24]

The Attorney Generals made the following observations:

1. Most fast food companies would ultimately like to go smoke free;

2. Many companies would prefer to wait until legislative smoking bans are enacted before ordering a smoke free policy for their customers;

3. The companies would not oppose legislation to ban smoking in restaurants and some even indicated a willingness to support such legislation;

4. The companies are concerned that they may lose business if they implement a smoke free policy before their competitors do;

5. The companies want to operate on a level playing field with respect to smoking policies.

Of course, it is anticipated that tobacco companies, tobacco industry PACs and their lobbyists will do everything legally possible to thwart such legislation banning smoking in restaurants and especially fast food chains. They are aware that tobacco smoke and secondary tobacco smoke kills, but they are more concerned about tobacco company and industry profits than the health and lives of children and restaurant workers.

One wonders how these tobacco company officials can look at themselves in the mirror and sleep at night. They should be asking themselves each night, "How many people today am I responsible for facilitating the death or serious illness?" Of course, one wonders how tobacco company officials − just like the commanders of the World War II concentration camps at Auschwitz, Belsen, Buchenwald, Dachau, Treblinka, and others - could live with their conscience whether sending millions of human beings to their deaths in gas chambers whether in these concentration camps or by the carcinogens and toxins of tobacco smoke and secondary tobacco smoke. As the British Royal College of Physicians of London stated in 1971 in its second report on "Smoking and Health Now," the annual death toll caused by cigarette smoking is the "present holocaust."[25] When former Winston Man David Goerlitz asked a tobacco company executive why he did not smoke, the executive replied, "Are you kidding? We reserve that right for the young, the poor, the black, and the stupid."[26]

The 15 State Attorney Generals made the following preliminary recommendations for implementing smoke-free policies in fast food restaurants:[27]

1. Implement a corporate smoke free policy in all corporate locations immediately, and a minimum of 10% of all corporately owned fast food restaurants initially and expand this policy by an additional 20% in each quarter thereafter;

2. Implement a smoke free policy in all newly opened corporate restaurants;

3. Require a smoke free policy as part of all new franchise agreements;

4. Encourage all franchise operators to implement a smoke free policy immediately;

5. Remove cigarette vending machines from all fast food restaurants;

6. Support legislation to ban smoking in restaurants;

7. Post a warning in corporate and franchise operated restaurants that are not smoke free of the dangers of smoking, especially to children.

The State Attorney General recommendations are sound food for thought suggestions. Parents and especially their children deserve a break today and every day from being exposed to the carcinogens and toxins of poisonous secondary tobacco smoke. Parents should be warned that a Big Mac attack may be the precursor of a smoking-induced asthma attack. Perhaps sample "cynical menus" to persuade state and local legislators to vote for smoking bans in restaurants could contain items such as carcinogen burgers, toxin burgers, poison dogs and a benzene shake. Dining and working in restaurants may be a sure fast track to Marlboro Country, the local cemetery, unless smoking is banned.

Word has gotten around to the big restaurant chains. For example, effective June 1, 1995, Dunkin' Donuts has banned smoking in its 3,000 shops.[28] Other large restaurant chains have and will follow the Dunkin' Donuts example.

2. Smoking in the Workplace

There is no question that smoking in the workplace is harmful. A health physicist who has specialized in indoor air pollution examined portions of two buildings containing federal offices in a large city downtown area where smoking was not permitted.[29] When asked what would happen if smoking were to be initiated in these office spaces, the physicist said that the work areas would be turned into "gas chambers" in one building because of the age and the shape and ventilating problems and in the other building because of serious air flow obstructions resulting from remodeling. The health physicist noted that the buildings he had examined were not atypical. It is unfortunate that many workers have to spend at least 40 of the 168 hours in a week in such unhealthy work environments.

The National Institute for Occupational Safety and Health (NIOSH) concluded in June 1991 that cigarette smoke causes cancer and possibly heart disease.[30] NIOSH recommended that employers "should minimize occupational exposure to environmental tobacco smoke by using all available preventive measures." The purpose of the report was to persuade many employers to impose or toughen smoking restrictions in the workplace and to assist the Occupational Safety and Health Administration (OSHA) to establish regulations for smoking in the workplace. OSHA has been reluctant to take meaningful steps to regulate passive smoking in the workplace.[31] Finally, in March 1994 OSHA took the first steps towards banning smoking in almost all workplaces.[32]

A study in the Journal of the American Medical Association concluded that where there were limited bans on smoking, nonsmokers in workplaces were 2.8 times more likely to be exposed to environmental tobacco smoke than those working in a smoke-free environment.[33] The author of this 1990 California Tobacco Survey conducted by the University of California-San Diego indicated "that the only way to protect non-smokers' health is with a smoke-free work site."[34]

Aside from the health and humanitarian reasons, it makes sense from a business economics standpoint to ban smoking in the workplace. Dr. William Weiss, Chairman of the Accounting Department of the University of Seattle Business School, estimates that a smoker costs an employer $4,611 each year broken down as follows:[35]

On the job time spent smoking	$1,820
Morbidity/Early Mortality	765
Property Damage	500
Maintenance	500
Effects on nonsmokers (secondhand smoke)	486
Medical care	230
Absenteeism	220
Insurance (excluding health)	90

In April 1994 Lockheed Aeronautical Systems followed a small group of companies such as Turner Broadcasting and Northwest Airlines that will no longer hire smokers.[36] A spokesman for the Marietta-based subsidiary of Lockheed Corp., a 10,000 person unit affected by this new policy, pointed out the policy will help cut health costs since smokers cost more on a long-term basis.[37] The company cited a study finding that 77% of Lockheed's employees who are cardiac patients also smoke.[38] Hopefully, other companies will follow the lead of Turner Broadcasting, Northwest Airlines, and Lockheed in an effort to both hold down health care costs and improve the health of the American worker by not hiring smokers. Such a step will be an important additional incentive for the nation's 46 million smokers to stop.

A growing number of insurance companies offer premium reductions for life, health, fire and casualty policies for companies that have smoke-free workplaces. Smoking in the workplace may result in higher worker's compensation case recoveries. Absenteeism for smokers is generally higher than nonsmokers. There is every reason from a health standpoint to have a smoke-free work environment.

It is surprising that it took so long for many hospitals to eliminate smoking. Day-care centers where parents entrust the safety and health of their children should have similar restrictions. Whether day-care center workers smoke should be high on the list of questions asked by any parent seeking a place to care for his or children each workday.

With approximately three fourths of workers being nonsmokers, the quarter minority subjecting the overwhelming majority to the carcinogens and toxins of secondary tobacco smoke is liable to create a great deal of resentment and animosity in the workplace. In a country where the majority rules, why should a minority be permitted to subject the overwhelming majority, including pregnant employees at particular risk, to major health risks? There is no excuse, even a union contract provision, for a working condition that subjects three quarters of the employees who care about the quality of the air they breathe to increased lung cancer, heart disease, emphysema, and other health risks.

Senator Frank Lautenberg from New Jersey and Representative Henry Waxman from California proposed legislation banning smoking in all public facilities to protect nonsmokers from exposure to poisonous secondary tobacco smoke.[39] The legislation was suggested not only by the American Lung Association, the Coalition on Smoking or Health, and the American Academy of Pediatrics, but also the Building Owners and Managers Association International which manages or owns more than five billion square feet of North American office space. The nation's more than 200 million nonsmokers should ascertain how their representatives stand on the bill or similar bills and how much tobacco PAC and industry money their representatives receive, if any. The voters should not be fooled by someone like New York Congressman Edolpus Towns who when questioned about how the $8,100 he got from the tobacco industry influenced his vote against the airline smoking ban, he glibly replied, "Not at all, I don't know who contributes to my campaign."[40]

The President should take the lead and issue an executive order banning smoking in all federal buildings. It would be consistent with the thrust of his health care reform program and most surely could be a cornerstone of any preventive health care effort designed to lower health care costs. The number one way to reduce health care costs in the long run is to reduce and eventually eliminate smoking. A seventy-five cent per pack cigarette tax increase as proposed by President Clinton to help pay for health care reform or the $1.25 a pack proposed by a House subcommittee will not, in itself, accomplish this critical objective.[41] Cessation of smoking in the workplace and other public facilities is an essential objective. A low cigarette tax increase should not be the trade-off to obtain tobacco-state Congressmen votes in return for their support of such measures as health care reform. The health of Americans and freedom from the carcinogens and toxins of poisonous tobacco smoke through a large cigarette tax increase should be able to stand on its own.

3. Athletics

It is annoying and unhealthy to go to a baseball game and other athletic events and sit through both the pre-game festivities and the game with cigarette, cigar and pipe smoke blowing in one's face for three to four hours.

Perhaps the January 1993 EPA report warning of the major health problems of environmental tobacco smoke for both adults and children may negate the need for more than 200 million nonsmoking Americans to sing the following chorus before attending another smoke-filled athletic event:

> Take me out to the ball game,
> But take me out of the smoke-infested crowd,
>
> Buy me a gas mask to shield the tobacco smoke,
> I hope the carcinogens won't make me choke,
>
> Gasp, gasp, gasp for the clean-air team,
> If they don't ban smoking its a shame,
>
> For its an asthma attack, tearing eyes,
> Itchy nose and sore throat,
>
> From breathing three hours of tobacco smoke,
> At the old ball game.

Since experiencing over three hours of tobacco smoke blowing in my face at a 1991 Northwestern-Notre Dame football game at smoky Soldier Field in Chicago, I have refused to go to any athletic stadium where smoking is permitted. Hopefully many of the other over 200 million nonsmokers will follow suit and heed the tobacco-twisted words of the take-me-out-to-the-ball-game melody.

More than half of the major league baseball stadiums have 100% smokefree seating. As of the fall of 1993, the Atlanta Braves, the Boston Red Sox, the Chicago Cubs, the Chicago White Sox, the Florida Marlins, the Kansas City Royals, the Milwaukee Brewers, the New York Mets, the New York Yankees, the Pittsburgh Pirates, the St. Louis Cardinals, and the San Francisco Giants had 100% smokefree seating.[42] A number of stadiums are also tobacco ad free.[43] Hopefully pressure by the paying public to all athletic events will result in all stadiums being 100% smokefree, including eating and restroom areas, and tobacco ad free. Parents with asthmatic children should consider keeping their children away from smoky sports facilities.

Many athletic events, including tennis and automobile racing, are sponsored by tobacco companies. There is no rational relationship between athletics, good health, and smoking. The nation's over 200 million non-smokers should boycott all tobacco-sponsored sporting events, just for the health of it.

Some unions have obstructed the enactment of a health and safety measure designed to benefit their bargaining unit members – banning smoking. As of June 15, 1993, tobacco use was banned in the minor leagues.[44] The ban applies to players, coaches, and umpires anywhere in the ballpark or on team buses. While officials can unilaterally put the ban into effect in the minor leagues, such a ban must be subject to collective bargaining with the major league union, the Major League Baseball Players Association.[45] For the sake of the health of major league ballplayers, their families, and the youth of this country who frequently emulate athletes, the major league union should be urged to follow the minor league ban.

Many years and decades ago athletics were supposed to encompass everything that is healthy about life. The multi-million dollar contracts, the influence of television, and the huge endorsement money for athletes has made the "health" aspect of athletics a myth.

Recently national columnist Mike Royko ran a column which painted then Philadelphia Philly first baseman John Kruk into a hero.[46] In response to my October 16, 1993 letter, Royko said:[47]

Next, I managed to anger Edward L. Koven of Highland Park, by recounting anecdotes about John Kruk, the wise-cracking Philadelphia baseball player.

One was when a female fan saw Kruk smoking and berated him, saying that an athlete should not use tobacco. Kruk responded, "Lady, I'm not an athlete, I'm a baseball player."

This prompted Mr. Koven to say that my "concept of a hero, John Kruk, is quite warped."

"Since tobacco is a drug containing at least 43 carcinogens and toxins, it should be added to the list of other drugs banned in baseball. Tobacco kills. Kruk and other ballplayers should spread that message – not poisonous tobacco smoke.

"Perhaps you could find other heroes, such as the physicians, nurses, and family members who care for and treat the millions of victims of tobacco smoke."

John Kruk was struck with cancer after the 1993 baseball season, has undergone treatment which appears to be successful, and came back to perform with the Phillies and the Chicago White Sox. The recently retired baseball player may now have some different views about smoking.

Bowling alleys are a nonsmoker's horror. Although I enjoyed bowling, I quit in my late teens because I could not stand the smoke-filled bowling alleys. It is amazing that one's lungs can survive until the fifth or beer frame. Local ordinances curtailing smoking in bowling alleys would protect youngsters as well as adults from the horrors of smoking.

4. OTHER PUBLIC PLACES

Most commercial airline flights in the United States have been smokefree since 1990 thanks to the courageous testimony of flight attendants who passed on their horror stories of colleagues being struck down by lung cancer from working in smoke-filled gas chamber type environments. Their stories were so emotionally overwhelming that tears were seen in the eyes of several members of Congress during the hearings leading up to the airline smoking ban. The tobacco companies and PACs were unable to prevent passage of the legislation in this highly emotional atmosphere. The International Civil Aviation Organization has recommended that all international flights be smokefree. The Clinton administration is reportedly attempting to speed up the process by revising its agreements with other nations directly.[48]

During the April 1992 National Collegiate Athletic Association final-four basketball weekend in Minneapolis the only motel available to me at the last minute was a recently refurbished dive that reeked of tobacco smoke compounded by an antique ventilation system. I should have slept outside in a sleeping bag. It would have been much healthier. Fortunately hotels are designating nonsmoking floors and rooms since tobacco smoke gets into the carpeting, curtains, and blankets and smells up the rooms. Hopefully in the foreseeable future all hotels and motels will be designated 100% smokefree.

A friend similarly complained of a rental car that made her ill from the residues of tobacco smoke. A renter frequently has an option of requesting a nonsmoking car.

Banks and other financial institutions have begun to institute total bans on smoking. One of the largest downtown banking institutions in Chicago, the Northern Trust Company, initiated a total smoking ban on July 1, 1993, for health and economic reasons.

The railroads in this country have frequently been slow to modernize and stay up to date with the times. Amtrak in 1993 finally decided to ban smoking on all trains with scheduled running time of less than 4-1/2 hours and on selected routes 6 hours or less, as well as trains within California and selected sleeping cars. This came more than three years after similar bans on domestic airline flights.[49]

A parent assumes when sending his or her son or daughter to college that the child is going to get a sound education in a healthy environment. All too frequently the son or daughter gets assigned to a smoking room-mate and thereby finds himself or herself in an unhealthy indoor air environment a significant portion of the time.

The Columbia University Center on Addiction and Substance Abuse chaired by former HEW Secretary Joseph A. Califano, Jr., issued a report in August 1993 urging the nation's colleges to create smokefree campuses, including a ban on the sale, advertising, and distribution of tobacco products on the nation's 3,535 college campuses containing 14 million students with almost 25% who smoke.[50] The report points out that since "virtually all Americans who smoke begin in their teens or early twenties" higher educational institutions should take steps to limit the opportunities to buy and consume cigarettes.[51] Besides calling for a ban on smoking in all campus facilities, vehicles, and dormitories, the report encouraged universities to offer treatment programs to help students quit smoking. The report said that besides improving the health of faculty and students, a smokefree campus would protect universities from possible future lawsuits from graduates asserting damages from secondary tobacco smoke and would reduce health care and cleaning costs.

A number of universities have already implemented no smoking policies. Indiana University at Bloomington was scheduled to become smoke-free as of November 1, 1993.[52] Smoking was banned in all indoor air space on campus including faculty, staff, student, and administrative offices, as well as University owned and leased housing.

The lead by universities such as Indiana should be followed by high school, grade school, nursery school, and day-care center faculties and support staff by banning smoking on school and center premises. Adults should lead by example.

Starting in the 1950s shopping malls sprouted up throughout the country. With the indoor malls, came the proliferation of smokers. With about a quarter of today's adult population smokers, one out of every four adult visitors to a shopping mall is a potential spreader of the carcinogens and toxins of secondary tobacco smoke. Those parents who have an asthmatic child or child with other bronchial problems, might be advised to boycott those indoor malls that permit smoking.

Many malls have banned smoking. The International Council of Shopping Centers has reported that many of the nation's 38,966 shopping centers visited by 179.4 million customers each month have announced plans to go smokefree.[53] The huge Mall of America in Bloomington, Minnesota, has had a no-smoking policy since it opened on August 11, 1992, which did not deter 35 million people from visiting it during the first year.[54]

Of the nation's 38,966 shopping centers, 1,835 are enclosed malls containing at least 400,000 square feet. Of the enclosed malls as of December 1993, 93 in New York, all centers in Houston, Fulton and DeKalb Counties in Georgia, Howard and Anne Arundel County in Maryland, and a few in New Jersey are smoke free.[55] The 103 centers operated by JMP were scheduled to become smoke free January 1, 1994.[56]

The shopping centers are visited by 179.4 million adults each month or 94% of the country's population of which 13% are 15 to 19 year olds.[57] Clearly, banning smoking in the nation's nearly 39,000 shopping centers will help make them a healthier place for all child and adult visitors.

ENDNOTES

[1] "Respiratory Health Effects of Passive Smoking: Lung Cancer and Other Disorders," U.S. Environmental Protection Agency, Office of Research and Development and Office of Air and Radiation, December 1992, pp. 1-4 to 1-6.

2 "U.S. Issues Guides to Curb Second-Hand Smoke," New York Times, 7/22/93, p. A-7.

3 Id.

4 "EPA Guidelines Suggest Policies for Avoiding Secondhand Smoke," Washington Post, 7/22/93, A-3.

5 "Indoor Air Facts No. 5" entitled "Environmental Tobacco Smoke," 6/89, p. 2.

6 Id. at pp. 2-3.

7 Id. at p. 2.

8 The Gallup Organization, survey dates March 14-18, 1987.

9 "Majority of Americans Say Cigarettes Spur Addiction," New York Times, 5/1/94, Sec. 1, p. 22.

10 "Trends in Cigarette Smoking Among U.S. Physicians and Nurses," Journal of the American Medical Association," Vol. 271, No. 16, 4/27/94, pp. 1273-1275.

11 Americans for Nonsmokers Rights, 3/92.

12 EPA Review Draft, Health Effects of Passive Smoking, 1990; Environmental Tobacco Smoke in the Workplace, NIOSH, 6/91 (Current Intelligence Bulletin 54).

13 "Smoking in the Workplace: 1991," Bulletin to Management, Bureau of National Affairs, 8/29/91.

14 "Study: Smoking bans don't hurt restaurants," Chicago Tribune, 5/19/95, Sec. 1, p. 8; Morbidity and Mortality Weekly Report, Centers for Disease Control and Prevention, 5/19/95, Vol. 44, No. 19, pp. 370-373.

15 Siegel, M., "Involuntary Smoking in the Restaurant Workplace: A Review of Employee Exposure and Health Effects," Journal of the American Medical Association, 7/28/93, p. 493.

16 Id.

17 Id.

18 Id.

19 Id.

20 Id.

21 "Smoke Signals, danger for restaurant help," Chicago Tribune, 11/22/93, Sec. 6, p. 1.

22 "Fast Food, Growing Children and Passive Smoke: A Dangerous Menu – Findings and Preliminary Recommendations for Implementing Smoke Free Policies in Fast Food Restaurants," by the Attorney Generals of Arizona, Connecticut, Idaho, Iowa, Massachusetts, Michigan, New Mexico, New York, Oklahoma, Oregon, Texas, Utah, Vermont, and Wisconsin, pp. 6-7.

23 Id. at p. 1.

24 Id. at 13.

25 Taylor, Peter, The Smoke Ring – Tobacco, Money & Multi-National Politics, Pantheon Books, 1984, p. xiv.

26 "Kids Say Don't Smoke" by Andrew Tobias and SmokeFree Educational Services, Inc., Workman Publishing Company, Inc., 1991.

27 See footnote 23 at pages 14-17.

28 Chicago Sun-Times, 5/31/94, p. 4.

29 The examination was conducted in July 1991 by James L. Repace, a health physicist and senior analyst in the Air Policy Office of the U.S. Environmental Protection Agency.

30 NIOSH Current Intelligence Bulletin, No. 54, 6/91, "Environmental Tobacco Smoke in the Workplace – Lung Cancer and Other Health Effects;" San Jose Mercury News, "Tobacco Smoke Called Job Hazard," 7/18/91, p. 9A.

31 The Nation's Health, 2/91, p. 20.

32 "The Butt Stops Here," Time, 4/18/94, p. 58; "Despite Growing Support New Laws on Smoking Unlikely This Year," New York Times, 4/18/94, Sec. A, p. 10.

33 "Protection From Environmental Tobacco Smoke in California – The Case for a Smoke-Free Workplace," Journal of the American Medical Association, 8/12/92, Vol. 268, No. 6, pp. 749-752.

34 Id.

35 American Lung Association, "Toward a Smoke-Free Workplace," 1985.

36 "No Smokers at Lockheed Unit," USA Today, 4/25/94, B1.

[37] "Smokers Need Not Apply," Chicago Sun-Times, 4/26/94, p. 43.

[38] Id.

[39] "Congressmen Aim to Ban Smoking in Public Places," Chicago Tribune, 10/30/93, Sec. 1, p. 2.

[40] See footnote 26.

[41] "The Butt Stops Here," Time, 4/18/94, p. 58.

[42] SmokeFree Air, Smoke Free Educational Services, Inc., "Most Major League Teams Play in Smoke Free Stadiums," Summer 1993, p. 7.

[43] Fall 1993, SmokeFree Air, p. 1.

[44] Id. at p. 2.

[45] Id.

[46] Chicago Tribune, 10/15/93, sec. 1, p. 3.

[47] Chicago Tribune, 10/29/93, Sec. 1, p. 3.

[48] SmokeFree Air, Fall 1993, p. 2.

[49] SmokeFree Air, Summer 1993, p. 2.

[50] "Panel Urges Colleges to Create Campuses that are Smoke Free," Wall Street Journal, 8/30/93, p. A5A.

[51] Id.

[52] "Indiana University to become smoke-free," Chicago Tribune - Evening, 9/22/93, p. 2.

[53] "More Malls are snuffing out smoking," USA Today, 8/5/93; International Council of Shopping Centers, 665 5th Avenue, New York, NY 10022.

[54] Id.

[55] International Council of Shopping Centers, supra at footnote 53.

[56] Id.

[57] Id.

PINPOINTING THE FUMES

A. ELIMINATE TOBACCO PACS

Acrucial ingredient to the continued flourishing of the tobacco industry has been its enormous success in getting Congress either to oppose or not act upon most legislation that might be unfavorable to industry interests. How is this accomplished? By money. Apparently it is all legal. Tobacco companies and their Political Action Committees (PACs) contribute to the campaigns of nearly half the members of the Senate and the House of Representatives. During the period January 1, 1991 through June 30, 1992, tobacco contributions to senators totalled $578,390 of which 88% went to the 27 senators seeking reelection in the fall of 1992.[1] Tobacco interests contributed $1,161,474 to House members during a recent election cycle with the top recipients being Richard A. Gephardt, former Democratic House Majority Leader from Missouri, with $26,198, and Virginia Republican Thomas J. Bliley, a funeral director by profession, with $23,500. Dan Rostenkowski, who had not been known as the champion of ethics in government, was the recipient of $17,000.[2]

It is inconceivable that an industry would hand out over a million and a half dollars to members of Congress without expecting something in return. The tobacco companies have reaped enormous financial benefits at the expense of the American taxpayer, the more than 200 million nonsmoking Americans, and hundreds of millions of foreigners who purchase American cigarettes and are exposed to these carcinogens and toxins in their products. The economic and health toll on Americans and peoples around the world have become secondary or tertiary concerns of amoral politicians who receive tobacco PAC and industry funds while closing their eyes and holding their nose from the putrid smell of the carcinogens and toxins in the tobacco smoke and secondary tobacco smoke they are spreading around the world. Each member of Congress who accepts a single tobacco PAC or industry dollar should be ashamed of an act facilitating the death of hundreds of thousands of Americans and millions throughout the world each year.

What has been the effect of the tobacco PAC and industry efforts? It has delayed or killed action on the following proposed measures designed to limit, reduce or end the devastation of poisonous tobacco smoke:[3]

1. Prohibiting smoking in federal buildings,

2. Eliminating the tobacco price support program,

3. Granting the Food and Drug Administration limited regulatory oversight over tobacco products for health and safety purposes,

4. Protecting millions of young children, including those suffering from asthma, in federally funded programs including Head Start and Women, Infants, and Children,

5. Restricting cigarette advertising and promotion, including that which targets children such as Joe Camel ads,

6. Requiring that exported cigarette packs contain U.S. health warnings in the importing country's language,

7. Reducing youth access to tobacco products by a large increase in cigarette excise taxes of $2 - $3 per pack, restrictions on distributors of free cigarette samples, elimination of candy cigarettes, increasing the minimum age to 19 for purchase of tobacco products, and strong restrictions on placement of cigarette vending machines.

8. Establishing a national information program on tobacco and health and adding tobacco education to the Drug-Free Schools and Communities Act of 1986 (now covering illegal drugs and alcohol only).

9. Partially repealing the federal preemption against state regulation of tobacco product billboard and local transit advertising.

In addition, Congress killed legislation that would have prohibited the sponsorship of sporting and other events using the brand name of a tobacco product, stronger health warnings on tobacco packages and advertisements such as "Cigarettes Kill" and "Tobacco is an Addicting Drug," reducing the federal tax deduction accorded tobacco advertising and promotional expenditures, and increasing the price of tobacco products sold in the military to civilian levels.

What is the solution to the problem of special interest money influencing legislative action or inaction which is detrimental to the health of every American and hundreds of millions of human beings throughout the world who use or are exposed to American tobacco products? The narrow answer would appear to be to ban tobacco PACs and industry contributions to any public office holder or candidate for public office. But similar problems appear to arise in many other areas including gun control and restrictions on alcohol. Term limit restrictions or at least limiting committee chairmanships to one term would force powerful tobacco interest Congressmen such as Representative Bliley, the funeral director from Virginia, and Senate Minority Whip Wendell Ford from Kentucky, to be less beholden to tobacco interests and less needy of the tainted tobacco money.

However, there is another solution which may at times be very effective – the coalescing of all or a portion of the country's more than 200 million nonsmokers to force legislative action despite overwhelming tobacco interest pressures. The best example resulted in Congressional passage of a smoking ban on most domestic passenger airline flights in 1987. Those present at the Congressional hearings pointed out that the determinative factor was the heroic and passionate testimony of surviving stewards and stewardesses who broke down when describing how their co-workers contracted lung cancer and died from working in gas-chamber type smoke-filled cabins. Their testimony was so moving that even some Congressmen shed tears. Nevertheless, the tobacco lobby was so strong that the bill passed the House by only a five-vote margin, 198-193, and the Senate by a voice vote. Perhaps if the tobacco PACs and industry had poured a few more dollars into Congressmen's war chests, crews and all passengers on American domestic flights would still be subject to the carcinogens and toxins of poisonous tobacco smoke on each flight today. Fortunately, that is not the case.

How much does a vote cost? Or, put another way, how many lives does a vote cost? A reader commented on the U.S. News & World Report April 18, 1994 cover story "Should Cigarettes Be Outlawed?" with the following letter published on May 2, 1994:[4]

Your article said that 419,000 Americans die annually from tobacco, and the industry employs nearly 47,000 people. That works out to killing nine people a year to preserve each of those jobs. Seems like a high price to pay.

Eliminate tobacco PACs and other PACs and we may never have to answer the question as to how many lives does a vote cost.

Of course, tobacco money is not just limited to influencing members of Congress. Tobacco money has permeated the coffers of the American Civil Liberties Union (ACLU), women's groups, minority organizations, and children's groups. The silence of these organizations when it comes to protecting the right of over 200 million nonsmoking Americans to live in a smoke-free environment void of the carcinogens and toxins from secondary tobacco smoke is deafening. Many child advocacy groups do not care that parents exposing children to poisonous tobacco smoke in the home or in a car is a form of child abuse. Many black organizations do not care if cigarette companies target black neighborhoods with their billboard advertising to help recruit new smokers to make up for the nearly half million Americans who prematurely die each year from tobacco smoke and secondary tobacco smoke.

Women's groups who do not hesitate to point up the need for better and more research on women's health issues have not come very far in expressing any concern about the exploitation of women through targeted cigarette advertising. The rapidly increasing health toll of tobacco smoke on women is quite alarming, but one would never know that smoking is a major health problem for women based on the silence of women's organizations who receive some of their funding from tobacco companies. Women's advocacy groups clearly have not come "a long way baby" on the smoking issues.

And would the ACLU be so willing to represent tobacco companies if it had not received funding from these companies? Perhaps the ACLU should be more concerned about the right of over 200 million nonsmoking Americans to breathe fresh air.

In the coming years, tobacco PACs will likely be directing their tainted money in efforts to hold down cigarette taxes both as a way of funding and as part of any health care reform, maintaining the tobacco price support programs, opposing bans on smoking in public places, opposing further restrictions on advertising including Joe Camel type ads, screaming against placing restrictions on tobacco exports, and opposing increasing public educational expenditures on the dangers of tobacco smoke and secondary tobacco smoke. Tobacco PACs are a cancer to the health of all Americans. They should be banned. The poisonous products from the tobacco companies they represent should be banned or be made available only by prescription just like other drugs.

B. TOBACCO EXPORTS – FOREIGN EXPLOITATION BY THE TOBACCO INDUSTRY

The United States has become a merchant of death throughout the world as American cigarette exports increased from $1.8 to $3.5 billion in a five-year period from the late 1980s to the early 1990s.[5] Nearly a half million Americans and about 2.5 million other human beings around the world will die prematurely from tobacco smoke and secondary tobacco smoke each year.[6] The World Health Organization estimates that by the year 2020 ten million human beings will die each year from tobacco smoke and secondary tobacco smoke.[7]

Since the Surgeon General's 1964 report entitled "Smoking and Health" concluded that smoking was a major cause of lung disease, the United States government has undertaken a health policy warning its citizens of the dangers of tobacco smoke and more recently secondary tobacco smoke. However, during this same period the United States has embarked on a trade policy urging foreigners to smoke American cigarettes.[8] The General Accounting Office in May 1990 found that "U.S. policy and programs for assisting the export of tobacco and tobacco products work at cross purposes to U.S. health policy and initiatives, both domestically and internationally."[9]

The United States has pried open Asian markets under threat of American trade sanctions.[10] American cigarettes in Japan and Taiwan are sold for about half the cost in the United States. As a result of the efforts of the American tobacco industry to make up for the loss in domestic sales, Asian countries report big increases in smoking particularly among women and young people, two of the groups exploited in the United States.[11]

President Clinton and many Americans protested Singapore's lashing of an 18-year-old American with a rattan cane for disfiguring two cars with eggs and spray paint.[12] The President's protest seemed quite hypocritical for a country that warns Americans of the dangers of smoking, but has a policy of aggressively encouraging foreigners to smoke poisonous American cigarettes. It is difficult to get agitated over several lashes for one criminal act while simultaneously encouraging huge increases in tobacco exports that contribute to the premature deaths of over 2.5 million human beings around the world each year. When the United States stops tobacco companies from exporting death, disease, and disability, perhaps nations will treat Americans more humanely and heed our human rights concerns.

A recent Reader's Digest 20-country investigation spanning four continents revealed that millions of children are being lured into addictive smoking by American cigarette manufacturers.[13] These American companies in several nations have been fighting legislation that curtails cigarette use by minors and creatively violates the spirit of those countries' advertising curbs.[14] The Reader's Digest concludes that the American tobacco company activities "show a cynical disregard for public health."[15]

There appears to be a moral inconsistency about a health policy of warning Americans of the dangers of smoking and a trade policy that encourages foreigners to smoke American cigarettes. Helping kill 2.5 million foreigners a year does not appear to be consistent with any moral principle upon which our country was founded and has endured for more than 200 years. It is consistent with the tobacco industry's big profit motive and this country's desire to reduce its balance of trade deficit. It is inconsistent with the Seventh Commandment which states "Thou Shalt Not Kill." And it is ruining the image of the United States abroad as an advanced nation with live saving technology and medicine and substitutes an image as a merchant of cancer especially in Asia.

We purport to be a nation that values the lives of human beings. Throughout the exploitation of peoples through cigarettes we have become an amoral government that encourages tobacco industry profits at the expense of 2.5 million foreign lives a year which is estimated to reach about 10 million a year by the year 2020. Our government's duplicity of warning Americans and discouraging them from smoking because of the carcinogens and toxins in poisonous tobacco smoke and secondary tobacco smoke on the one hand and pushing the lethal product off on citizens of countries around the world on the other hand is shameful. It is difficult to understand how a nation of purported high moral values and principles can do this.

It has often been said that instruction will be geared to the level of the lowest member of the group. Teachers sometimes gear their instructions to the weakest student in the class. The tobacco industry's propaganda appears to have been geared to the most vulnerable potential victims such as our youth, slim conscious women, and the poorly educated of other countries. The tobacco industry's abysmal track record on health issues in producing the only consumer product that when used as intended causes premature death and serious illness has infiltrated the nation's trade policy. The United States is the merchant of death. We somehow have a clear conscience that warning Americans of the dangers of smoking relieves us of all moral responsibility in helping kill 2.5 million foreigners a year.

There are some answers. In the long run educating our children may help create an awareness. There are legislative steps that can be taken such as taxing all cigarettes, whether sold domestically or exported, at $2 to $3 a pack. And eventually this country should ban the growth, manufacture, sale, and exportation of cigarettes.

In connection with the 5th World No-Tobacco Day (1992), then African National Congress leader Nelson Mandela had these thoughts about the cessation of smoking:[16]

Sunday May 31, is World No-Tobacco Day. It is a Day with a single aim – to build a world in which no one smokes, chews or sniffs tobacco.

It is a Day on which to remember that a human life is lost every eleven seconds to tobacco-related disease. The World Health Organisation's experts estimate that tobacco kills at least 3 million people each year worldwide.

It is a Day on which to stop smoking. For if we do not then the annual global death rate is forecast to increase to ten million in the next few decades. Most of these deaths will be in Africa and Asia.

It is a day on which to recall that tobacco ranks alongside AIDS, famine and pestilence as a threat to the health of the world's people.

For these reasons I gladly accepted the National Council Against Smoking's invitation to help them celebrate World No-Tobacco Day.

I am pleased to add my voice to the cause of health through non-smoking. Smoking is a problem both for the individual and for society.

Smokers can no longer ignore the frightening facts about tobacco. But many are caught in a trap. They worry about their health, yet they also worry about how to live without cigarettes! They think they "should" stop, but feel they "can't". So it is easier to continue smoking than to try to stop.

Stopping smoking is difficult. It requires energy, time and effort. Yet millions have quit and so regained control of their lives and their health.

On May 31, I appeal to smokers to quit for one day, as a first step to conquering their habit. They say the hardest part about stopping smoking, is making the decision to do it. Make that decision for one day on May 31.

I also appeal to the rest of our society to take up the challenge of building a healthier world through non-smoking:

* Women – because of cultural traditions few of you smoke. Remain non-smokers. Prize your growing independence and do not chain yourself to cigarettes.
* Children – do not start, smoking is a dirty habit, not a fashionable or grown-up one. The best sportsmen and sportswomen do not smoke.
* Advertising agencies: devote your communication skills to sell health, not ill health.
* Agriculturists – use your green fingers to finding economic alternatives to tobacco growing.
* Athletes, and public figures – you are role models for young people. Set an example of non-tobacco use and publicise the fact.
* Health workers – you have the duty to inform yourselves and others of the risks. Help people quit the habit, and do so yourself if you smoke.
* Journalists and the media – spread the news so that no one can claim not to know of the dangers. Find new and exciting ways to educate people.
* Politicians – my own calling. Let us as soon as we are able pass legislation aimed at ensuring the right of people to live free from tobacco hazards.
* Teachers – encourage self-confidence in the child and help young people formulate values which lead to healthy decisions. Are you setting the right example?
* Tobacco farmers – start to reduce your dependence on tobacco crops.
* Unions – work will be safer and healthier in an environment free from tobacco. Protect workers from air polluted with tobacco smoke.

Health is a basic human right. Let us all work, to help everyone, everywhere, attain health. Let us build a tobacco free world.

At the Seventh World Conference on Tobacco and Health sponsored by the American Cancer Society and several allied organizations, Richard Peto, a renowned Oxford University epidemiologist, predicted that "without large reductions in early smoking (starts) or smoking persistence, there will probably be over ten million deaths per year during the second quarter (2025-2049) of the next century."[17] During the 1990s, Peto said, "the epidemic in slow motion" will kill roughly one million people a year in less-developed countries and about two million a year in the industrialized nations. But "probably sometime in the 2020s," when global tobacco mortality begins to exceed 10 million annually, about 7 million of the deaths – 70% – will be in the less-developed nations where, thanks in part to American tobacco exports, cigarette consumption is increasing rapidly.[18]

An Australian public health official stated that "this is the greatest human disaster of our times" and "future generations will find it simply unbelievable that our government failed to respond, knowing they could have prevented tens of millions of deaths."[19]

Hopefully we live in a world where human life, whether American or foreign, is more important than tobacco industry profits and balances of trade. This nation's more than 200 million nonsmokers should follow the advice of Nelson Mandela. We can attempt to elect public officials who are more responsive to the needs of our children and human beings around the world than campaign contributions from tobacco companies, PACs, and other lobbyists.

C. SUBSIDIZING TOBACCO

There is a concern among the more than 200 million nonsmoking Americans that we are subsidizing the farmers who grow a poisonous product that prematurely kills nearly a half million Americans and 2.5 million foreigners each year.

Tobacco is produced in 21 states and Puerto Rico.[20] Six states – North Carolina, Kentucky, Tennessee, Virginia, South Carolina, and Georgia – accounted in 1987 for 91% of the $1.9 billion in farm cash receipts from tobacco.[21] Cigarette exports are up, but there is a downward trend in United States consumption.

Government programs influencing the supply and price of American tobacco began with the passage of the Agricultural Adjustment Act of 1933. The Act designated tobacco as a basic (storable) commodity and provided cash payments to tobacco growers who restricted their production through 1935.[22] The current tobacco program has its origin in the Agricultural Adjustment Act of 1938 which established a supply control and price support program for tobacco that remains very much the same today. The Agricultural Act of 1949 authorized tobacco price supports.[23]

The tobacco price support program consists of marketing quotas and nonresource loans.[24] A national marketing quota is divided among tobacco farms, which must restrict production and sales to a farm quota level. The marketing quota serves to limit supplies and thereby raise market prices above the loan rate. The Department of Agriculture records show that from 1933 to 1991 the Commodity Credit Corporation has loaned about $9 billion in its tobacco price support operations.[25] The administrative cost of managing the price support program was about $14.1 million in fiscal year 1992.[26]

A critical tobacco industry vote occurred in 1985 when a proposal, the Petri Amendment, was introduced in the House of Representatives to eliminate the tobacco price control program that has been in place since the early 1930s when the Agricultural Adjustment Act first designated tobacco as a basic commodity and authorized payments to growers who reduced production.[27] These quotas, which are still in place today, restrain tobacco production, thereby raising the prices that growers receive.[28] The current program uses a combination of support loans and supply controls.

The tobacco PACs poured nearly a million dollars into the coffers of Congressmen who voted down the Petri Amendment by a 230-195 margin. As a result, the eventual annual cost to American taxpayers will be between $660 and $900 million dollars.[29]

It is unconscionable that the American taxpayers should be subsidizing an industry that produces an agricultural product that is responsible for the premature death of nearly a half million Americans and 2.5 million foreigners each year. Tobacco kills. American taxpayers should not be aiding and abetting in this slaughter through tobacco subsidies. The only financial assistance that should be contemplated is to assist tobacco growers in the transition of utilizing their land for other uses.

D. EXPLOITATION OF BLACKS – "THEY USED TO MAKE US PICK IT. NOW THEY WANT US TO SMOKE IT."

In attempting to make up for the nearly half million Americans dying prematurely each year from poisonous tobacco smoke and secondary tobacco smoke, the tobacco industry has effectively exploited another group, the American black community. Although the tobacco industry results among blacks have met with a great deal of success, they have not always been as successful as the exploitation of foreigners.

The National Black Leadership Initiative on Cancer and Harlem Hospital in New York City launched an ad campaign with two anti-smoking organizations in 1992.[30] The ad, which depicts a skeleton cowboy lighting the cigarette of a 10-year-old black child, reads:

> They used to make us pick it.
> Now they want us to smoke it.

The ad attempts to highlight several disturbing trends – tobacco companies disproportionately target blacks, blacks have the highest American tobacco addiction rate, and blacks have the highest American rate of smoker's cancer. A study published in the May 1991 *New Jersey Medicine* found that 76% of billboards in minority communities advertise tobacco and alcohol compared to only 42% in white communities. In the 1991 trial of Chicago billboard activist Reverend Michael Pfleger arrested for painting over tobacco billboards, the Chicago Lung Association testified that Chicago's minority areas have about three times as many tobacco billboards as predominantly white areas. Pfleger was acquitted by a judge who apparently found his acts to be less harmful to the community than the tobacco ads. The Detroit Free Press found similar targeting in that city.[31]

According to American Lung Association and National Cancer Institute statistics, the lung cancer rates among blacks has increased four times faster than among whites in the past 30 years.[32] The National Medical Association which represents black surgeons in America voted unanimously to endorse the "pick-it, smoke-it" ad.[33] Smokefree Educational Services President Joseph Cherner said the ad "isn't a question of black versus whites." He stressed that "this ad is a question of blacks versus the tobacco industry. And the black community is 100% right."

Former United States Health and Human Services Secretary Dr. Louis W. Sullivan alarmingly stated, "At a time when our people (black) desperately need the message of health promotion, the (Tobacco Industry's) message is more disease, more suffering, and more death to a group already bearing more than its share of smoking-related illness and mortality."[34]

The silence of most of the nation's black leaders and organizations while the blacks have been exploited by the tobacco companies is most notable. Many black leaders have apparently been bought off with tobacco company money just like many members of Congress, women's advocacy groups, child advocacy groups, and the American Civil Liberties Union.

In his November 28, 1993 New York Times column, Tobacco Dollars – Buying the Silence of black leaders," black columnist Bob Herbert concluded:[35]

> The tobacco companies are buying the silence of the black leaders. And by accepting the money, and not speaking out against the awful dangers of smoking, these leaders are selling out their people.

Mr. Herbert noted the comment of one tobacco company non-smoking executive who said that "we reserve that right (to smoke) for the poor, the young, the black and the stupid." The columnist had access to a "internal use" only lengthy list of organizations that received contributions from Philip Morris U.S.A. in 1988. Because of the grouping of recipient organizations, Mr. Herbert concluded that "Philip Morris has been a bonanza for black groups and politicians."[36] The columnist noted that in 1988 Philip Morris gave to the NAACP, the Urban League, Associated Black Charities, the United Negro College Fund, and many others.

However, the contributions are not just from Philip Morris. In 1989, the United Negro College Fund received $285,500 from RJR Nabisco and $200,500 from Philip Morris.[37] The National Urban League received $4.4 million from cigarette concerns over a recent three-year period.[38] Similar contributions are made to Hispanic organizations such as a $50,000 contribution in 1989 from tobacco companies to the Hispanic Congressional Caucus for an internship program in public policy.

Tobacco companies operate in more subtle ways often linking promotional activities to African-American music and black history month activities.[39]

What can be done to stop this exploitation of the black community by the tobacco companies? An example occurred when R.J. Reynolds in 1989 spent $10 million developing a high-tar menthol cigarette called Uptown to test-market in Philadelphia's African-American community. The company overlooked the strong reaction of the African-American community leaders. It resulted in a swift and powerful backlash that forced the company to cancel its plans for a quicker exploitation of the black community and continue down the road of more subtle exploitation – contributing to political leaders, black organizations, and black oriented promotional activities such as music festivals.

Other things might be done. A boycott against tobacco industry products spearheaded by leaders such as those in the black community in Philadelphia that forced the cancellation of Uptown cigarettes might be successful. Blacks have successfully used boycotts in the past to counter exploitation. They should consider boycotting all non-tobacco goods sold by cigarette companies such as Philip Morris' Kraft Foods and Oscar Mayer products, as well as RJR Nabisco's crackers and cookies.

All chairmen of American tobacco companies are white males, some or all of whom do not smoke.[40] For the most part the tobacco companies have effectively bought the silence of the black leaders and organizations. However, the black community and this nation cannot afford to have the white-dominated tobacco industry and their political cohorts exploit them any longer. Likewise, the black community cannot afford to have elected black officials let their votes on tobacco/health issues be influenced by tobacco industry or PAC campaign contributions to their political coffers. As Bob Herbert concluded in his perceptive column, "How many black bodies is a political contribution worth?"[41] Whether the question pertains to blacks, Hispanics, women, or foreigners, the answer in an alleged moralistic society that believes in the Seventh Commandment (Thou Shalt Not Kill), has to be "none."

E. EXPLOITATION OF WOMEN BY THE TOBACCO INDUSTRY

The line "It's hard to be a woman" in country-music star Tammy Wynette's rendition of "Stand By Your Man" in the movie "Sleepless in Seattle" is borne out by the tobacco industry's exploitation of women through preying on their weight control concerns, status symbols, and other socio-cultural factors. Through a combination of slick target advertising and promotion of activities such as sporting events (Virginia Slims) the tobacco industry has succeeded in persuading women to more than make up its proportional share of the nearly half million Americans who die prematurely each year from tobacco smoke and secondary tobacco smoke.

During the 1800s and prior to World War I, tobacco use by women was socially unacceptable.[42] As women became more emancipated through suffrage and dress reform, smoking became more acceptable.[43] Women started smoking in public as a sign of emancipation and equality though they smoked considerably less than men (2.4 versus 7.2 cigarettes per day in the United States in 1929).[44] Women smoking became more fashionable in the 1930s, especially in the cities. In 1935, 18.1% of women and 52.5% of men smoked.[45] By World War II, one-third of American women smoked cigarettes.[46]

The tobacco industry has publicly acknowledged that it is directing much of its contemporary advertising to the female market.[47] A front page 1981 *Advertising Age* article headlined "Women top cig target" quotes the president and chief executive of R.J. Reynolds as describing the women's market as "probably the largest opportunity" for the company.[48] In recent years, a number of cigarette brands targeted specifically to women have been introduced, the most successful of which has been Philip Morris' Virginia Slims.[49]

Following the 1970 ban on radio and television advertising, the number of cigarette advertisements in women's magazines increased dramatically.[50] Of the 17 leading women's magazines in 1984, only *Good Housekeeping* refused to accept cigarette advertisements.[51] It has been suggested that the editorial policy of women's magazines that accepted cigarette advertising limits the amount of space devoted to reporting the health hazards of smoking.[52]

In a manner similar to its largely silencing black leaders and black organizations, the tobacco industry on the health horrors of smoking issues
effectively bought off female leaders and organizations for many years.
For example, *Ms. Magazine* with a circulation of just over a half million in
1984 accepted a sizeable share of its advertising budget from cigarette
companies, but for years failed to print a story on smoking despite its in-
clusion of numerous health related articles.[53] The National Organization
for Women has had its meeting programs partly underwritten by Philip
Morris and in the mid-1980s refused to print in its national newsletter an
advertisement taking *Ms. Magazine* to task on the cigarette smoking issue.[54] By their silence on the issue of tobacco company exploiting and endangering the health of millions of American women, the leaders of the
women's movement as well as the publishers of women's magazines
played right into the hands of the amoral tobacco industry.

Numerous women's organizations have received financial support from
tobacco companies.[55] A Harvard University Institute for the Study of
Smoking behavior and Policy study in the 1980s revealed that of 53 wom-
en's organizations contacted, 13 responded that they presently received
funding from the tobacco industry totalling in excess of $300,000.[56] The
primary recipients of tobacco industry funding appear to be women's leadership groups. Of those leadership organizations, the primary targets are
political, business, professional, and minority women.[57]

However, there have been some significant recent changes. The
National Organization of Women stopped accepting tobacco industry
contributions several years ago.[58] And, in February 1987, *Ms. Magazine*,
without a single tobacco or alcohol advertisement, devoted the entire issue
reporting the results of a readership survey on addictive behaviors, including cigarette smoking.[59]

The medical data is frightening on the enormous increased risk of
smoking for women than for men. A recent Yale University School of
Medicine study revealed that women at the highest smoking levels had 82
times the lung cancer risk as men. Overall, female smokers showed twice
the risk that male smokers have for a given number of cigarettes smoked in
a lifetime.[60] Lung cancer most often caused by smoking has surpassed
breast cancer as the leading cancer killer of women.[61] Women who smoke
double the risk of cervical cancer, smokers enter menopause an average of
three years earlier than nonsmokers probably because smoking lowers
estrogen levels, smoking increases a women's risk for the brittle-bone
disease osteoporosis, and smoking causes premature wrinkling due to
decreased blood flow to the skin and damages connective tissues.[62]
Smoking can contribute to premature birth, low birth rate, and still-births.[63]

Women have come a long way in this country during the twentieth century. However, thanks in part to the tobacco industry, women health-wise still have a long way to go. It was projected by 1995 that 240,000 American women will die prematurely from tobacco each year.[64] In 1990, 22.8% of adult women smoked.[65] The number of women smokers lagged behind men until women smoking became more socially acceptable. Likewise, the related health problems from smoking showed a similar lag. It appears that women's smoking-related health problems which often take decades to fully develop will enormously increase in the next decade.

ENDNOTES

[1] Wolfe, Sidney, et al., "The Congressional Addiction to Tobacco: How the Tobacco Lobby Suffocates Federal Health Policy," A Report by Public Citizen's Health Research Group and the Advocacy Institute, 10/92.

[2] *Id.* at p. 6.

[3] *Id.*

[4] U.S. News & World Report, 5/2/94, p. 6.

[5] "Smoking America's Image," San Francisco Examiner, 1/27/92, p. A-18; "Merchant of Cancer," Chicago Tribune, 1/30/92, Sec. 1, p. 23.

[6] "The Global Tobacco Epidemic," Scientific American, May 1995, pp. 44, 46.

[7] "Tobacco Roads – Delivering Death to the Third World," by Morton Mintz, Progressive, 5/91, pp. 24-26, at 25.

[8] *Id.*

[9] Trade and Health Issues, "Dichotomy Between U.S. Tobacco Export Policy and Antismoking Initiatives, General Accounting Office, p. 5.

[10] "U.S. Government Criticized for Helping to Export a Deadly Epidemic of Tobacco Addiction," Journal of the American Medical Association, 6/24/92, vol. 267, no. 24, pp. 3256-3258.

[11] *Id.*

[12] "Justice in Six Lashes," Newsweek, 4/11/94, p. 40.

[13] "America's New Merchants of Death," Readers Digest, 4/93, pp. 50-53.

[14] *Id.*

[15] *Id.*

[16] Message from Nelson Mandela to mark the 5th World No-Tobacco Day (1992).

[17] See footnote 7 at p. 24.

[18] *Id.*

[19] *Id.*

[20] "U.S. Agricultural Policy on Tobacco," Fran DuMelle, Office of Government Relations, American Lung Association, at Tobacco Use in America Conference, January 27-28, 1989, p. 43.

[21] *Id.*

[22] National Food Review, U.S. Department of Agriculture, Jan.-March 1990, p. 66.

[23] *Id.*

[24] Congressional Research Report for Congress, "Tobacco Programs of U.S. Department of Agriculture: Their Operation and Cost," p. 1.

[25] *Id.*

26 *Id.*

27 "Short-Changed – How Congress and Special Interests Benefit at the Expense of the American People," by Jean Coble, The Center for Public Integrity, 1991, p. 20.

28 *Id.*

29 *Id.*

30 Smoke-Free Air, Fall, 1992, p. 6. The two organizations are Smoke-Free Educational Services and the Coalition for a Smoke-Free City.

31 *Id.*

32 *Id.*

33 *Id.*

34 "African Americans and Smoking – At a Glance," Centers for Disease Control, Public Health Service, Department of Health and Human Services.

35 "Tobacco Dollars," New York Times, 11/28/93, Sec. E, p. 11; "Have tobacco firms bought off black leaders," by Bob Herbert, South Bend Tribune, 11/30/93, p. A-12.

36 *Id.*

37 "Tobacco Stains – cigarette firms buy into African-American Groups," by Danny R. Johnson, The Progressive, 12/92, pp. 26, 28.

38 *Id.*

39 *Id.*

40 Smoke-Free Air, Fall 1992, p. 6.

41 See footnote 35 – "Tobacco Dollars."

42 Women and Tobacco, World Health Organization, Geneva, 1992, p. 4.

43 *Id.*

44 *Id.* at p. 5.

45 *Id.*

46 "Mixed messages for women, a social history of cigarette smoking and advertising," New York State Journal of Medicine, July 1985, pp. 335, 337.

47 *Id.* at 337.

48 *Id.* at 337 at article footnote 30.

49 *Id.*

50 *Id.* at 339.

51 *Id.*

52 *Id.*; Whelan, E. M. et al., Analysis of Coverage of tobacco hazards in women's magazines, Journal of Public Health Policy, 1981: 2:28, p. 35.

53 See footnote 46 at page 349.

54 *Id.* at 340.

55 Not Far Enough: Women vs. Smoking: A workshop for Women's Group and Women's Health Leaders. Convened by the Advocacy Institute in Cooperation with the National Cancer Institute and the Harvard Institute for the Study of Smoking Behavior and Policy, 2/4/87, "Tobacco Industry Funding of Women's Organizations," by Andrea M. Berman, p. 20.

56 *Id.*

57 Among the leading women's groups that received tobacco contributions are the National Women's Political Caucus, the Women's Campaign Fund, the Women's Research and Education Institute, the American Association of University Women, the American Federation of Business and Professional Women's Clubs, Wider Opportunities for Women, the League of Women Voters Education Fund, the Center for Women Policy Studies, and Women Executives in State Government. "Tobacco's Hold on Women's Groups," Washington Post, 11/14/91, pp. A1, A38.

58 "Women, Girls and Tobacco" – Briefing Paper from American Medical Association Conference, 2/93, by Michele Bloch, M.D., Ph.D., Deborah McLellan, MHS.

59 See footnote 55. "Which Women Smoke and Why? – Cigarette Smoking as a Woman's Issue," by Ellen R. Girtz, Ph.D., pp. 15, 18.

[60] "Smoking may hold more risk for women," Chicago Tribune, 9/22/93, Sec. 1, p. 20; "Women Smoker's Risk," Chicago Sun-Times, 9/22/93, p. 6.

[61] "Cover Story: Lung Cancer is women's most deadly – Smoking doubles cancer risks," USA Today, 11/11/93, pp. 1D, 2D.

[62] *Id.* at 2D.

[63] *Id.*

[64] "Women, Girls and Tobacco," Briefing Paper for 2/93 AMA Conference, Draft 5, by Michele H. Bloch, M.D., Ph.D., Deborah McLellan, p 1.

[65] *Id.*

Conclusion

Approximately 472,000 Americans die prematurely each year from the carcinogens and toxins of tobacco smoke and secondary tobacco smoke – more human beings than the population of Albuquerque, Atlanta, Austin, Charlotte, Cincinnati, Denver, Fort Worth, Honolulu, Kansas City, Minneapolis, Oakland, Oklahoma City, or St. Louis.[1]

The broader challenge facing the United States is to bring to a halt what some have termed "the present holocaust" or smoking holocaust. On a larger scale some have suggested classifying cigarettes as a drug and banning their sale,[2] others have suggested limiting the sale of cigarettes in the same manner as other prescription drugs available only in pharmacies, and a professor of medicine at the University of California at San Francisco recently suggested setting decreasing limits of nicotine in cigarettes over the next 20 years.[3]

A friend who is quite interested in the substance of the smoking problem and means of combatting the problem suggested that it might be helpful to provide the nation's 46 million smokers, as well as concerned friends, co-workers, and family members, with some suggestions as to how the nation's smokers individually might stop smoking since many of them apparently wish to do so after being exposed to all the data related to the dangers of cigarette smoke. The suggestion was well-founded since in 1990 there were 44 million American former adult smokers compared to 46 million current adult smokers.[4]

At the outset each smoker should seek the advice of his or her physician or a reliable medical person knowledgeable in smoking cessation. There has been some indication, for example, that persons who continue to smoke while using the patch may be risking a heart attack, especially if they do not follow their doctor's directions.[5]

It has been found that individuals with serious smoking-related health problems such as cardiac and pulmonary disease are most likely to quit.[6] About 40% of persons with serious health problems attribute quitting to having a serious smoking-related health problem while just 7% who quit for a year or more attributed it to doctors advice and about the same number quit on their own.[7] A study published in the Journal of Applied Psychology at the University of Iowa found that the best aids for quitting were hypnosis, aversion therapy, acupuncture, and cessation programs that take a multifaceted approach to the problem.[8]

Although addiction to smoking kills 419,000 Americans a year, the problem is too infrequently mentioned by doctors or therapists to their patients.[9] It has been pointed out that doctors, psychologists, and other health professionals have an ethical responsibility to address nicotine addiction.[10] Nicotine masks two diagnosable disorders – depression and anxiety.[11]

A spokesperson for the Centers for Disease Control in Atlanta reported that the majority of smokers who manage to kick the habit do so "cold turkey" and are more likely to resort to self-help methods than to participate in formal programs.[12] However, smoke-cessation programs have higher success rates than self-help methods and are more likely to attract heavy smokers.[13] The Centers for Disease Control spokesperson reported that about 90% who quit smoking do so on their own using self-help kits offered by such organizations as the American Heart Association and the American Cancer Society.[14] The observation is consistent with my acquaintances who have quit – most either quitting cold turkey or having cut back due to a no-smoking policy at work which forced them to reduce cigarette consumption to the point where they decided to quit "cold turkey" for health reasons.

The highest smoking-cessation success rate I ever heard of was through hypnosis. A friend's husband succeeded in quitting after two hypnosis sessions with a Chicago suburban psychologist. The psychologist advised me that he has seen over 8,000 smokers. He reported a 92% success rate after two 45-minute group or individual sessions spaced two days apart. Follow-ups indicated that more than half remained nonsmokers two years later. Of course, the success rate could vary on such factors as the skill of the hypnotist and the motivation of the smoker to stop.

When I was in the Army, one of the significant factors in making those rough moments in basic training more palatable was the fact that everyone else was going through the same horrendous experience. Participation in the annual Great American Smokeout each November which has been held since 1976 encourages cigarette smokers to stop smoking for at least 24 hours.[15] During the Great American Smokeout in 1992, an estimated 3.3 million smokers reported quitting and 7.5 million reduced the number of cigarettes smoked that day.[16] As a runner, I can attest that training for marathons was a lot easier when I ran in the morning darkness with a friend than when I ran alone. I would imagine stopping smoking might be easier if it were initiated in a group setting such as a smokeout or with friends.

There has been a lot written about the use of nicotine patches, nicotine gum and sprays, pills, and inhalers.[17] Consultation with a physician is critical before embarking on any of these methods.   '

The patch, typically worn on the upper arm, pumps nicotine into the bloodstream of smokers who are "weaned of their addiction by decreasing the dosage over time."[18] However, doctors and researchers report that patches may not affect the psychological dependency that may be responsible for the inability to quit, prescriptions are given without enough consideration for the initial dose, patients fail to follow instructions by smoking when wearing the patch thereby overdosing on nicotine and risking heart attacks, withdrawal symptoms such as dizziness and nausea may be experienced, and problems may result from overdosing by sticking on extra patches.[19]

The greatest concern about stopping smoking is weight gain. For women one of the greatest deterrents to giving up smoking is the fear of gaining weight. It has been estimated that this concern keeps two-thirds of women from trying to stop, while half of men report this concern.[20] Tobacco ads stressing glamor, independence, sexiness and thinness reinforce this link between smoking and appearance.[21] The average woman who quits smoking gains six to eight pounds.[22] This is consistent with a 1993 study by researchers at San Francisco General Hospital who reported that men who smoked burned 5% more calories when smoking.[23] A combination of proper diet and where permissible exercise may help offset any tendency to gain weight by substituting fattening snacks for cigarettes. Of course, a physician should be consulted regarding the commencement of any exercise program or dietary change.

The surest way to end smoking is never to start. Our nation's youth must be educated starting in kindergarten that the Joe Camel product spreads a fatal tobacco plague. Our children must be persuaded that they should never start smoking.

The key to persuading people to stop smoking is education. What parent would rationally want to expose his or her child to the carcinogens and toxins of poisonous tobacco smoke or secondary tobacco smoke and the numerous diseases and illnesses resulting therefrom? Who would want to endanger the health of a co-worker on the job or risk initiating an asthma attack of a young child in a fast-food restaurant? Discussing the smoking cessation problem with one's physician, participating in a smokeout, and reading up-to-date information on the health hazards of smoking are important steps in the process of stopping. A good starting point would be to contact the American Cancer Society or American Heart Association for smoke-quitting kits or information.

A recent New York Times/CBS News poll of 1,215 adults conducted April 21-23, 1994 with a three percentage point sampling error margin revealed a strong concern of the American public regarding smoking and that something should be done about it.[24] Contrary to tobacco industry contentions, 91% of those surveyed, including 87% of those who said they smoked, believed cigarettes are addictive.[25] Over two-thirds or 67% favored a ban on smoking in public places and 61% believed tobacco companies encourage teenagers to smoke.

The American Medical Association has recently recommended the following 14 steps be taken in opposing tobacco use:[26]

1. Additional efforts should be made to educate physicians, the public and policy-makers regarding the consequences of tobacco use, the predatory nature of the tobacco industry, and ways smokers can break their addiction to tobacco.

2. Medical schools and research institutions, as well as individual researchers, should refuse any funding from the tobacco industry and its subsidiaries to avoid giving them an appearance of credibility.

3. Politicians should not accept money from the tobacco industry and those who accept tobacco PAC or industry contributions should be identified publicly.

4. The Occupational Safety and Health Administration should move forward with its proposal to require smoke-free workplaces nationwide.

5. Local communities should continue efforts to control smoking in public places.

6. State legislatures should assume responsibility for ensuring smoke-free areas.

7. Tobacco purchases should be strictly limited to adults with severe penalties for violators. All tobacco advertising should be eliminated, and a vigorous counteradvertising campaign should be instituted.

8. The Department of Justice should enforce the ban against indirect tobacco advertising such as displayed in televised sporting events.

9. Tobacco should be considered a drug delivery vehicle and placed under the oversight of the Food and Drug Administration, with appropriate regulation as for other life-threatening drugs.

10. State and federal excise taxes on tobacco products should be greatly increased, both to help pay for the costs of tobacco-induced illnesses and to deter minors from becoming addicted.

11. The federal government should ban the export of tobacco to other countries.

12. The continued contribution to knowledge of the control of tobacco by the National Cancer Institute should be strongly supported.

13. Physicians and the public should support legal actions against the tobacco industry to recover billions of dollars in excess medical costs from tobacco-related diseases borne by Medicaid, Medicare, and the Department of Veterans Affairs.

14. All avenues of individual and collective redress should be pursued through the judicial system.

The concern encompassed by these recommendations from the nation's largest medical organization should serve as a warning of a pending national health disaster if strong steps are not taken to limit or curb smoking.

As the New York Times/CBS News poll shows, the overwhelming majority of the American public wants something to be done to limit or curb smoking. The best suggestions I have heard to minimize the withdrawal problems of the nation's 46 million smokers is to limit the sale of cigarettes in the same manner as other presumption drugs or under the Food and Drug Administration control by setting decreasing levels of nicotine in cigarettes over the next five to 20 years. Hopefully the tobacco companies and Congressmen who accept their money will not thwart the will of the overwhelming majority of the American people. If the

American public prevails, the smoke-free United States will be a much healthier place for more than 200 million nonsmoking American children and adults to live.

Unlike Prohibition, where a large percentage of Americans drank alcoholic beverages, only about 26% of American adults and less than 20% of all Americans smoke. Moreover, a reasonable amount of consumption of alcoholic beverages does not normally harm others; however, secondary tobacco smoke kills thousands of innocent victims each year and renders many more seriously ill.

Perhaps one or more of the myriad of observations, thoughts, facts and ideas throughout this book may serve as a motivator to stop smoking and to set in motion a chain of forces that will result in a lower level of contamination of our indoor and outdoor atmospheres from tobacco smoke and secondary tobacco smoke. If one life is saved or one less child experiences an asthma attack, all the effort that went into this book will have been worth it. For smokers, their families, and friends may experience the benefits of healthier, longer, and higher quality lives as we approach a smoke-free society by the year 2,000. The villains in this health scenario, the tobacco companies and the public official recipients of their tainted money, will be the ones who are fuming as the health of Americans will improve while tobacco sales and profits plummet. Then, tobacco profits will no longer be drawn from the blood of Americans.

Tobacco morality is the spreading of death, disability, and disease. It is disregard for human life. Tobacco morality is amorality.

The United States purports to be a moral nation that values the lives of human beings and attempts to eradicate disease and illness. The values of the tobacco industry and the overwhelming majority of Americans cannot coexist. The basic decency of a moral nation demands that every reasonable step be taken to safeguard the health of more than 200 million nonsmoking Americans. It is the moral or right thing to do.

ENDNOTES

[1] The World Almanac 1993, p. 392.
[2] "Should Cigarettes be Outlawed?", U.S. News & World Report, 4/18/94, pp. 32-43.
[3] Quindlen, Anna, "Second-State Smoke," New York Times, 4/30/94, p. A15.
[4] "Smoke Signals – Clinics May Be Best for Snuffing Habit," Chicago Sun-Times, 9/4/92, p. 8.
[5] "Smoking while using nicotine patch may be risky," Columbus Dispatch, 6/12/92; "A Rough Patch in the Road – Smoking while you quit may make you sorry," Newsweek, 7/6/92, p. 53.
[6] "Taking their chances – Health problems, not warnings, motivate smokers to quit," Chicago Tribune, 11/22/92, Sec. 5, p. 8.
[7] Id.

[8] *Id.*

[9] "Doctors have responsibility to discourage smoking," South Bend Tribune, 11/8/93, p. A-8 (Editorial – Mary J. Loftus).

[10] *Id.*

[11] *Id.*

[12] "Smoke Signals – Clinics May be Best for Snuffing Habit," Chicago Sun-Times, 9/4/92, p. 8.

[13] *Id.*

[14] *Id.*

[15] "MMWR – Morbidity and Mortality Weekly Report, Centers for Disease Control, "The Great American Smokeout, November 18, 1993," Centers for Disease Control, 11/12/93, vol. 42, no. 44, p. 853; "Smokeout Helps Cut Smoking," Chicago Sun-Times Editorial, 11/18/93, p. 33.

[16] *Id.*

[17] "After Nicotine Patches: Sprays, Pills, Inhalers?", Wall Street Journal, 11/8/93, pp. B-1, 9; "Nicotine patch may help smokers who want to quit," Milwaukee Journal 4/24/91, pp. 1, 5.

[18] "Nicotine Patch," USA Today Weekend, 7/31/92 – 8/2/92, p. 12.

[19] *Id.*

[20] "Women and Smoking – a deadly combination," by Leslie Laurence, McCalls, February 1993, pp. 45, 54.

[21] *Id.* at 54.

[22] *Id.*

[23] "Smokers who quit burn fewer calories," USA Today, 5/4/93, p. 1.

[24] "Majority of Americans Say Cigarettes Spur Addiction," New York Times, 5/1/94, A16.

[25] *Id.*

[26] "The Brown and Williamson Documents – Where Do We Go From Here?," Journal of the American Medical Association, 7/19/95, Vol. 274, No. 3.

SUBJECT INDEX

A

Abused Spouses, 117
ACLU, 166
Advertising, Ban On, 139
Advertising, Cigarette, 129, 130
Advertising, Misleading, 125
Advertising, Tobacco, 123
Agricultural Act Of 1949, 171
Agricultural Adjustment Act Of 1933, 171
Agricultural Adjustment Act Of 1938, 171
Akins, Claude, 38
Arnaz, Desi, 38
Arteriosclerosis, 23
Asian Markets, 167
Asthma, 25
Asthmatic Children, 149
Athletics, 156

B

Back, 28
Ball, Lucille, 39
Ban On Advertising, 139
Bernstein, Leonard, 39
Bigelow V. Virginia, 127
Blacks, 172
Blakey Art, 39
Bogart, Humphrey, 6
Broken Bones, 27
Brynner, Yul, 8, 40

Buerger's Disease, 31

C

Califano, Joseph A. Jr., 7, 159
Cancer Linkage, Smoking-Lung, 19
Cancer, Colon, 21
Cancer, Rectal, 21
Capitol Broadcasting Co. V. Mitchell, 127
Castano V. American Tobacco Company, 102
Chewing Tobacco, 79, 126
Children , Asthmatic, 149
Children, 25, 70, 78, 116
Chronic Bronchitis, 24
Chronic Obstructive Pulmonary Disease, 24
Cigarette Advertising, 129, 130
Cigarette Billboard Advertising, 104
Cigarette Tax, 92
Cipollone V. Liggett Group, 99
Clinton, Bill, 11
Colon Cancer, 21
Columbus, 4
Commercial Airline Flights, 158
Cooper, Gary, 41

D

Davis, Sammy, Jr. 41
Dental, 30

Depression, 29
Diabetes, 23
Dirksen, Everett Mckinley, 7, 55
Douglas, Kirk, 42

E

Education, 135, 183
Emphysema, 23, 24
Environmental Protection
    Agency, 148
Esophagus, 32
Exports, Tobacco, 88, 167
Eyes, 30

F

Federal Buildings, Smoking
    In, 156
Federal Tax Deduction, 165
Feldon, Barbara, 43
Ford, Glenn, 44

G

Gabor, Eva, 45
Gatlin, Larry, 46
Godfrey Arthur, 5
Goerlitz, David, 57
Graves Disease, 32
Great American Smokeout, 182

H

Hagman, Larry, 46
Heart Disease, 22
Helling V. Mckinney, 99
High Blood Pressure, 24
Hypnosis, 182

I

Indoor Air Pollution, 109, 118

J

Jennings, Waylon, 47
Joe Camel, 78, 88, 124, 128, 134
Johnson, Lyndon Baines, 56

K

Kendricks, Eddie, 12, 47
Kessler, David, 12, 69
King James I, 13, 17, 119
King, Larry, 59
Kirkland, Sally, 48
Koop C. Everett, 59
Kruk, John, 158

L

Landers, Alan, 58
Landers, Ann, 68
Landon, Michael, 48
Legislation, 165
Lehrer, Jim, 61
Lemon, Chris, 48
Leukemia, 22
Liquormart, Inc. V. Rhode
    Island, 104, 128
Lobbyists, Tobacco, 144
Loveless, Patty, 49
Lung Cancer 4, 19

M

Maclaine, Shirley, 49
Malls, 160
Mandela, Nelson, 169
Manslaughter, 110
Marlboro Man, 12, 85

Mathis, Johnny, 50
Medical Cost Third Party
   Liability Suits, 104
Misleading Advertising, 125
Money, Pac, 143
Money, Special Interest, 165
Murrow, Edward R., 60

N
Nat "King" Cole 6, 40
National Association of
   Broadcasters V.
   Kleindienst, 405
Neck Problems, 28
Neuberger, Richard, 6
Newsweek, 130
Nicotine Patches, 183
Nixon, Patricia, 56

O
O'neill, Jennifer, 51
Oslin, R.T., 51
Osteoporosis, 26

P
Pac Money, 143
Pacs, 166
Parental Smoking, 115
Parents, 135, 139
Passive Smoke, 85
Penn Advertising Of Baltimore,
   Inc. V. Mayor & City Council
   Of Baltimore, 128
Penn Advertising Of Baltimore,
   Inc., V. Schmoke, 104
Peripheral Muscular Disease, 22

Petri Amendment, 172
Posadas De Puerto Rico V.
   Tourism Company Of Puerto
   Rico, 128
Pregnancy, 19
Pregnant Women, 116
Public Places, 147

Q
Quality Of Life, 77

R
R.J. Reynolds Tobacco Co. V.
   Mangini, 104, 128
Randall, Tony, 52
Reasoner, Harry, 60
Rectal Cancer, 21
Restaurants 66, 150
Restaurants, Smoking In, 67
Reynolds, Patrick, 9
Rheumatoid Arthritis, 29
Robertson, Cliff, 52
Rolfe 4

S
Secondary Tobacco Smoke 23,
   25, 117, 155
Shirley Maclaine 49
Smoke, Passive 85 (See also
   secondary smoke)
Smoke, Secondary Tobacco 23,
   25, 117, 155
Smoke-Free Policies, 152
Smoking In Federal Buildings, 156
Smoking In Restaurants, 67
Smoking In The Workplace, 153

Smoking, Parental, 115
Smoking, Underage, 138, 144
Smoking-Lung Cancer
    Linkage, 19
Special Interest Money, 165
Stroke, 23
Subsidizing Tobacco, 171
Sudden Infant Death
    Syndrome, 19, 75
Sullivan, Louis, 10
Surgeon General's
    Warning, 8, 108

T
Talman, William, 7
Teenagers, 133, 140
Tobacco Advertising, 123
Tobacco Exports 88, 167
Tobacco Industry 86, 112
Tobacco Lobbyists, 144

U
Uecker , Bob 59
U.S. 1000 (1972), 127
Underage Smoking, 138, 144
Universities, 160

V
Vaughn, Sarah, 53

W
Wayne Mcclaren, 12, 58, 85
Wayne, John, 7, 54
Weight Gain, 183
Wells, Mary, 54
Wilks V. American Tobacco
    Co., 100
Williams, Hank, Jr. 55
Women, 27, 68, 127, 175
Women's Groups, 166, 176
Women, Pregnant, 116
Workplace, Smoking in
    the, 153